NURSING NEGLIGENCE

For George
with love, respect, and gratitude

NURSING NEGLIGENCE

Analyzing Malpractice in the Hospital Setting

Janet Pitts Beckmann, Ph.D, R.N.

SAGE Publications
International Educational and Professional Publisher
Thousand Oaks London New Delhi

For information address:

 SAGE Publications, Inc.
2455 Teller Road
Thousand Oaks, California 91320
E-mail: order@sagepub.com

SAGE Publications Ltd.
6 Bonhill Street
London EC2A 4PU
United Kingdom

SAGE Publications India Pvt. Ltd.
M-32 Market
Greater Kailash I
New Delhi 110 048 India

Printed in the United States of America

Library of Congress Cataloging-in-Publication Data

Beckmann, Janet Pitts, 1946-
    Nursing negligence: Analyzing malpractice in the hospital setting/
Janet Pitts Beckmann.
        p. cm.
    Includes bibliographical references and index.
    ISBN 0-7619-0225-2 (cloth: acid-free paper).—ISBN 0-7619-0226-0
(pbk.: acid-free paper)
    1. Nursing errors—Case studies. 2. Nurses—Malpractice—Case
studies. I. Title.
RT85.6.B43   1996
346.7303'32—dc20   95-41787
Y347.306332

This book is printed on acid-free paper.

97 98 99 00 10 9 8 7 6 5 4 3 2

Sage Production Editor: Diane S. Foster

Contents

Tables

Figures

Introduction

THE PROBLEM OF NURSING MALPRACTICE

Nursing malpractice is beginning to haunt the nursing profession. It is a major problem that negatively affects the delivery of health care in the United States by causing unnecessary injury or death. Major nursing organizations such as the American Nurses' Association do in fact acknowledge that nursing malpractice cases are becoming more numerous. This is made abundantly clear in the study by the Risk Management Foundation of the Harvard Medical Institutions, which examined open and closed malpractice claims over a 12-year period (April 1, 1976, to December 31, 1987). The study found that malpractice claims in which the nurse was named as defendant had risen dramatically. Specifically, the data indicated that malpractice claims against nurses had increased 100% over previous years (McDonough & Rioux, 1989, pp. 4-5, 12).

The increasing number of adverse nursing care outcomes engendering malpractice action underscores the seriousness of the problem. A risk-free health care system is impossible, but many of the unnecessary risks can be eliminated or reduced through knowledge and application of the accepted standards of care. Valuable lessons can be learned from examining adverse nursing care outcomes.

When human error is systematically studied, safety is improved. The airline industry, for example, is far ahead of the health care industry and especially the nursing profession in this regard. The professional

1

airline pilot organization, the Air Line Pilots Association (ALPA), for many years has encouraged its members to report all errors, even those not causing an accident. Investigative protocols are used to retrieve comprehensive information immediately after an accident. ALPA studies errors and communicates preventative strategies to the pilots through numerous established channels. One of the primary purposes of ALPA is promoting passenger safety. A large portion of *Air Line Pilot,* the professional publication of this organization, is devoted each month to safety issues. A similar approach should be used in the nursing profession.

No comprehensive, systematic, or authoritative source of information is currently available to describe either the etiology of nursing malpractice or the morbidity and mortality associated with it. There is an obvious need to define and analyze nursing-care-related injury. The purpose of this book is to improve patient care and safety in the hospital setting by preventing or at least reducing nursing-care-related injury. Only through the examination of adverse nursing care outcomes can strategies for their prevention be developed.

Nursing negligence and associated health care delivery problems are not readily discussed or made known to the public. For example, the results of hospital accreditation surveys by the Joint Commission on Accreditation of Health Care Organizations (JCAHO) are confidential. Companies that insure health care agencies and professionals against malpractice generally purposefully guard claims data. However, in recent years the media—newspapers, magazines, and television—have increasingly reported incidents of malpractice in the hospital setting. As a matter of fact, within a period of 1 month, one national newspaper reported on four catastrophic cases of negligence: injury caused by amputation of the wrong foot, death caused by a massive overdose of a chemotherapeutic medication, death caused by removing a ventilator-dependent patient from mechanical ventilation, and a persistent vegetative state caused by failure to recognize and treat tension pneumothorax.

The mantle of secrecy has been raised in part also by malpractice litigation. When a lawsuit is filed, the complaint, along with all evidentiary documents (including the medical record in a malpractice action), becomes public record, with only very rare exceptions. In many instances, it is the lawsuit that exposes unsafe patient care practices. In a number of cases, if it had not been for litigation, unsafe nursing care practices would have been essentially ignored and allowed to continue indefinitely. The malpractice litigation in these cases made the hospitals safer by exposing and deterring the substandard care.

A report on some of the nation's largest jury verdicts revealed that two out of the four medical malpractice cases cited involved nursing care problems ("1993's Largest Verdicts," 1994, pp. S1, S8-9). One of the cases concerned a 16-year-old admitted to the hospital for the delivery of her first child. A fetal monitor demonstrated signs of fetal distress, but the monitor was discontinued. The nurses failed to apprise the physician of the situation. The child was eventually delivered but suffered severe brain damage. On October 21, 1993, a jury awarded the plaintiff $72.65 million (*Washington v. New York City Health and Hospitals Corp.*).

The other case involved a 32-year-old man who slipped, fell, and dislocated a knee. He was admitted to the hospital for surgical repair of the torn ligaments and tendons in the left knee. Postoperatively, the patient complained of pain, numbness, and loss of sensation in the left lower extremity. The patient said that the nurses ignored his complaints. Within 4 days, the popliteal artery in the left leg had become totally occluded, and this necessitated a below-the-knee amputation. The popliteal artery had been damaged, as is not uncommon after this type of injury. The patient had exhibited classical signs and symptoms of neurovascular embarrassment, but the nursing staff failed to obtain adequate care for the patient. At trial, the jury found both the nurses and physician liable, with the hospital 80% at fault because of inadequate nursing care and the physician 20% at fault. The jury awarded the plaintiff $15 million (*Donahue v. Port,* 1993).

Research clearly indicates that 75% of all malpractice incidents occur in hospitals and that a sizable portion of the claims stem from the negligence of supervised health care personnel (referring primarily to the nursing staff). The Harvard Medical Practice Study, published in 1990, reported that nearly 4% of patients discharged from hospitals in New York State were harmed in the hospital and that 1% suffered negligent injury. Fourteen percent of the patients harmed in hospitals died. The study was designed to be representative of hospitals throughout the United States.

By applying these data to the total number of hospital admissions in the United States, as supplied by the American Hospital Association (1993, p. 20), it can be estimated that annually 1.33 million patients will suffer injury and 150,000 will die as the result of an adverse health care outcome. Over 300,000 of these adverse outcomes will be the result of actual negligence by a health care provider.

To put this problem in a broader perspective, malpractice by health care providers in the hospital setting has caused more deaths in 1 year than all of the United States' combined casualties in the Korean war, the Vietnam war, and the Persian Gulf war. Looking at this problem in another way, the total number of deaths in 1994 in the United States attributed to both murder and accident (e.g., caused by motor vehicles, poisonings, fires, etc.) was less than the number of deaths caused by malpractice in hospitals (U.S. Bureau of Statistics, 1993, pp. 97-105). Table 1.1 summarizes comparative data on causes of death in the United States.

The hospital is one of the most dynamic and complex organizations in our society. Functions of the hospital include (a) patient care services (prevention, diagnosis, treatment, rehabilitation), (b) education, and (c) research. Care administered by hospitals still constitutes the single largest component of the health care industry. Hospital services account for the largest portion of the health care dollars that are spent.

The nursing department is the mainstay of the organization in fulfilling its objectives in relation to patient care. Nurses constitute the largest single group of health care professionals in the hospital setting.

The primary purpose of the nursing department in the hospital is to provide safe, individualized, comprehensive, and effective care to patients through the use of the nursing process. Nursing interventions are guided by policies and procedures established by the hospital in accordance with accepted standards of care.

The nurse is the only member of the health care team responsible for the hospitalized patient over the course of a 24-hour day. Over all, nurses are well educated, and they provide competent patient care throughout hospitals in the United States. Despite best efforts to give quality nursing care, some accidents and injuries are inevitable. However, it is recognized by the American Nurses' Association and others that many patient injuries are unnecessary and are the result of nursing malpractice.

Over the years, I have reviewed many cases in which nursing malpractice in the hospital setting was alleged and was found to be the cause of injury and death. Surprisingly, the majority of these cases involved the neglect of basic nursing care practices. Failure to apply fundamental principles of nursing practice to patient care resulted in serious injury and death. Interestingly, the nurses who provided sub-

TABLE 1.1 Selected Causes of Death in the United States, 1991

Cause of Death	No. of Deaths
Medical/nursing malpractice (hospitals only)	85,000
Accidental deaths	
Motor vehicles	43,500
Falls	12,200
Poison (solid, liquid)	5,600
Poison (gas)	800
Drowning	4,600
Fires, burns	4,200
Firearms	1,400
Other	12,000
Murder	24,700
Disease	
Hypertensive heart disease	23,400
Atherosclerosis	18,000
Carcinoma, breast	44,500
Leukemia	19,600
Diabetes mellitus	50,000
Suicide	30,200
Acquired immunodeficiency syndrome (AIDS)	22,675

SOURCE: Figures for accidental deaths, murder, and disease are taken from the *World Almanac and Book of Facts* (1993, pp. 223, 946, 948). The malpractice figure is extrapolated from the malpractice deaths/hospital admissions ratio supplied by the Harvard Medical Practice Study (1990), as applied to the hospital admissions numbers for 1991 reported by the American Hospital Association (AHA, 1993).

standard care were graduates of nationally accredited nursing programs and were licensed by the state. In addition, these cases of nursing malpractice occurred at well-funded, well-respected, and JCAHO-accredited hospitals. In almost every case in which a nurse clearly provided negligent care, no remedial or disciplinary action was taken by the hospital or the licensing body. That is, the system permits the nurse to continue practicing as if nothing has happened.

MEDICAL MALPRACTICE RESEARCH

Major malpractice research studies are summarized in this section. This body of research is referred to in the literature as *medical malpractice research* because physician negligence and negligence claims arising in the hospital setting are examined.

Adverse nursing care outcomes and adverse physician care outcomes causing and/or contributing to "negligence claims filed against the hospital" are not differentiated or addressed in the research studies. Nursing malpractice, if mentioned, is generally referred to in one sentence noting the existence of "negligence of supervised health care personnel." There are no comprehensive, systematic research studies addressing the problem of nursing negligence.

Researchers in the United States during the 1960s observed an increase in both the number of malpractice suits against physicians and the size of the malpractice payments made to patients or their estates. Negligence claims filed against hospitals increased over 75% from 1967 to 1970 (Pabst, 1973, p. 610). By the 1970s, it was documented that the number of malpractice claims against physicians had risen dramatically. Largely motivated by economics and the high cost of malpractice insurance, physicians initiated serious study of the problem. One of the major outcomes of their efforts was the improvement of patient care.

The Commission on Medical Malpractice was established by the president of the United States in 1971. The major objectives of the commission were to identify the critical elements of the medical malpractice problem and to make recommendations for possible solutions (Freeland, 1973, pp. 3, 6). Nine major projects were developed, along with a number of staff studies.

More than 800 medical records at two hospitals, representative of American hospitals, were examined by medical-legal experts. Their purpose was to determine the incidence of iatrogenic injury. Analysis revealed that approximately 7.5% of the patients suffered iatrogenic injury. Using these data, projections regarding the incidence of iatrogenic injury were made for both of the hospitals. Of the 23,750 patients discharged in 1972, it was determined that 1,780 patients suffered iatrogenic injury. In addition, review of medical records clearly indicated that 517 of the injuries were caused by negligence. However, only 31 malpractice claims were made by patients (Pocincki, Dogger, & Schwartz, 1973, pp. 50, 62-63).

Another phase of the commission's fact-finding function was review of closed malpractice insurance claim files. Insurance industry experts judged that 46% of all the closed malpractice claim files were meritorious and that the majority of negligence claims had a firm basis. It was also noted that for 1970, 50% of the claim files opened by insurance companies in anticipation of malpractice action closed without resulting in a lawsuit and 45% of the remaining claims terminated either by a settlement or by a trial verdict in favor of the plaintiff. In addition, it was determined that 75% of all malpractice incidents occurred in hospitals (Rudov, Myers, & Mirabella, 1973, p. 609).

Initiated by the commission, another investigation concluded that a sizable portion of malpractice claims and suits against hospitals stemmed from negligence of the supervised health care personnel (Pabst, 1973, p. 9). This study, however, contained no significant quantitative or qualitative data regarding malpractice claims involving nursing care.

Finally, the commission estimated that 7,738 malpractice claims were filed against all hospitals for adverse health care outcomes during 1970. This translated into 1.9 claims annually per hospital or 1.2 claims per 100 hospital beds. Thus, on the basis of these data, there were 3.1 claims per 10,000 hospital admissions and 3.8 claims filed per 10,000 patient census days (Pabst, 1973, pp. 9, 610).

In 1975, the Medical Insurance Feasibility Study was commissioned by the California Medical Association and the California Hospital Association. This was a major step forward in research concerning health-care-induced injury. It was the first study of its kind and magnitude to examine medical injury in hospitals representative of the state of California as a whole (Mills, 1977, pp. 10-12).

A panel of experts reviewed medical records for injury related to medical care. The sample consisted of the medical records for 20,864 California hospital inpatients discharged in 1974. Researchers found 970 potentially compensable events—that is, incidents of medical injury. Sixty percent of the potentially compensable events caused the patient only minor or temporary disability. However, nearly 10% (9.7%) of the adverse events led to death. It was determined that an overall rate of 4.65 medical injuries occurred per 100 hospitalizations. This meant that the hospitalized person had a 4.65% chance of being injured or killed in the course of treatment. Negligence was clearly evident in 17% of the records in which a medical-care-related injury was present. Forty-two percent of the medical-care-related deaths were associated with negligence.

Researchers also determined that only 5% of the adverse outcomes resulted in actual malpractice claims. Thus it was estimated that only 1 in 10 patients injured through health care negligence filed a claim for damages. On the basis of these data, malpractice legal actions represented only the tip of the iceberg.

A study in 1981 of legal cases involving medication administration suggested that in the average 300-bed hospital there were as many as 130,000 medication errors per year. Along with this, it was estimated that 140,000 hospitalized patients were dying each year from drug-related disorders (Patterson & Robinson, 1982, pp. 2-6).

The number of malpractice claims against physicians and hospitals continued to rise. In 1984, according to the U.S. General Accounting Office and the National Association of Insurance Commissioners, there were 73,472 closed malpractice claims. This represented a significant increase when compared to the 24,158 claims filed between July 1, 1975, and June 30, 1976. It was noted that the figures did not reflect the total number of malpractice incidents because many were not recognized and many were not reported. In addition, the numbers did not include all of the claims in the years studied because of the time lag between the date of an incident and the date the claim was reported to the insurance company. This averaged 21 months (U.S. General Accounting Office, 1986, pp. 28-30).

Researchers in 1985, using data from the California Medical Insurance Feasibility Study, came to the conclusion that approximately 1 in 126 hospital admissions resulted in patient injury caused by medical negligence. It was again noted that most malpractice claims had their origins in the hospital setting. The study went on to document that the malpractice problem was not simply one of litigious patients because only 1 in 10 of injuries due to health care negligence led to a malpractice claim (Danzon, 1985, pp. 52-56).

The Harvard Medical Practice Study, published in 1990, was executed under contract by the state of New York to provide information about medical-care-related injury and medical malpractice. Medical records from hospitals in New York State were scientifically sampled, and adverse events (unintended injury caused by medical management rather than by the disease process) were identified. On the basis of the data from record analysis, it was estimated that of the 2,671,863 patients discharged from hospitals in New York in 1984, 98,609, or 3.7%, experienced an injury that resulted from medical intervention. In that group, 27.6%, or 27,179, of the injuries clearly resulted from negligence. In other words, 1% of all patients discharged from hospitals in New York State experienced negligent injury (Harvard Medical Practice Study, 1990, pp. 11-13; Brennan et al., 1991, pp. 370-376).

According to the Harvard study, the majority of the adverse events (57%), occurring in New York State hospitals in 1984 resulted in minimal or transient disability. However, about 2,500 of the patients suffered permanent total disability because of medical injury. Approximately 14% of the patients experiencing an adverse event died. Medical injury, then, contributed at least in part to the deaths of more than 13,000 patients in that year. Negligence was clearly evident in 51% of the deaths due to medical injury. Medication complications were the most common adverse events, followed by wound infections and technical complications (Harvard Medical Practice Study, 1990, pp. 11-46; Leape et al., 1991, pp. 377-384).

The researchers then estimated that eight times as many patients suffered an injury from negligence (27,179) as filed malpractice claims (3,750) in New York State. Their conclusion, consistent with previous research data, was that malpractice litigation provides infrequent compensation for those injured by medical negligence because so few claims are filed. Sixteen times as many patients suffered from an injury due to negligence as received compensation from the tort liability system. Providers of substandard care were rarely identified and held accountable for negligent care (Localio et al., 1991, pp. 245-251). Net compensable losses of $894 million (in 1984 dollars) were in fact suffered by hospitalized patients in New York State in 1984 (Hiatt et al., 1989, p. 480).

Finally, a study based on the closed malpractice claims of a major insurance company contradicts the myth that malpractice verdicts depend on the whims of a jury. Analysis of malpractice claims in the state of New Jersey from 1977 to 1992 revealed that the physician as defendant prevailed in a malpractice case when the care rendered to the patient was consistent with the standard. Conversely, the injured plaintiff prevailed when the care did not conform to the standard. The research was designed so that the results of study could be generalizable to the entire United States (Taragin, Willett, Wilczek, Trout, & Carson, 1992, pp. 780-784).

All of the research on medical malpractice demonstrates that health care negligence is currently a widespread problem and that most of it occurs in the hospital setting. Clearly, a substantial number of injuries and deaths are related to medical care, and many are in fact the result of substandard care.

Some attempts to collect specific nursing malpractice data are being made. In 1987, the American Nurses' Association established the National Nurses Claims Data Base to collect information on nursing malpractice claims. This database relies on voluntary reporting by the individual nurse involved in a professional negligence claim. The U.S. government established the National Practitioner Data Bank (NPDB) to collect information on malpractice payments and professional disciplinary actions. This organization was mandated by the Health Care Quality Improvement Act of 1986 and was implemented in the summer of 1990. To date, accessible information regarding nursing malpractice has not been made available by these organizations. Thus no comprehensive database regarding nursing-care-related patient injury is available to the nursing profession.

STRATEGY FOR THE EXAMINATION OF NURSING MALPRACTICE

This book examines nursing negligence in the hospital setting. It is intended to improve patient care and safety by providing nurses and all persons concerned with the delivery of quality health care with an increased awareness of the problems associated with substandard care.

Adverse outcomes—that is, nursing-care-related patient injuries or deaths due to negligence—are examined qualitatively and quantitatively. Specifically, the book addresses common adverse nursing care outcomes, characteristics of patients experiencing negative outcomes, nursing care problems, frequent departures from the standard of nursing care that cause injury and death, mechanisms of injury, and costs associated with nursing malpractice.

The hospital was chosen as the focus because it is where the majority of the malpractice incidents occur. This book analyzes such incidents in the emergency department and in selected inpatient settings where nursing care is delivered. Nonsurgical patient care settings include the medical unit for care of the adult patient with a physiological problem and the psychiatric unit for care of the patient experiencing a primary psychosocial problem. Perioperative patient care settings are the operating room, the recovery room, and the surgical unit for care of the postoperative adult patient. This book also examines the pediatric unit for children requiring medical or surgical intervention and the patient care settings associated with childbirth—namely, the labor room, delivery room, and newborn nursery.

I constructed a database for the examination of nursing negligence in the hospital. This was necessary because no comprehensive source of information about nursing-care-related patient injury is available to the nursing professional.

Malpractice cases, the only source of public domain information concerning nursing-care-related patient injury, were used for the database. The body of civil court case decisions and jury verdict reports provided the facts for the objective examination of nursing-care-related injury.

Malpractice cases were obtained from the LEXIS-NEXIS service, a full-text on-line computerized database. Cases in the LEXIS database are derived from published U.S. federal civil court case decisions, state court case decisions, and jury verdict reports.

The legal database (LEXIS) was searched for cases (a) involving nursing negligence that caused or contributed to a negative patient care outcome, (b) occurring in the defined clinical settings of the hospital, and (c) resulting in a settlement or verdict in favor of the plaintiff. The computerized search covered a 5-year period from 1988 to 1993 and yielded 747 usable cases from 45 states. Cases were abstracted, summarized, and analyzed.

A comprehensive picture of nursing malpractice in the hospital setting is provided in Chapter 3. It is based on results of the analysis of the 747 malpractice cases in the 10 clinical areas. Characteristics of patients experiencing a negative nursing care outcome are addressed. Adverse outcomes, mechanisms of injury, and associated departures from the standard of nursing care are defined. Nursing care problems are examined in relation to communication, medication administration, nursing intervention, nursing assessment, environmental safety, inadequate care by the physician, equipment and products, and nosocomial infection. Finally, data concerning malpractice payment to the plaintiff are presented.

Nursing negligence in each of the defined clinical settings is addressed in Chapters 4 through 13. The format for the examination of nursing malpractice in these chapters follows that of Chapter 3. However, case studies to illustrate common nursing care problems and risk prevention strategies unique to the clinical setting are included in each of these chapters, which are written in a modular form and can be read independently. In each chapter, the percentages do not always sum to 100 because of rounding.

Common, recurrent, and preventable nursing care problems in the hospital setting are identified in Chapter 14. This knowledge is applied to the development of strategies to improve patient care. Recommendations are made for the prevention of common nursing care adverse outcomes. The risk prevention strategies, consistent with the standard of care, are not intended to be exhaustive or to cover every clinical circumstance.

This book provides the only qualitative and quantitative examination of nursing malpractice in the hospital setting.

2

Legal Aspects
of Malpractice

A brief discussion of malpractice is presented in this chapter because it is important to understand the issue in the legal context. An overview of negligence and malpractice is offered along with a brief explanation of the civil judicial process. The discussion is intended for the nonlawyer and is not confined to the laws applicable in any one state. Comments regarding malpractice and the judicial process are valid for most states, even though some state laws may vary on particular issues.

THE NATURE OF NEGLIGENCE
AND MALPRACTICE

When a person is harmed because another person fails to exercise the care that a reasonable and prudent person would use under the same circumstances, *negligence* is said to have occurred. *Malpractice* is negligence caused by a professional person in conducting a professional activity. Any person can be negligent, but only a professional person may be accused of malpractice.

Nursing malpractice, then, occurs if a nurse departs from the prevailing professional standard of patient care and causes harm to a person. A nursing standard is a criterion that is established to determine quality. That is, it is an agreed-upon measure of quality. Standards of care are broad in scope and are established by the nursing profession. They serve as guidelines for the assurance of quality in rendering patient care and thereby hold the nursing profession responsible and accountable to the consumer for the quality of its services.

Before a person can be held liable or responsible for negligence, certain prerequisites are required. The four elements of negligence are (a) duty owed, (b) breach of duty, (c) injury or damage (adverse outcome), and (d) causation. Thus, for negligence to occur, a person must be responsible for a particular duty, there must be failure to perform that duty, and the failure to perform the duty must in and of itself cause an injury or damage.

In terms of nursing practice, the nurse has a duty to the patient to provide nursing care. The care in turn must conform to the prevailing professional standard of nursing care. Nursing malpractice occurs when a patient is harmed because the nurse fails to provide nursing care or renders nursing care that departs from the prevailing professional standard.

A nurse is not negligent, however, if an error in judgment is made when providing nursing care. To establish that an error in judgment was made, two requirements must be met. It must be demonstrated (a) that the nurse possesses knowledge and skills comparable to those of the average nurse and (b) that the nursing care conformed to the prevailing professional standard.

A lawsuit is a mechanism whereby one party makes a legal complaint against another party. To establish liability, the party making the complaint (plaintiff) must demonstrate that the party defending the complaint (defendant) was negligent. Ordinarily, in a malpractice action, the plaintiff must prove by a preponderance of evidence (weight of the evidence more likely than not in the plaintiff's favor) all four of the elements of negligence. In a nursing malpractice suit, then, the actions of the allegedly negligent nurse are examined in relation to the four elements. That is, the nursing care is evaluated in relation to (a) what the standard of nursing care was at the time of the incident (duty owed), (b) whether the nurse deviated from the standard of care (breach of duty), (c) whether the patient was harmed (adverse outcome), and (d) whether the injury was caused by the breach of duty (causation). Each party produces facts and evidence to support its respective position. This process requires the neutral forum of a court. Facts and evidence are presented to a judge or jury (trier of fact).

THE JUDICIAL PROCESS

The judicial process functions to settle disputes peacefully. Specific procedural rules govern the transactions so that the process will be effective in resolving the complaint.

The actual process of a malpractice lawsuit is complex and requires many steps. First, the worthiness of a malpractice claim will be evaluated by an attorney. If the attorney feels that a person suffered an adverse outcome because of a health care professional's departure from the prevailing standard of care, a complaint will be filed. However, in some states, presuit screening is required before a complaint can be filed in a further attempt to eliminate cases without merit.

The complaint is a statement of facts supporting what the plaintiff intends to prove to the trier of fact. A summons is then issued to notify the party (or parties) named in the complaint (defendant[s]) of the charges and accusations. The defendant in turn is required to answer the complaint. Here the defendant admits or denies the allegations in the complaint. At this time, the defendant may add a counterclaim and/or a cross-complaint and/or file a motion for summary judgment (for a case in which the defense feels that the facts are not in dispute and that legal principles dictate a decision in favor of the defendant).

If the complaint is not dismissed, the pretrial discovery period commences. This is where both parties (plaintiff and defense) to the lawsuit gather information, facts, and evidence to develop the case. Discovery devices are the legal procedures for obtaining information and may include

1. *Interrogatories*—lists of questions to be answered in writing and made under oath
2. *Requests for production*—requests to obtain pertinent records and documents
3. *Depositions*—recorded oral examinations under oath taken outside of court and often intended to discover facts
4. *Subpoenas or subpoenas duces tecum*—a process for requiring a witness to give testimony or produce documents for inspection

The complexity of nursing care issues in a malpractice case often requires the services of a nursing expert. The expert witness may testify to assist the parties in understanding technical facts, issues, and evidence that are not a matter of common knowledge. Specialized knowledge based on education and/or experience sets the expert apart from the layperson. The expert witness is thus qualified to express an opinion on a technical subject because of this specialized knowledge. A nursing expert witness, then, evaluates the actual nursing care provided to a patient, using prevailing professional standards, and renders an opinion about the quality of the care.

After the discovery period, a pretrial hearing generally occurs. At this time, both parties present issues for the court to clarify or limit. An attempt to resolve the case without resorting to trial is usually made at a settlement conference. If the case is not resolved, preparation for trial commences.

By the time a malpractice case reaches the trial stage, more than a year has generally passed since the alleged incident. Initially, there is usually a delay between the time of the incident and the time a complaint is filed. Next, the discovery process takes time to uncover systematically pertinent information for the case. In addition, there is frequently a long wait for a trial date because the courts are so busy. As time passes, the medical record becomes increasingly important. Memories may fade or fail with the passage of time, but a written record remains. The medical record is a witness that never dies.

At the trial, all relevant facts are presented to the judge (who renders a decision) or the jury (who render a verdict). A judge will decide questions of fact as well as law if the plaintiff does not choose a jury trial. However, in most malpractice actions, the plaintiff asks for a jury trial, and the first step then is to impanel a jury. Prospective jurors are questioned by the attorneys for each party (plaintiff and defense) to determine possible bias. This process is known as *voir dire*. Each party attempts to select jurors who will be fair and impartial to the issue at hand.

After jury selection, an opening statement is made by the attorneys representing the plaintiff and the defense. At this time, each party has the opportunity to provide a preview of the facts that will be presented during trial. This essentially serves as a road map for the jury.

The plaintiff then presents evidence believed necessary to prove the case. This is done primarily through the testimony of witnesses, with direct examination by the plaintiff's attorney and cross-examination by the defendant's attorney. The purpose of the direct examination is to communicate facts supporting the plaintiff's case; the cross-examination by the defendant's attorney is to define or impute the direct testimony of the witness. Documentary evidence such as reports by experts may also be used in presenting a case.

At the conclusion of the plaintiff's case, either party may make a motion for a directed verdict. If the plaintiff makes the motion, the judge is asked to rule that the evidence or law presented is so clearly in favor of the plaintiff that it is not necessary for the trial to proceed. If the judge grants the motion, the judgment is made in favor of the plaintiff. On the other hand, if the defense makes a motion for a directed verdict, the judge is asked to rule that the plaintiff has no case—that is, that insufficient evidence has been presented. If the judge grants the defendant's motion, the case is said to be *dismissed with prejudice,* and the defendant has prevailed.

If there is no motion for a directed verdict or if the motion is denied by a judge, the defense presents its case. Testimony of witnesses and documentary evidence are used in the same way as for the plaintiff's presentation. At the end of the defendant's case, the plaintiff may rebut evidence presented by the defendant. Either party may again ask for a directed verdict. If the motion is not made or is denied, each party makes a closing statement. This is a summary of the case along with what each party believes the evidence has demonstrated.

In a jury trial, the judge instructs the jury about points of law applicable to the case. This provides a point of reference for the jury to weigh the evidence. After deliberation, the jury returns a verdict. Under some conditions, the judge may (a) remove the case from the jury by directing a verdict in favor of one party, (b) declare a mistrial, or (c) declare a nonsuit if the plaintiff has failed to present a sufficient case. If a jury cannot agree on a verdict, a hung jury is declared, and a new trial is ordered.

Finally, either the plaintiff or defendant, depending upon the verdict, may appeal to a higher court. The basis for the appeal is alleged error(s) made by the trial court. One of three outcomes may occur in the appellate court: (a) The court may affirm the verdict, (b) it may reverse the verdict (in whole or part), or (c) it may send the case back to lower court for a new trial (*remand*).

3

Nursing Malpractice
in the Hospital Setting

Nurses play an indispensable role in providing society with comprehensive health care. Their knowledge, gained through education and clinical practice, forms the basis for safe and effective nursing care. Nursing practice involves promotion of health, prevention of disease, restoration of health, and palliative care to the dying.

Nurses in the hospital setting are responsible for the patient 24 hours a day. Thus they coordinate the plan of care and initiate and control all nursing care measures. The nursing process is the framework for organizing the elements of nursing practice. The nursing process encompasses patient assessment, nursing diagnosis or definition of patient problem(s), statement of nursing care goal(s), plan of action, and evaluation of nursing care outcome(s). A nursing care plan, which is a written statement of the nursing process, is developed for each patient. Nursing care is planned around the individual biopsychosocial needs of the patient, and the nursing care plan is modified as the patient's condition dictates.

One of the vital responsibilities of the nurse is that of patient observation or assessment. It is fundamental to the delivery of systematic, scientifically based, effective nursing care. In addition, it is essential to developing a therapeutic relationship with the patient as well as determining the teaching needs of the patient. Systematic assessment begins with the nurse's first contact with the patient and continues as long as the patient is under the nurse's care.

Nursing assessments are useless, of course, unless they are communicated both verbally and in writing. An important obligation is to communicate verbally to the physician important nursing assessment data as well as any change in the patient's condition. This communication forms the foundation for appropriate medical decision making and action because the physician usually attends the hospitalized patient for only a brief period of time each day.

Written communication in the form of documentation of patient care in the medical record is fundamental to safe patient care. The maintenance of an accurate and timely medical record is as critical to patient care as the actual care provided. Documentation is a strategic part of each and every nursing action, and it is thus inseparable from the actual nursing care rendered.

The physician is expected to develop a comprehensive medical treatment plan for the hospitalized patient. Appropriate and timely patient care interventions prescribed and/or executed by the physician are fundamental to the treatment plan. Inadequate care of the patient by the physician must be recognized and addressed. The nurse is obligated to secure appropriate care by a physician under the guidance of and consistent with established hospital policies and procedures.

The nurse is responsible for executing various treatments and procedures when providing patient care. Nursing interventions must be performed in accordance with prevailing professional standards. Some interventions involve independent actions initiated by the nurse. Actions such as assessment and skin care do not require a physician's order. Dependent nursing interventions, on the other hand, such as medication administration, are executed with the physician's order. Many nursing interventions in the hospital setting require the use of a wide variety of products as well as equipment. The nurse must be knowledgeable about the safe use of various patient care products and types of equipment.

A safe patient care environment is fundamental to providing nursing care in the hospital setting. Maintaining a safe biological environment is an important nursing consideration. Nosocomial infection still remains a serious threat to the hospitalized patient. Along with this, the integrity of the physical environment is of concern because the nurse is obligated to protect the patient from avoidable injury. Hospitalized patients are especially prone to falls because of a weakened and/or impaired state of health.

Through assessment, planning, communication, intervention, and the maintenance of a safe environment, the nurse helps the patient toward therapeutic goals. However, when any component of nursing care is omitted or when nursing care is not delivered in accordance with the accepted standards, the patient may experience a nursing-care-related adverse outcome.

A comprehensive picture of nursing negligence in the hospital setting is provided in this chapter. It is based on data from 747 cases of nursing malpractice in 10 selected clinical settings of the hospital: the emergency department; nonsurgical patient care settings of the medical and psychiatric units; perioperative patient care settings of the operating room, the recovery room, and the surgical unit; the pediatric unit; and patient care settings associated with childbirth—namely, the labor room, delivery room, and newborn nursery.

This chapter first presents data concerning adverse outcomes, characteristics of patients experiencing an adverse outcome, nursing care problems, and mechanisms of injury. Then it analyzes each nursing care problem. Next, it addresses documentation problems and malpractice payment data. The chapter concludes with a summary.

GENERAL ADVERSE OUTCOMES

Adverse patient care outcomes due to nursing negligence were particularly severe in a large number of the 747 nursing malpractice cases. General adverse outcomes—namely, those of death and injury—are examined first.

Nursing negligence either caused or contributed to a death in 29.31% (219 of 747) of the cases. The primary departures from the standard of care resulting in death were inadequate communication with the physician regarding nursing assessment data (76; 34.70%), inadequate nursing assessment (46; 21.00%), and medication administration error (42; 19.17%).

Serious injury accounted for the remaining 70.68% (528 of 747) of the adverse nursing care outcomes. The majority of the injuries were due to inadequate communication with the physician regarding nursing assessment data (124; 23.48%), an unsafe environment (87; 16.47%), inadequate nursing intervention (91; 17.23%), and medication administration error (98; 18.56%). General adverse nursing care outcomes along with associated departures from the standard of care are summarized in Table 3.1.

Fetal/newborn deaths accounted for 27 of the 219 deaths. The term *fetal/newborn* is used in this book for cases of pregnancy in which there is a childbirth-induced/associated adverse outcome that involves only the fetus or the newborn infant. Inadequate communication with the physician regarding nursing assessment data caused or contributed to 81.48% of the fetal/newborn deaths. Nursing-care-related fetal/newborn injuries were responsible for 114 of the 528 injuries. Again, inadequate communication of nursing assessment data was the primary cause of fetal/newborn injury. Fetal/newborn adverse nursing care outcomes and associated departures from the standard of care are summarized in Table 3.2.

Patient deaths excluding fetal/newborn deaths accounted for 192 of the 219 deaths. Inadequate communication with the physician regarding nursing assessment data, inadequate nursing assessment, and medication administration error were the major departures from the standard of nursing care causing or contributing to patient deaths. Nursing-care-related patient injuries were responsible for 414 of the 528 injuries. Most of these injuries were due to an unsafe environment, inadequate nursing intervention, or medication error. Table 3.3 summarizes patient adverse outcomes and associated departures from the standard of care.

The highest percentage of nursing-care-related deaths in the database occurred in the recovery room, and the delivery room setting had the highest percentage of database injuries. Table 3.4 presents the general adverse outcomes of injury and death by clinical setting.

PATIENT CHARACTERISTICS

The age of patients experiencing a nursing care adverse outcome ranged from fetal/newborn to 95 years. The mean age for database patients was 31.64, and the median was 34.00 years. Maternal age was used for computational purposes in cases of fetal/newborn death or injury. Age data for all cases, according to adverse outcome, are presented in Table 3.5.

The widest age range of patients in the database was found in the emergency department. The greatest mean and median ages occurred

TABLE 3.1 Nursing Malpractice Adverse Outcomes and Associated
Departures From the Standard of Care

Adverse Outcome Category	Departure From the Standard of Care Causing an Adverse Outcome	No. of Cases	% of Category	% of Total
Death		219	100.00	29.31
	Inadequate nursing assessment	46	21.00	
	Medication administration error	42	19.17	
	Inadequate communication with the physician regarding nursing assessment	76	34.70	
	Inadequate care by the physician	21	9.58	
	Unsafe environment	7	3.19	
	Inadequate nursing intervention	17	7.76	
	Inadequate infection control	3	1.36	
	Improper use of equipment/products	7	3.19	
Injury		528	100.00	70.68
	Unsafe environment	87	16.47	
	Inadequate nursing assessment	58	10.98	
	Inadequate nursing intervention	91	17.23	
	Medication administration error	98	18.56	
	Inadequate communication with the physician regarding nursing assessment	124	23.48	
	Inadequate care by the physician	35	6.62	
	Inadequate infection control	11	2.08	
	Improper use of equipment/products	24	4.54	

TABLE 3.2 Fetal/Newborn Nursing Malpractice Adverse Outcomes and
Associated Departures From the Standard of Care

Adverse Outcome Category	Departure From the Standard of Care Causing an Adverse Outcome	No. of Cases	% of Category	% of Total
Fetal/newborn death		27	100.00	19.14
	Inadequate communication with the physician regarding nursing assessment	22	81.48	
	Inadequate care by the physician	3	11.11	
	Inadequate nursing intervention	2	7.40	
Fetal/newborn injury		114	100.00	80.85
	Inadequate communication with the physician regarding nursing assessment	49	42.98	
	Inadequate nursing assessment	21	18.42	
	Inadequate care by the physician	19	16.66	
	Medication administration error	15	13.15	
	Inadequate nursing intervention	6	5.26	
	Unsafe environment	2	1.75	
	Improper use of equipment/products	2	1.75	

TABLE 3.3 Patient Adverse Outcomes Due to Nursing Malpractice and Associated Departures From the Standard of Care

Adverse Outcome Category	Departure From the Standard of Care Causing an Adverse Outcome	No. of Cases	% of Category	% of Total
Patient death[a]		192	100.00	31.68
	Inadequate nursing assessment	46	23.95	
	Medication administration error	42	21.87	
	Inadequate communication with the physician regarding nursing assessments	54	28.12	
	Inadequate care by the physician	18	9.37	
	Unsafe environment	7	3.64	
	Inadequate nursing intervention	15	7.81	
	Inadequate infection control	3	1.56	
	Improper use of equipment/products	7	3.64	
Patient injury[a]		414	100.00	68.31
	Unsafe environment	85	20.53	
	Inadequate nursing assessment	37	8.93	
	Inadequate nursing intervention	85	20.53	
	Medication administration error	83	20.04	
	Inadequate communication with the physician regarding nursing assessment	75	18.11	
	Inadequate care by the physician	16	3.86	
	Inadequate infection control	11	2.65	
	Improper use of equipment/products	22	5.31	

a. Excludes fetal/newborn population.

TABLE 3.4 Injury and Death Due to Nursing Malpractice, by Clinical Setting

Clinical Setting	Adverse Outcome (N = 747)									
	Patient Injury		Patient Death		Fetal/Newborn Injury		Fetal/Newborn Death		Total	
	No.	%	No.	%	No.	%	No.	%	No.	%
Psychiatric	21	60.00	14	40.00	0	0.00	0	0.00	35	100.00
Emergency dept.	34	48.57	26	37.14	5	7.14	5	7.14	70	100.00
Medical	95	64.19	53	35.81	0	0.00	0	0.00	148	100.00
Surgical	113	72.90	42	27.10	0	0.00	0	0.00	155	100.00
Pediatric	33	62.26	20	37.73	0	0.00	0	0.00	53	100.00
Labor room	8	6.25	5	3.90	94	73.43	21	16.40	128	100.00
Delivery room	5	23.80	0	0.00	15	71.42	1	4.76	21	100.00
Newborn nursery	44	84.61	8	15.38	0	0.00	0	0.00	52	100.00
Operating room	40	90.90	4	9.09	0	0.00	0	0.00	44	100.00
Recovery room	21	51.21	20	48.78	0	0.00	0	0.00	41	100.00

in the medical setting. Age data summarized by clinical setting are found in Table 3.6.

Age data by the adverse outcomes of injury and death for each clinical setting are presented in Table 3.7.

In terms of age distribution, the greatest number of adverse outcomes related to nursing care were in the fetal/newborn-through-20-year age group (279 of 747; 37.34%). This age group was followed by groups aged 21 through 40 years (182; 24.35%), 41 through 60 years (160; 21.41%), 61 through 80 years (103; 13.78%), and 81 through 100 years (23; 3.07%). Table 3.8 shows the age distribution for all patients (including the fetal/newborn) experiencing an adverse outcome of nursing care.

Patients experiencing death as a negative outcome of nursing care were primarily between 21 and 40 years of age (72 of 219; 32.87%). Sixty-two patients (28.30%) and 55 patients (25.10%) were clustered in the age groups of newborn to 20 and 41 to 60 years, respectively. Only 13.68% (30 of 219) of the patients suffering death were between 61 and 100 years. The age distribution of patients (including the fetal/newborn) experiencing death as an adverse outcome of nursing care is shown in Table 3.9.

In cases of nursing-care-related injury, the majority of the patients were distributed in the age category of fetal/newborn to 20 years (217 of 528; 41.08%). The remaining injured patients were clustered in the following age distributions: 21 through 40 years (110; 20.82%), 41 through 60 years (105; 19.88%), 61 through 80 years (75; 14.20%), and 81 through 100 years (21; 3.97%). Table 3.10 presents age distribution data for patients (including the fetal/newborn) experiencing injury as an adverse outcome of nursing care.

Four hundred and sixty-three (61.98%) of the 747 patients experiencing a nursing-care-related adverse outcome were female; 38.01% (284) were male. Cases of fetal/newborn adverse outcome were coded as female (using the mother as proxy). Excluding labor and delivery room patients, gender distribution was more evenly divided between male (284; 47.49%) and female (314; 52.50%). Table 3.11 summarizes gender data.

Excluding the labor, delivery, and newborn nursery settings, the majority of both male and female negative outcomes occurred in the medical and surgical settings. Table 3.12 summarizes gender data by clinical setting.

TABLE 3.5 Age of Patients Experiencing a Nursing-Care-Related Adverse Outcome

Age	All Cases (N = 747)	Cases of Death (N = 192)[a]	Cases of Injury (N = 414)[a]
Range	Fetal/newborn to 95 yr.	2 mo. to 82 yr.	3 mo. to 95 yr.
Mean[b]	31.64 yr.	31.31 yr.	31.58 yr.
Median[b]	34.00 yr.	40.50 yr.	33.00 yr.

a. Excludes fetal/newborn population.
b. Maternal age used for computation.

TABLE 3.6 Age of Patients Experiencing a Nursing-Care-Related Adverse Outcome, by Clinical Setting

Clinical Setting	Age Range	Mean Age (Years)	Median Age (Years)
Psychiatric	15 to 79 yr.	40.31	37.00
Emergency dept.[a]	2 mo. to 93 yr.	33.18	31.50
Medical	18 to 95 yr.	54.62	54.50
Surgical	18 to 88 yr.	48.87	47.00
Pediatric	Newborn to 17 yr.	4.97	2.00
Labor room[a]	16 to 38 yr.	24.97	26.00
Delivery room[a]	18 to 43 yr.	27.00	27.00
Newborn nursery	Newborn	Newborn	Newborn
Operating room	1.5 to 75 yr.	46.22	47.00
Recovery room	5 mo. to 77 yr.	36.35	38.00

a. Maternal age used for computation.

TABLE 3.7 Age of Patients Experiencing the Adverse Outcome of Death or Injury, by Clinical Setting

Clinical Setting	Death			Injury		
	Age Range	Mean Age (Years)	Median Age (Years)	Age Range	Mean Age (Years)	Median Age (Years)
Psychiatric	16 to 79 yr.	31.70	44.50	15 to 70 yr.	36.52	34.00
Emergency[a]	2 mo. to 80 yr.	33.74	33.00	3 mo. to 93 yr.	34.90	32.50
Medical	24 to 81 yr.	50.53	50.00	18 to 95 yr.	56.89	58.00
Surgical	22 to 82 yr.	46.11	43.00	18 to 88 yr.	49.89	48.00
Pediatric	3 mo. to 15 yr.	5.42	3.50	Newborn to 17 yr.	4.69	1.00
Labor room[a]	18 to 33 yr.	24.48	26.50	20 to 38 yr.	26.30	26.25
Delivery room[a]	43 yr.	43.00	43.00	18 to 36 yr.	27.46	28.50
Newborn nursery	Newborn	Newborn	Newborn	Newborn	Newborn	Newborn
Operating room	1.5 to 58 yr.	37.37	45.00	3.5 to 75 yr.	47.11	47.00
Recovery room	23 to 67 yr.	40.80	38.00	5 mo. to 77 yr.	32.12	38.00

a. Maternal age used for computation.

TABLE 3.8 Age Distribution of Database Population Experiencing an
Adverse Outcome of Nursing Care ($N = 747$)

Age (Years)	No. of Cases	% of Cases
Fetal/newborn to 10	253	33.86
11 to 20	26	3.48
21 to 30	87	11.64
31 to 40	95	12.71
41 to 50	91	12.18
51 to 60	69	9.23
61 to 70	58	7.76
71 to 80	45	6.02
81 to 100	23	3.07

TABLE 3.9 Age Distribution of Database Population Experiencing Death
as an Adverse Outcome of Nursing Care ($N = 219$)

Age (Years)	No. of Cases	% of Cases
Fetal/newborn to 10	53	24.20
11 to 20	9	4.10
21 to 30	34	15.52
31 to 40	38	17.35
41 to 50	31	14.15
51 to 60	24	10.95
61 to 70	13	5.93
71 to 80	15	6.84
81 to 100	2	0.91

TABLE 3.10 Age Distribution of Database Population Experiencing Injury
as an Adverse Outcome of Nursing Care ($N = 528$)

Age (Years)	No. of Cases	% of Cases
Fetal/newborn to 10	200	37.87
11 to 20	17	3.21
21 to 30	53	10.03
31 to 40	57	10.79
41 to 50	60	11.36
51 to 60	45	8.52
61 to 70	45	8.52
71 to 80	30	5.68
81 to 100	21	3.97

The greatest frequencies of male deaths and injuries occurred in the medical and surgical settings, respectively. On the other hand, the greatest frequencies of female deaths and injuries occurred in the surgical and medical settings, respectively. Table 3.13 presents gender data by adverse nursing care outcome.

The most frequent presenting problems, representing 49.11% (367 of 747) of the database, were pregnancy/childbirth, including associated fetal/newborn problems (23.82%; 178); musculoskeletal problems (13.25%; 99); and gastrointestinal problems (12.04%; 90).

The most common presenting problem in cases of nursing-care-related death was pregnancy/childbirth with associated fetal/newborn problems (42 of 219; 19.17%). This presenting problem was followed by gastrointestinal problems (33; 15.06%), cardiovascular problems (25; 11.41%), neurological problems (19; 8.67%), respiratory problems (18; 8.21%), infectious problems (18; 8.21%), musculoskeletal problems (16; 7.30%), and psychiatric problems (15; 6.84%).

Like nursing-care-related death, pregnancy/childbirth with associated fetal/newborn problems was the most frequent presenting problem in cases of injury (136 of 528; 25.75%). Other frequent presenting problems associated with injury as an adverse outcome included musculoskeletal problems (83; 15.71%), gastrointestinal problems (57; 10.79%), newborn status (44; 8.33%), neurological problems (43; 8.14%), and cardiovascular problems (37; 7.00%). Table 3.14 presents data concerning the presenting problems of patients experiencing an adverse outcome.

Presenting problems summarized by clinical setting are found in Table 3.15.

ADVERSE NURSING CARE OUTCOMES

Adverse outcomes as a function of nursing negligence were quite varied. However, a most notable finding was that 59.43% (444 of 747) of the patients suffered brain damage or death as a result of substandard nursing care. A fracture, wound, sprain, or dislocation (73; 9.77%) was the next most frequent nursing care induced adverse event, followed by neurovascular/peripheral nerve damage (36; 4.81%), amputation (28; 3.74%), retained sponge or other foreign object (28; 3.74%), paralysis (26; 3.48%), burn (26; 3.48%), and infection (25; 3.34%). Adverse outcomes of lesser frequency are

TABLE 3.11 Sex of Patients Experiencing a Nursing-Care-Related Adverse Outcome

Cases of Adverse Outcomes	Male		Female		Total	
	No.	%	No.	%	No.	%
Cases, all[a]	284	38.01	463	61.98	747	100.00
Cases (excluding labor and delivery)	284	47.49	314	52.50	598	100.00
Cases, death (excluding fetal/newborn)	95	51.63	89	48.36	184	100.00
Cases, injury (excluding fetal/newborn)	163	44.05	207	55.94	370	100.00

a. Includes maternal gender for fetal/newborn adverse outcomes.

TABLE 3.12 Sex of Patients Experiencing a Nursing-Care-Related Adverse Outcome, by Clinical Setting

Clinical Setting[a]	Male (N = 258)		Female (N = 288)	
	No.	%	No.	%
Psychiatric	21	8.13	14	4.86
Emergency dept.	34	13.17	36	12.50
Medical	62	24.03	86	29.86
Surgical	78	30.32	77	26.73
Pediatric	32	12.40	21	7.29
Operating room	14	5.42	30	10.41
Recovery room	17	6.58	24	8.33

a. Excludes labor, delivery, and nursery settings.

TABLE 3.13 Sex of Patients Experiencing Injury or Death as an Adverse Outcome, by Clinical Setting

Clinical Setting[a]	Male				Female			
	Death (N = 95)[b]		Injury (N = 163)[b]		Death (N = 89)[b]		Injury (N = 207)[b]	
	No.	%	No.	%	No.	%	No.	%
Psychiatric	10	10.52	11	6.74	4	4.49	10	4.83
Emergency dept.	17	17.89	17	10.42	9	10.11	17	8.21
Medical	30	31.57	32	19.63	23	25.84	63	30.43
Surgical	17	17.89	61	37.42	25	28.08	52	25.12
Pediatric	12	12.63	20	12.26	8	8.98	13	6.28
Labor room	0	0.00	0	0.00	5	5.61	8	3.86
Delivery room	0	0.00	0	0.00	0	0.00	5	2.41
Operating room	1	1.05	13	7.97	3	3.37	27	13.04
Recovery room	8	8.42	9	5.52	12	13.48	12	5.79

a. Nursery setting excluded.
b. Fetal/newborn injury and death excluded.

TABLE 3.14 Diagnoses/Presenting Problems of Patients Experiencing a Nursing-Care-Related Adverse Outcome

Patient Diagnosis/ Presenting Problem	Adverse Outcome					
	All Cases (N = 747)		Death (N = 219)		Injury (N = 528)	
	No.	%	No.	%	No.	%
Psychiatric/mental	37	4.95	15	6.84	22	4.16
Pregnancy/childbirth (includes associated fetal/newborn problems)	178	23.82	42	19.17	136	25.75
Neurological	62	8.29	19	8.67	43	8.14
Gastrointestinal	90	12.04	33	15.06	57	10.79
Respiratory	30	4.01	18	8.21	12	2.27
Cardiovascular	62	8.29	25	11.41	37	7.00
Infectious (local and systemic)	46	6.15	18	8.21	28	5.30
Musculoskeletal	99	13.25	16	7.30	83	15.71
Multiple trauma	20	2.67	6	2.73	14	2.65
Thermoregulatory	1	0.13	0	0.00	1	0.18
Neoplasia	9	1.20	2	0.91	7	1.32
Endocrine-metabolic	6	0.80	3	1.36	3	0.56
Genitourinary	30	4.01	6	2.73	24	4.54
Ear, nose, throat	8	1.07	5	2.28	3	0.56
Plastic/reconstructive	7	0.93	1	0.45	6	1.13
Eye	5	0.66	1	0.45	4	0.75
Wound/integument	5	0.66	1	0.45	4	0.75
Newborn (excludes fetal/ newborn childbirth-associated problems)	52	6.96	8	3.65	44	8.33

included in Table 3.16, which summarizes all nursing-care-related injuries.

Central nervous system damage and death were the most frequent nursing-care-related adverse outcomes occurring in all clinical settings except the medical setting, delivery room, and operating room. For the medical setting, death followed by a wound, fracture, sprain, or dislocation was the most common consequence of nursing negligence. The most frequent nursing-care-related negative outcomes in the delivery room were brain damage and peripheral nerve injury. The largest class of adverse events due to nursing negligence in the operating room was that of a retained foreign body or surgery on the wrong body part. Adverse outcomes summarized by clinical setting are presented in Table 3.17.

TABLE 3.15 Diagnoses/Presenting Problems of Patients Experiencing a Nursing-Care-Related Adverse Outcome, by Clinical Setting

Diagnosis/ Presenting Problem	No. of Cases, by Clinical Setting									
	Psych.	Emer.	Med.	Surg.	Ped.	Labor	Deliv.	Nurs.	Oper.	Recov.
Psychiatric/mental	35	1	1	0	0	0	0	0	0	0
Pregnancy/ childbirth (includes associated fetal/ newborn problems)	0	13	0	6	0	128	21	0	0	10
Neurological	0	12	35	6	7	0	0	0	2	0
Gastrointestinal	0	10	29	28	3	0	0	0	10	10
Respiratory	0	10	14	6	0	0	0	0	0	0
Cardiovascular	0	7	24	21	5	0	0	0	5	0
Infection (local and systemic)	0	6	17	3	19	0	0	0	0	1
Musculoskeletal	0	4	11	50	9	0	0	0	15	10
Multiple trauma	0	4	5	9	2	0	0	0	0	0
Thermoregulatory	0	1	0	0	0	0	0	0	0	0
Neoplasia	0	0	8	0	1	0	0	0	0	0
Endocrine-metabolic	0	0	3	2	1	0	0	0	0	0
Genitourinary	0	0	1	13	0	0	0	0	11	5
Ear, nose, throat	0	0	0	4	2	0	0	0	1	1
Plastic/reconstructive	0	0	0	4	1	0	0	0	0	2
Eye	0	0	0	3	0	0	0	0	0	2
Wound/integument	0	2	0	0	3	0	0	0	0	0
Newborn (excludes fetal/newborn childbirth-associated problems)	0	0	0	0	0	0	0	52	0	0

NOTE: Psych. = psychiatric, Emer. = emergency room, Med. = medical, Surg. = surgical, Ped. = pediatric, Labor = labor room, Deliv. = delivery room, Nurs. = newborn nursery, Oper. = operating room, Recov. = recovery room.

GENERAL NURSING CARE PROBLEMS

Two nursing care problem areas—namely, communication and medication administration—were responsible for 45.91% (343 of 747) of the adverse outcomes experienced by patients. Failure to inform the physician of a change in the patient's condition or of abnormal assessment data was responsible for 27.17% (203) of the incidents, and failure to administer medication(s) properly caused 18.74% (140) of the adverse outcomes.

Nursing intervention problems due to the failure to perform a nursing treatment or procedure properly were responsible for 14.45%

TABLE 3.16 Type of Adverse Outcome Caused by Nursing Malpractice
(N = 747)

Adverse Outcome Caused by Nursing Malpractice	No. of Cases	% of Cases
Death	219	29.31
Brain damage	225	30.12
Multiple trauma	5	0.66
Fracture, wound, sprain, dislocation	73	9.77
Rape	2	0.26
False imprisonment	1	0.13
Emotional distress	9	1.20
Subdural hematoma	1	0.13
Hemiplegia, paraplegia, quadriplegia	26	3.48
Burn: thermal, chemical, electrical	26	3.48
Amputation: limb, digits	28	3.74
Infection	25	3.34
Sensory loss: hearing, sight	13	1.74
Myocardial infarction	1	0.13
Thrombophlebitis	1	0.13
Neurovascular/peripheral nerve damage	36	4.81
Kidney, ureter, bladder damage	6	0.80
Duodenal ulcer hemorrhage	1	0.13
Respiratory system damage	5	0.66
Cerebrovascular accident	4	0.53
Bowel perforation or necrosis	3	0.40
Inadvertent T-tube removal	1	0.13
Surgery on the wrong body part	4	0.53
Retained sponge or other object	28	3.74
Uterine perforation, rupture	4	0.53

(108) of the nursing malpractice incidents. Nursing interventions involving medication administration and patient assessment, however, are treated as separate problem areas because of their key importance in the delivery of nursing care.

Patient assessment problems—namely, the failure to observe the patient systematically—accounted for 13.92% (104) of the incidents, and failure to provide a safe environment led to 94 (12.58%) cases of nursing negligence. Other major problem areas included inadequate patient care by the physician with failure by the nurse to obtain appropriate care for the patient (53; 7.09%), negligent use of equipment and/or products (31; 4.14%), and the failure to prevent infection

TABLE 3.17 Type of Adverse Outcome Due to Nursing Negligence, by Clinical Setting

Adverse Outcome	No. of Cases, by Clinical Setting									
	Psych.	Emer.	Med.	Surg.	Ped.	Labor	Deliv.	Nurs.	Oper.	Recov.
Death	14	31	53	42	20	26	1	8	4	20
Central nervous system damage: brain damage, paralysis, cerebrovascular accident	9	15	18	33	23	97	11	32	2	16
Multiple trauma	5	0	0	0	0	0	0	0	0	0
Fracture, wound, sprain, and/or dislocation	2	8	38	20	1	0	1	0	2	1
Emotional distress, including rape and false imprisonment	3	3	1	1	0	0	0	3	1	0
Burn: electrical, chemical, and/or thermal	1	0	12	4	2	0	0	2	6	1
Amputation: digit, foot, limb	1	3	7	10	2	1	0	3	0	1
Infectious process	0	4	2	16	0	1	0	1	1	0
Sensory loss: sight, hearing	0	2	3	2	1	1	0	2	0	0
Peripheral nervous system damage	0	2	11	15	4	0	4	0	0	0
Cardiovascular system damage	0	2	0	0	0	0	0	0	0	0
Genitourinary system damage	0	0	2	3	0	2	1	0	1	1
Gastrointestinal system damage	0	0	1	3	0	0	0	0	0	1
Respiratory system damage	0	0	0	4	0	0	0	1	0	0
Surgery on the wrong body part or a retained sponge (or other foreign object)	0	0	0	2	0	0	3	0	27	0

NOTE: Psych. = psychiatric, Emer. = emergency room, Med. = medical, Surg. = surgical, Ped. = pediatric, Labor = labor room, Deliv. = delivery room, Nurs. = newborn nursery, Oper. = operating room, Recov. = recovery room.

(14; 1.87%). Table 3.18 summarizes nursing care problem areas and the corresponding departures from the standard of care.

Examination of nursing care problems by clinical setting revealed that in both the psychiatric and recovery room settings, the most common problem was that of nursing assessment. The departure from the standard of care causing negative outcomes was failure to assess the patient systematically. The most frequent problem in the medical setting as well as the pediatric setting was medication administration error. Failure to inform the physician of a change in the patient's condition or of abnormal assessment data was the dominant departure from the standard of care in the emergency department, surgical setting, labor room, and delivery room. Finally, problems associated with nursing intervention predominated in the operating room and the newborn nursery setting. The frequency of nursing malpractice problems and the corresponding departures from the standard of care by clinical setting are presented in Table 3.19.

MECHANISMS OF INJURY

Inadequate communication was the mechanism of injury responsible for the greatest number of adverse events. Failure by the nurse to communicate nursing assessment data to the physician caused 22.22% (166 of 747) of the negative outcomes. Inadequate communication of an existing unresolved patient problem or of a new patient problem prior to discharge from the hospital accounted for 4.41% (33 of 747) of the adverse nursing care outcomes.

Medication errors caused 139 or 18.57% of the nursing-care-related negative outcomes. Specifically, mechanisms of injury included administration of the wrong dose of a medication or intravenous infusion solution (38; 5.08%), incorrect parenteral medication administration technique (35; 4.68%), failure to assess medication toxicity or allergy status (28; 3.74%), administration of the wrong medication or intravenous infusion solution (27; 3.61%), failure to administer medication(s) (10; 1.33%), and administration of medication at the wrong time (1; 0.13%).

Inadequate nursing assessment was the mechanism of injury to 100 patients, representing 13.38% of the database, and inadequate execution of nursing treatments or procedures was responsible for 91 (12.18%) of the adverse outcomes. Less common mechanisms of injury are found in Table 3.20, which summarizes all mechanisms of injury involved in adverse patient outcomes.

The dominant mechanism of injury in three clinical settings was inadequate communication. Failure to communicate nursing assessment

TABLE 3.18 Frequency of Nursing Care Problems and Associated
Departures From the Standard of Care

Problem Area	Departure From the Standard of Care	Adverse Outcome (N = 747)	
		No.	%
Communication	Failure to inform the physician of a change in the patient's condition or of abnormal assessment data	203	27.17
Medication administration	Failure to administer medication(s) properly	140	18.74
Nursing intervention	Failure to perform a nursing procedure or treatment properly	108	14.45
Nursing assessment	Failure to assess the patient systematically	104	13.92
Environmental safety	Failure to provide a safe environment	94	12.58
Inadequate physician care	Failure to obtain help for a patient not receiving adequate care from a physician	53	7.09
Equipment and products	Failure to use equipment/products properly	31	4.14
Nosocomial infection	Failure to prevent infection	14	1.87

data to the physician was the most common mechanism of injury in the surgical setting and labor room; the inadequate communication of a new or existing patient problem prior to discharge was the most common mechanism of injury in the emergency department. In the operating room, an inadequate or absent sponge and/or instrument count was the most common mechanism of injury.

Medication administration error dominated as the mechanism of injury in the medical as well as the pediatric setting. In the psychiatric setting as well as the recovery room, inadequate patient assessment problems were commonly responsible for adverse incidents.

The major mechanism of injury in the newborn nursery, on the other hand, was failure by the nurse to execute a nursing treatment or procedure properly. In the delivery room, both inadequate communication of assessment data and failure to execute a nursing treatment and/or procedure properly were responsible for the majority of nursing-care-related injuries. Table 3.21 presents a summary of all mechanisms of injury by clinical setting.

TABLE 3.19 Nursing Care Problem Areas and Frequency of Departures From the Standard of Care, by Clinical Setting

Problem Area	Departure From the Standard of Care	No. of Cases, by Clinical Setting									
		Psych.	Emer.	Med.	Surg.	Ped.	Labor	Deliv.	Nurs.	Oper.	Recov.
Nursing assessment	Failure to assess the patient systematically	13	7	7	18	5	22	0	9	4	19
Environmental safety	Failure to provide a safe environment for the patient	7	9	47	20	0	2	0	9	0	0
Medication administration	Failure to administer medication(s) properly	8	7	50	19	18	23	0	8	1	6
Nursing intervention	Failure to perform a nursing treatment or procedure properly	2	2	11	31	8	6	6	13	24	5
Communication	Failure to inform the physician of abnormal assessment data or of a change in the patient's condition	5	42	23	43	15	52	11	7	0	5
Inadequate physician care	Failure to obtain help for a patient not receiving adequate care from a physician	0	3	5	10	1	23	1	2	6	2
Nosocomial infection	Failure to prevent infection	0	0	4	9	0	0	0	1	0	0
Equipment and products	Failure to use equipment and/or products properly	0	0	1	5	6	0	3	3	9	4

NOTE: Psych. = psychiatric, Emer. = emergency room, Med. = medical, Surg. = surgical, Ped. = pediatric, Labor = labor room, Deliv. = delivery room, Nurs. = newborn nursery, Oper. = operating room, Recov. = recovery room.

TABLE 3.20 Mechanisms of Injury Responsible for Adverse
Nursing-Care-Related Adverse Outcomes

	Adverse Outcome (N = 747)	
Mechanism of Injury	%	No.
Wrong dose of medication or intravenous infusion solution	5.08	38
Wrong medication or intravenous infusion solution	3.61	27
Medication toxicity or allergy status not monitored or assessed	3.74	28
Wrong time of medication administration	0.13	1
Incorrect parenteral medication administration technique	4.68	35
Medication(s) not administered	1.33	10
Inadequate assessment of the patient	13.38	100
Inadequate execution of the physician's orders	0.40	3
Inadequate restraint application/maintenance	2.54	19
Inadequate communication of nursing assessment data to the physician	22.22	166
Inadequate or delayed cardiopulmonary resuscitation	0.26	2
Inadequate communication of a patient problem prior to discharge	4.41	33
Fall	9.23	69
Inadequate care by the physician	7.09	53
Incorrect/inadequate execution of a nursing treatment and/or procedure	12.18	91
Inadequate patient supervision	0.66	5
Inadequate or absent sponge and/or instrument count	3.21	24
Delay in transfer to appropriate unit or facility	0.66	5
Improper use of equipment and/or products	4.14	31
Inadequate identification of the patient	0.93	7

ANALYSIS OF SPECIFIC
NURSING CARE PROBLEM AREAS

Communication Negligence

Communication negligence was responsible for 27.17% (203 of 747) of the adverse events in the database. Failure to inform the physician of a change in the patient's condition or of abnormal assessment data caused 18.11% of the patient injuries, 42.98% of the fetal/newborn injuries, 28.12% of the patient deaths, and 81.48% of the fetal/newborn deaths. The majority, or 67.30%, of the communication problems occurred in three clinical settings: the labor room

(25.60%), surgical setting (21.10%), and emergency department (20.60%).

Sixty-nine percent of the patients in this subgroup were female, and 31.00% were male (excluding fetal/newborn cases). The mean age was 28.75 years, and the median was 29.50 years (excluding fetal/newborn cases). The majority of these patients presented to the hospital because of pregnancy/childbirth (38.42%), a surgical problem (28.07%), or a medical problem (27.09%). Newborn infants accounted for 3.44% of the admissions in this subgroup, and psychiatric problems were responsible for 2.95%.

Nursing-care-related injuries because of communication negligence were varied. However, the most common adverse events were death (39.40%) and brain damage (34.97%). Other nursing-care-related injuries included paralysis (hemiplegia, paraplegia, quadriplegia; 8.37%), amputation (5.91%), peripheral nerve damage (3.94%), other neurological injury (2.95%), newborn Erb's palsy (0.98%), small bowel necrosis (0.98%), sensory loss (0.98%), infection (0.98%), and pneumonia (0.49%).

The mechanism of injury common to all cases in this subgroup was inadequate communication by the nurse with the physician. Specifically, there was failure to inform the physician of fetal distress (26.60%), lack of improvement in a patient's condition prior to discharge from the hospital (19.70%), a neurological status change (16.25%), a respiratory status change (10.83%), a neurovascular status change (7.88%), a circulatory status change (6.40%), obstetrical delivery status (3.44%), a gastrointestinal status change (2.95%), a high-risk delivery status (1.97%), a psychosocial status change (1.47%), abnormal maternal assessment (0.98%), symptoms of infection (0.98%), or a genitourinary status change (0.49%).

The largest mean malpractice payments that were made because of communication negligence were in the newborn nursery and labor room settings. The mean payments, respectively, were $5,530,000 and $4,340,826. Malpractice payment data for communication negligence by clinical setting are summarized in Table 3.22.

Medication Administration Negligence

Medication administration negligence caused 18.74% (140) of the adverse events in the database. Failure to administer medication(s) properly accounted for 20.04% of the patient injuries, 13.15% of the

TABLE 3.21 Mechanisms of Injury Responsible for Nursing-Care-Related Adverse Outcomes, by Clinical Setting

Mechanism of Injury	No. of Cases, by Clinical Setting									
	Psych.	Emer.	Med.	Surg.	Ped.	Labor	Deliv.	Nurs.	Oper	Recov.
Wrong dose of medication or intravenous infusion solution	3	1	16	5	6	3	0	2	1	1
Wrong medication or intravenous infusion solution	3	1	8	2	5	1	0	5	0	2
Medication toxicity or allergy status not monitored or assessed	2	2	2	2	3	15	0	0	0	2
Wrong time of medication administration	0	0	0	1	0	0	0	0	0	0
Incorrect parenteral medication administration technique	0	3	17	7	4	2	0	1	0	1
Medications not administered	0	0	6	2	0	2	0	0	0	0
Inadequate patient assessment	13	7	7	18	5	22	0	9	0	19
Inadequate execution of the physician's orders	1	0	1	0	0	0	0	1	0	0
Inadequate restraint application or maintenance	4	0	5	10	0	0	0	0	0	0
Inadequate communication of nursing assessment data to the physician	5	9	23	43	15	52	7	7	0	5

fetal/newborn injuries, and 21.87% of the patient deaths. In terms of clinical setting, most of the medication administration problems (35.70%) occurred in the medical setting.

Sixty percent of the patients in this subgroup were female, and 40% were male (excluding fetal/newborn cases). The mean age of patients was 34.75, and the median was 37.00 (excluding fetal/newborn cases). The most frequent presenting problems in this group were medical (46.42%) and surgical (25.71%). However, other reasons for hospital

TABLE 3.21 *Continued*

Mechanism of Injury	No. of Cases, by Clinical Setting									
	Psych.	Emer.	Med.	Surg.	Ped.	Labor	Deliv.	Nurs.	Oper.	Recov.
Inadequate or delayed cardiopulmonary resuscitation	0	1	0	0	0	0	0	1	0	0
Inadequate communication of a patient problem prior to discharge	0	33	0	0	0	0	0	0	0	0
Fall	0	9	41	19	0	0	0	0	0	0
Inadequate care by the physician	0	3	5	10	1	23	1	2	6	2
Inadequate or incorrect execution of a nursing treatment or procedure	3	1	12	30	8	6	7	15	4	5
Inadequate patient supervision	1	0	4	0	0	0	0	0	0	0
Inadequate or absent sponge/instrument count	0	0	0	0	0	0	3	0	21	0
Delay in transfer to appropriate facility or unit	0	0	0	0	0	2	0	3	0	0
Improper use of equipment or products	0	0	1	6	6	0	3	3	8	4
Inadequate identification of the patient	0	0	0	0	0	0	0	3	4	0

NOTE: Psych. = psychiatric, Emer. = emergency room, Med. = medical, Surg. = surgical, Ped. = pediatric, Labor = labor room, Deliv. = delivery room, Nurs. = newborn nursery, Oper. = operating room, Recov. = recovery room.

admission included pregnancy/childbirth (16.42%), newborn status (5.71%), and psychiatric problems (5.71%).

Injuries due to nursing negligence in the subgroup were diverse. The majority of adverse outcomes, however, were death (30.00%) and brain damage (34.28%). Other nursing-care-related injuries included peripheral nerve damage (11.42%), chemical burns or tissue necrosis (10.00%), amputation (3.57%), sensory loss (2.85%), respiratory system damage (1.42%), paralysis (paraplegia or hemiplegia; 1.42%), emotional distress (1.42%), uterine rupture (0.71%), cerebrovascular

accident (0.71%), infection (0.71%), renal failure (0.71%), and gastrointestinal hemorrhage (0.71%).

The majority of medication-related negative outcomes were due to
three mechanisms of injury: (a) administration of the wrong dose of a
medication or intravenous infusion solution (28.57%), (b) incorrect
parenteral medication administration technique (24.28%), and (c)
administration of a medication when contraindicated (22.14%). Other
mechanisms of injury related to medication administration negligence
causing harm to the patient were administration of the wrong medication or intravenous infusion solution (16.42%), failure to administer
medication(s) (7.85%), and administration of medication at the wrong
time (0.71%).

The largest mean malpractice payment in this subgroup for medication administration negligence was $3,746,565. This payment was
made in the labor room setting. Malpractice payment data for medication administration negligence are summarized by clinical setting in
Table 3.23.

Nursing Intervention Negligence

Nursing intervention negligence was responsible for 14.45% (108
of 747) of the adverse events in the database. Failure to perform a
nursing treatment or procedure properly caused 20.53% of the patient
injuries, 5.26% of the fetal/newborn injuries, 7.81% of the patient
deaths, and 7.40% of the fetal/newborn deaths. Slightly over half of
the nursing intervention problems occurred in the surgical setting
(28.70%) and the operating room setting (22.20%).

Fifty-seven percent of the patients in this subgroup were female, and
43% were male (excluding fetal/newborn cases). The mean and median ages of patients respectively were 33.00 and 36.00 years (excluding fetal/newborn cases). Patients in this subgroup presented to
the hospital with surgical problems (60.18%), medical problems
(14.81%), psychiatric problems (1.85%), and pregnancy/childbirth
(11.11%). Newborns made up 12.03% of the admissions.

Nursing intervention negligence led to a number of adverse outcomes, including the need for additional surgery (21.29%); brain
damage (19.44%); death (13.88%); emotional distress (6.48%); decubitus ulcer (6.48%); musculoskeletal system injury (5.55%); peripheral nerve injury (4.62%); perforated bladder (3.70%); other genitourinary system damage (3.70%); injury associated with a tube, drain,

TABLE 3.22 Malpractice Payments Involving Communication Negligence, by Clinical Setting

Clinical Setting	Communication Negligence Payments (N = 203)			
	No. (%)	Range ($)	Mean ($)	Median ($)
Psychiatric	5 (2.40)	755,000 to 3,610,000	1,352,600	900,000
Emergency dept.	42 (20.60)	4,000 to 16,500,000	1,764,286	862,500
Medical	23 (11.30)	75,000 to 10,000,000	1,498,260	900,000
Surgical	43 (21.10)	20,000 to 15,000,000	1,684,721	700,000
Pediatric	15 (7.30)	200,000 to 9,000,000	2,188,000	1,100,000
Labor room	52 (25.60)	3,000 to 72,650,000	4,340,826	1,665,000
Delivery room	11 (5.40)	220,000 to 12,500,000	3,629,000	2,100,000
Newborn nursery	7 (3.40)	500,000 to 19,190,000	5,530,000	3,650,000
Operating room	0 (0.00)	0	0	0
Recovery room	5 (2.40)	367,000 to 9,000,000	3,473,400	1,000,000

TABLE 3.23 Malpractice Payments Involving Medication Administration Negligence, by Clinical Setting

Clinical Setting	Medication Administration Negligence Payments (N = 140)			
	No. (%)	Range ($)	Mean ($)	Median ($)
Psychiatric	8 (5.70)	412,000 to 12,300,000	2,880,625	675,000
Emergency dept.	7 (5.00)	3,000 to 11,150,000	2,594,143	740,000
Medical	50 (35.70)	12,000 to 11,000,000	831,780	399,000
Surgical	19 (13.50)	65,000 to 3,580,000	874,105	500,000
Pediatric	18 (12.80)	1,000 to 6,500,000	1,360,777	980,000
Labor room	23 (16.40)	150,000 to 22,000,000	3,746,565	1,840,000
Delivery room	0 (0.00)	0	0	0
Newborn nursery	8 (5.70)	90,000 to 2,340,000	676,375	417,500
Operating room	1 (0.70)	1,930,000	1,930,000	1,930,000
Recovery room	6 (4.20)	250,000 to 1,860,000	782,666	455,000

and/or catheter (2.77%); paralysis (paraplegia or quadriplegia; 2.77%); infection (1.85%); respiratory system damage (1.85%); amputation (1.85%); stillbirth (1.85%); sensory loss (0.92%); and newborn Erb's palsy (0.92%).

Mechanisms of injury in this subgroup were quite varied because nurses are responsible for executing a large number of different dependent and independent nursing interventions. The most common mechanisms of injury, however, were inadequate insertion, management, or removal of a tube, drain, or catheter (23.14%) and an incorrect or absent sponge/instrument count (22.22%). Other mechanisms of injury included inadequate execution of independent nursing treatments (19.40%), improper airway management (9.25%), improper positioning or immobilization (9.25%), inadequate skin care (5.50%), improper application of pressure (3.70%), failure to execute a physician's order (2.77%), incorrect patient identification procedure (2.77%), and delay in cardiopulmonary resuscitation (1.85%).

The largest mean malpractice payment of $6,542,923 for nursing intervention negligence was in the newborn nursery setting. Malpractice payments for failure to perform a nursing treatment or procedure properly are summarized in Table 3.24.

Nursing Assessment Negligence

Nursing assessment negligence was responsible for 13.92% (104 of 747) of the adverse events in the database. Failure to assess the patient systematically caused 18.42% of the fetal/newborn injuries, 8.93% of the patient injuries, and 23.95% of the patient deaths. The majority, or 56.60%, of the nursing assessment negligence cases occurred in three clinical settings: the labor room (21.10%), recovery room (18.20%), and surgical setting (17.30%).

Sixty-three percent of the patients in this subgroup were female, and the remaining 37.00% were male (excluding fetal/newborn cases). The mean and median ages respectively were 31.50 and 32.00 years (excluding fetal/newborn cases). Presenting problems or reasons for hospital admission were related to surgical problems (41.34%), pregnancy/childbirth (25.00%), medical problems (12.50%), psychiatric problems (12.50%), and newborn status (8.65%).

The most common adverse outcomes due to nursing assessment negligence were death (43.26%) and brain damage (41.34%). Other nursing-care-related injuries due to failure to assess the patient systematically included multiple trauma (5.76%), surgery on the wrong body part (3.84%), emotional distress (1.92%), dislocated teeth (0.96%), uterine rupture (0.96%), amputation (0.96%), and infection (0.96%).

The mechanism of injury for all of the cases in this subgroup was inadequate systematic assessment. Specifically, there was failure to assess respiratory status (19.23%), fetal status (19.23%), circulatory status (16.34%), vital signs (15.38%), psychosocial status (12.50%), neurological status (8.65%), body part identity (3.84%), blood sugar level (2.88%), neurovascular status (0.96%), and wound status (0.96%).

The two largest mean payments for failure to provide systematic nursing assessment occurred in the newborn nursery ($2,493,888) and

TABLE 3.24 Malpractice Payments Involving Nursing Intervention Negligence, by Clinical Setting

Clinical Setting	Nursing Intervention Negligence Payments (N = 108)			
	No. (%)	Range ($)	Mean ($)	Median ($)
Psychiatric	2 (1.80)	35,000 to 2,000,000	1,017,500	1,017,500
Emergency dept.	2 (1.80)	15,000 to 8,636,733	4,318,366	4,318,366
Medical	11 (10.10)	75,000 to 1,250,000	536,000	360,000
Surgical	31 (28.70)	10,000 to 16,500,000	1,315,258	450,000
Pediatric	8 (7.40)	130,000 to 10,350,000	3,420,000	1,815,000
Labor room	6 (5.50)	200,000 to 7,500,000	2,250,000	1,037,500
Delivery room	6 (5.50)	50,000 to 1,240,000	449,500	168,500
Newborn nursery	13 (12.00)	22,000 to 56,000,000	6,542,923	500,000
Operating room	24 (22.20)	20 to 935,000	187,583	105,000
Recovery room	5 (4.60)	268,000 to 9,130,000	2,200,000	487,000

TABLE 3.25 Malpractice Payments Involving Nursing Assessment Negligence, by Clinical Setting

Clinical Setting	Nursing Assessment Negligence Payments (N = 104)			
	No. (%)	Range ($)	Mean ($)	Median ($)
Psychiatric	13 (12.50)	17,000 to 3,000,000	892,462	540,000
Emergency dept.	7 (6.70)	40,000 to 2,000,000	806,571	475,035
Medical	7 (6.70)	100,000 to 3,000,000	1,151,714	1,200,000
Surgical	18 (17.30)	112,000 to 4,090,000	917,444	826,000
Pediatric	5 (4.80)	75,000 to 6,875,000	1,375,000	800,000
Labor room	22 (21.10)	55,000 to 8,440,000	2,061,545	1,860,000
Delivery room	0 (0.00)	0	0	0
Newborn nursery	9 (8.60)	375,000 to 5,640,000	2,493,888	1,500,000
Operating room	4 (3.80)	25,000 to 230,000	115,000	102,500
Recovery room	19 (18.20)	150,000 to 4,000,000	1,540,578	1,200,000

labor room setting ($2,061,545). Malpractice payment data for nursing assessment negligence are summarized by clinical setting in Table 3.25.

Environmental Safety Negligence

Environmental safety negligence was responsible for 12.58% (94 of 747) of the adverse events in the database. Failure to provide a safe environment caused 20.53% of the patient injuries, 1.75% of the fetal/newborn injuries, and 3.64% of the patient deaths. Half of the environmental safety negligence cases occurred in the medical unit setting.

Sixty-five percent of the patients in this subgroup were female, and the remaining 35.00% were male (excluding fetal/newborn cases). The mean age of patients was 50.00 years, with a median of 59.00 years (excluding fetal/newborn cases). Reasons for admission to the hospital included medical problems (59.57%), surgical problems (21.27%), newborn status (9.57%), psychosocial problems (7.44%), and pregnancy/childbirth (2.12%).

The most frequent injury due to failure by the nurse to provide a safe environment and prevent avoidable injury was a fracture, sprain, and/or dislocation (65.95%). Other adverse events caused by environmental safety negligence included brain damage (10.63%), death (5.31%), amputation of a digit or limb (5.31%), sensory loss (3.19%), paraplegia or triplegia (2.12%), peripheral nerve damage (2.12%), rape (2.12%), burn (2.12%), and infection (1.06%).

The predominant mechanism of injury to patients in this subgroup was a fall (73.40%). Other environmental-safety-related mechanisms of injury included inadequate or inappropriate restraint application (6.38%), inappropriate or delayed transfer to a needed facility or unit (6.38%), hot liquid spill or other burn (4.25%), dropped baby (4.25%), elopement (2.12%), finger amputated by door closing (1.06%), fingers amputated due to constricting tape application (1.06%), and finger amputated by careless use of scissors (1.06%).

Mean malpractice payments in the labor room ($5,345,000) and newborn nursery ($1,341,111) were large because of the severe nature of the adverse outcomes. Mean payments in the other clinical settings, especially in the emergency department, were relatively low because most nursing-care-related injuries in this subgroup involved a fall and were not severe. Table 3.26 contains malpractice payment data for environmental safety negligence by clinical setting.

Nursing Negligence Associated With Inadequate Care by the Physician

Nursing negligence associated with inadequate care by the physician was responsible for 7.09% (53 of 747) of the adverse events in the database. Failure to obtain help for a patient not receiving adequate care from a physician caused 16.66% of the fetal/newborn injuries, 3.86% of the patient injuries, 11.11% of the fetal/newborn deaths, and 9.37% of the patient deaths. The greatest number (43.30%) of incidents due to nursing negligence in relation to inadequate care by the physician occurred in the labor room setting.

TABLE 3.26 Malpractice Payments Involving Environmental Safety
Negligence, by Clinical Setting

| Clinical Setting | Environmental Safety Negligence Payments (N = 94) | | | |
	No. (%)	Range ($)	Mean ($)	Median ($)
Psychiatric	7 (7.40)	20,000 to 1,850,000	472,143	300,000
Emergency dept.	9 (9.50)	3,000 to 510,000	111,333	26,000
Medical	47 (50.00)	1,000 to 1,600,000	183,553	68,000
Surgical	20 (21.20)	2,000 to 4,700,000	514,700	210,000
Pediatric	0 (0.00)	0	0	0
Labor room	2 (2.10)	450,000 to 10,240,000	5,345,000	5,345,000
Delivery room	0 (0.00)	0	0	0
Newborn nursery	9 (9.50)	50,000 to 2,900,000	1,341,111	1,350,000
Operating room	0 (0.00)	0	0	0
Recovery room	0 (0.00)	0	0	0

Sixty-three percent of the patients in this subgroup were female, and
37.00% were male (excluding fetal/newborn cases). Mean and median
ages respectively were 37.37 and 40.00 years (excluding fetal/newborn
cases). Reasons for admission to the hospital were pregnancy/childbirth
(45.28%), surgical problems (39.62%), medical problems (11.32%),
and newborn status (3.77%).

Adverse outcomes due to nursing negligence in relation to inadequate care by the physician were severe. The majority of them involved
either death (33.96%) or brain damage (47.16%). Other nursing-care-
related injuries associated with failure by the nurse to obtain help for
a patient not receiving adequate care by the physician were need for
additional surgery (5.66%), infection (5.66%), peripheral nerve damage (1.88%), amputation (1.88%), cerebrovascular accident (1.88%),
and quadriplegia (1.88%).

Two mechanisms of injury were responsible for all of the nursing-
care-related adverse outcomes in this subgroup. In 69.81% of the
cases, there was failure by the physician to treat a patient when
problems were reported to him or her by the nurse. In the remaining
30.18% of the cases, the physician did not respond to the nurse's
telephone calls concerning the condition of a patient. In both situations, the nurse was negligent by failing to secure the care by a
physician that the patient needed.

Payment data for nursing negligence in relation to inadequate care
by the physician are summarized by clinical setting in Table 3.27. The
largest mean malpractice payments involving inadequate care by the

physician occurred in the emergency department ($4,733,333) and the labor room ($4,640,043).

Equipment and Product Negligence

Negligent use of equipment and/or products by the nurse was responsible for 4.14% (31 of 747) of the adverse events in the database. Failure to use equipment and/or products properly caused 5.31% of the patient injuries, 1.75% of the fetal/newborn injuries, and 3.64% of the patient deaths. Most of the equipment and product negligence occurred in the operating room (29.00%), the pediatric setting (19.30%), and the surgical setting (16.10%).

Patients in this subgroup were evenly divided by gender (excluding fetal/newborn cases). The mean age was 34.16 years, and the median was 37.50 years (excluding fetal/newborn cases). Hospital admissions in the subgroup were related to surgical problems (67.74%), medical problems (12.90%), pregnancy/childbirth (9.67%), and newborn status (9.67%).

Negligent use of equipment and/or products by the nurse resulted in devastating patient outcomes. The majority of the adverse events were either death (25.80%) or brain damage (29.03%). Other nursing-care-related injuries included burns (29.03%), peripheral nerve injury (6.45%), lumbar injury (6.45%), and cerebrovascular accident (3.22%).

Mechanisms of injury were varied. However, the most common one was failure to activate a monitor alarm (22.58%). Other equipment and/or product mechanisms of injury included the use of products in conflict with the manufacturer's intended purpose (16.20%); application of a heating pad to a child (12.90%); improper use of electrocautery equipment or use of malfunctioning electrocautery equipment (12.90%); failure to secure required equipment (6.45%); nonfunctional monitor (6.45%); inadequate maintenance of surgical instruments, causing instrument failure (6.45%); failure to provide proper lighting (3.22%); use of equipment in conflict with the manufacturer's intended purpose (3.22%); insertion of cardiac monitor leads into a standard wall electrical outlet (3.22%); securing and providing the wrong laser tip to the surgeon (3.22%); and failure to respond to monitor alarms (3.22%).

Malpractice payment data related to negligent use of equipment and products are summarized by clinical setting in Table 3.28. The largest

TABLE 3.27 Malpractice Payments for Nursing Negligence in Relation to Inadequate Care by the Physician, by Clinical Setting

Clinical Setting	Payments for Inadequate Care by the Physician and Associated Nursing Negligence (N = 53)			
	No. (%)	Range ($)	Mean ($)	Median ($)
Psychiatric	0 (0.00)	0	0	0
Emergency dept.	3 (5.60)	1,200,000 to 8,000,000	4,733,333	5,000,000
Medical	5 (9.40)	460,000 to 2,930,000	1,210,800	1,050,000
Surgical	10 (18.80)	130,000 to 25,250,000	3,387,900	1,125,000
Pediatric	1 (1.80)	600,000	600,000	600,000
Labor room	23 (43.30)	200,000 to 49,200,000	4,640,043	1,500,000
Delivery room	1 (1.80)	3,500,000	3,500,000	3,500,000
Newborn nursery	2 (3.70)	850,000 to 6,620,000	3,735,000	3,735,000
Operating room	6 (11.30)	55,000 to 3,000,000	1,202,500	680,000
Recovery room	2 (3.70)	250,000 to 2,000,000	1,125,000	1,125,000

TABLE 3.28 Malpractice Payments Involving Equipment and Product Negligence, by Clinical Setting

Clinical Setting	Equipment and Product Negligence Payments (N = 31)			
	No. (%)	Range ($)	Mean ($)	Median ($)
Psychiatric	0 (0.00)	0	0	0
Emergency dept.	0 (0.00)	0	0	0
Medical	1 (3.20)	760,000	760,000	760,000
Surgical	5 (16.10)	125,000 to 6,500,000	1,621,000	292,000
Pediatric	6 (19.30)	104,000 to 8,100,000	1,777,933	911,000
Labor room	0 (0.00)	0	0	0
Delivery room	3 (9.60)	66,000 to 49,300,000	18,120,000	4,400,000
Newborn nursery	3 (9.60)	35,000 to 1,270,000	551,666	350,000
Operating room	9 (29.00)	45,000 to 2,890,000	870,000	701,000
Recovery room	4 (12.90)	500,000 to 12,000,000	5,722,500	5,195,000

mean payment ($18,120,000) for equipment and product negligence was in the delivery room.

Nosocomial Infection

Nosocomial infection due to nursing negligence was responsible for 1.87% (14 of 747) of the adverse events in the database. Failure to control or prevent infection caused 2.65% of the patient injuries and 1.56% of the patient deaths. Nursing-care-related nosocomial infections occurred in the surgical setting (64.20%), the medical setting (28.50%), and the newborn nursery (7.10%).

Excluding newborns, 54.00% of the patients in this subgroup were male, and 46.00% were female. The mean and median ages of patients were 49.00 and 48.00 years, respectively. Hospital admission was related to surgical intervention (64.28%), medical intervention (21.42%), psychiatric intervention (7.14%), and newborn status (7.14%).

Nursing-care-related adverse outcomes due to the development of a nosocomial infection were wound infection (57.14%), death (21.42%), and metastatic infection (21.42%). Causes of nosocomial infection included inadequate observation of a surgical wound or failure to report symptoms of wound infection (42.85%), inadequate care of the intravenous infusion site (35.71%), inadequate care of a surgical wound (14.28%), and poor hand-washing technique (7.14%).

The largest mean payment for a hospital-acquired infection occurred in the medical setting and was $1,845,000. Malpractice payments involving nosocomial infection are summarized in Table 3.29.

DOCUMENTATION PROBLEMS

Documentation problems occurred in the majority of the nursing malpractice cases. Documentation of nursing care in the medical record was described as inadequate, incomplete, or absent in 61.98% (463 of 747) of the cases. Reference to alteration of the medical record was made in 46.98% (351 of 747) of the cases examined. All or part of a medical record was referred to as missing in 29.98% (224 of 747) of the cases. Notably, the parts of the medical record missing most frequently (91.96%; 206 of 224) dealt with the aspects of nursing care at issue in the litigation.

MALPRACTICE PAYMENTS

Malpractice payments to the patient in the 747 cases were substantial. Payment for a nursing-care-related adverse outcome ranged from $20 to $72,650,000. The mean payment was $2,170,313, and the median was $825,000. Table 3.30 summarizes malpractice payment data by adverse outcome.

Malpractice payments in cases of patient injury (excluding fetal/newborn injury) were larger than in cases of death. The mean payment for patient injury (414 of 747) was $1,889,125, compared to $971,111 for patient death (192 of 747). The difference is due to

TABLE 3.29   Malpractice Payments Involving Nosocomial Infection, by
             Clinical Setting

Clinical Setting	Nosocomial Infection Payments (N = 14)			
	No. (%)	Range ($)	Mean ($)	Median ($)
Psychiatric	0 (0.00)	0	0	0
Emergency dept.	0 (0.00)	0	0	0
Medical	4 (28.50)	600,000 to 3,500,000	1,845,000	1,640,000
Surgical	9 (64.20)	130,000 to 6,560,000	1,329,556	377,000
Pediatric	0 (0.00)	0	0	0
Labor room	0 (0.00)	0	0	0
Delivery room	0 (0.00)	0	0	0
Newborn nursery	1 (7.10)	1,000,000	1,000,000	1,000,000
Operating room	0 (0.00)	0	0	0
Recovery room	0 (0.00)	0	0	0

TABLE 3.30   Malpractice Payments, by Death and Injury

Adverse Outcome	Malpractice Payments			
	No. (%)	Range ($)	Mean ($)	Median ($)
Death (patient)	192 (25.70)	4,000 to 11,000,000	971,111	724,000
Death (fetal/ newborn)	27 (3.61)	3,000 to 3,000,000	741,285	300,000
Injury (patient)	414 (55.43)	20 to 56,000,000	1,889,125	627,500
Injury (fetal/ newborn)	114 (15.26)	50,000 to 72,650,000	4,735,298	2,145,000
All deaths and injuries	747 (100.00)	20 to 72,650,000	2,170,313	825,000

the fact that many injuries were severe and payment was made for lifelong assistance related to the activities of daily living.

Malpractice payments for fetal/newborn injury (114 of 747) were greater than those for fetal/newborn death (27 of 747). The mean payment for fetal/newborn injury was $4,735,298 compared to that of $741,285 for fetal/newborn death. Nursing negligence caused brain damage in a large number of cases, with the consequent need for lifelong assistance related to activities of daily living.

The greatest number of malpractice payments were made for communication negligence because the nurse failed to inform the physician of abnormal assessment data or of a change in the patient's condition. Equipment and product negligence was responsible for the largest mean payment ($4,203,299). Table 3.31 presents malpractice payment data by nursing care problem area.

The largest median payment for patient injury (excluding pregnancy/childbirth-associated fetal/newborn cases) occurred in the recovery room setting. Table 3.32 summarizes malpractice payment data for patient injury by clinical setting.

The operating room was the site of the largest median payment in cases of patient death. Malpractice payments by clinical setting for patient deaths are presented in Table 3.33.

Fetal/newborn deaths and injuries associated with pregnancy/childbirth occurred in three clinical settings: the emergency department, labor room, and delivery room. Payment data by clinical setting are summarized in Tables 3.34 and 3.35.

The majority of the 747 payments were distributed in two groups: $20 through $800,000 (396; 52.98%) and $800,001 through $10,000,000 (327; 43.75%). Of the remaining payments, 19, or 2.52%, were between $10,000,001 and $26,000,000, and 5, or 0.66%, were between $26,000,001 and $75,000,000. The distribution of malpractice payments for the database is presented in Table 3.36.

In cases of injury (528 out of 747), 49.98% of the malpractice payments (264 cases) were between $20 and $800,000, and 45.80% (242 cases) were between $800,001 and $10,000,000 (Table 3.37).

In cases of death (219 of 747), 60.70% (133) of the payments were between $1,000 and $800,000, and 36.51% (80) were between $800,000 and $4,000,000 (Table 3.38).

When all adverse events in the database are combined, the largest mean malpractice payments are shown to occur in three clinical settings: the delivery room ($4,754,952), labor room ($3,812,023), and newborn nursery ($3,342,673). Table 3.39 summarizes all malpractice payments by clinical setting.

SUMMARY

Nursing negligence in the hospital setting caused or contributed to patient injury in 70.68% (528) of the 747 malpractice cases of the database. Nursing care that fell below accepted standards caused a death in the remaining 29.31% (219 of 747) of the cases. Inadequate communication was the most common nursing care problem. Failure to inform the physician of a change in the patient's condition or of abnormal nursing assessment data was the departure from the standard of care responsible for the greatest number of injuries as well as

TABLE 3.31 Malpractice Payments, by Nursing Care Problem Area

| Problem Area | Malpractice Payments (N = 747) | | | |
	No. (%)	Range ($)	Mean ($)	Median ($)
Nursing assessment	104 (13.90)	17,000 to 8,440,000	1,261,578	826,000
Environmental safety	94 (12.58)	1,000 to 10,240,000	1,327,973	255,000
Nursing intervention	108 (14.45)	20 to 56,000,000	2,223,713	493,500
Medication administration	140 (18.74)	1,000 to 22,000,000	1,741,892	675,000
Inadequate physician care	53 (7.09)	55,000 to 49,200,000	2,681,619	1,125,000
Communication	203 (27.17)	3,000 to 72,650,000	2,829,010	1,000,000
Infection	14 (1.87)	130,000 to 6,560,000	1,391,518	1,000,000
Equipment and products	31 (4.14)	35,000 to 49,300,000	4,203,299	760,000

TABLE 3.32 Malpractice Payments for Patient Injuries, by Clinical Setting

| Clinical Setting | Payments for Patient Injuries (N = 414)[a] | | | |
	No. (%)	Range ($)	Mean ($)	Median ($)
Psychiatric	21 (5.00)	20,000 to 12,300,000	1,728,095	755,000
Emergency dept.	34 (8.20)	3,000 to 16,000,000	2,264,206	471,000
Medical	95 (22.90)	1,000 to 10,000,000	639,232	200,000
Surgical	113 (27.20)	2,000 to 25,250,000	1,453,593	500,000
Pediatric	33 (7.90)	1,000 to 10,350,000	2,487,333	1,500,000
Labor room	8 (1.90)	150,000 to 8,000,000	2,175,125	1,150,000
Delivery room	5 (1.20)	66,000 to 1,240,000	518,200	215,000
Newborn nursery	44 (10.60)	22,000 to 56,000,000	3,877,227	1,300,000
Operating room	40 (9.60)	20 to 2,890,000	385,200	110,000
Recovery room	21 (5.00)	150,000 to 12,000,000	3,363,047	2,000,000

a. Excluding fetal/newborn.

TABLE 3.33 Malpractice Payments for Patient Deaths, by Clinical Setting

| Clinical Setting | Payments for Patient Deaths (N = 192)[a] | | | |
	No. (%)	Range ($)	Mean ($)	Median ($)
Psychiatric	14 (7.20)	17,000 to 4,000,000	747,143	486,500
Emergency dept.	26 (13.50)	4,000 to 4,500,000	1,016,115	725,500
Medical	53 (27.60)	75,000 to 11,000,000	988,302	690,000
Surgical	42 (21.80)	20,000 to 10,000,000	1,031,571	750,000
Pediatric	20 (10.40)	130,000 to 7,000,000	1,087,150	850,000
Labor room	5 (2.60)	500,000 to 2,2600,000	991,000	600,000
Delivery room	0 (0.00)	0	0	0
Newborn nursery	8 (4.10)	90,000 to 606,000	402,625	387,500
Operating room	4 (2.00)	935,000 to 3,000,000	1,633,750	1,300,000
Recovery room	20 (10.40)	180,000 to 2,200,000	842,350	723,000

a. Excluding fetal/newborn.

TABLE 3.34 Malpractice Payments for Fetal/Newborn Injuries, by Clinical Setting

Clinical Setting	No. (%)	Range ($)	Mean ($)	Median ($)
		Payments for Fetal/Newborn Injuries (N = 114)		
Psychiatric	0 (0.00)	0	0	0
Emergency dept.	5 (4.38)	500,000 to 5,820,000	2,954,000	2,000,000
Medical	0 (0.00)	0	0	0
Surgical	0 (0.00)	0	0	0
Pediatric	0 (0.00)	0	0	0
Labor room	94 (82.45)	55,000 to 72,650,000	4,834,361	2,145,000
Delivery room	15 (13.15)	50,000 to 49,271,000	6,417,583	2,700,000
Newborn nursery	0 (0.00)	0	0	0
Operating room	0 (0.00)	0	0	0
Recovery room	0 (0.00)	0	0	0

TABLE 3.35 Malpractice Payments for Fetal/Newborn Deaths, by Clinical Setting

Clinical Setting	No. (%)	Range ($)	Mean ($)	Median ($)
		Payments for Fetal/Newborn Deaths (N = 27)		
Psychiatric	0 (0.00)	0	0	0
Emergency dept.	5 (18.50)	160,000 to 2,610,000	718,000	300,000
Medical	0 (0.00)	0	0	0
Surgical	0 (0.00)	0	0	0
Pediatric	0 (0.00)	0	0	0
Labor room	21 (77.70)	3,000 to 3,000,000	505,857	200,000
Delivery room	1 (3.70)	1,000,000	1,000,000	1,000,000
Newborn nursery	0 (0.00)	0	0	0
Operating room	0 (0.00)	0	0	0
Recovery room	0 (0.00)	0	0	0

deaths. The highest percentage of deaths occurred in the recovery room setting, and the highest percentage of total injuries occurred in the delivery room.

The age of patients experiencing a nursing care adverse outcome ranged from fetal/newborn to 95 years. The mean age was 31.64, and the median was 34.00 years (maternal age used for computation of fetal/newborn cases). The majority of the patients were distributed in four age categories: fetal/newborn through 10 years (253; 33.86%), 21 through 30 years (87; 11.64%), 31 through 40 years (95; 12.71%), and 41 through 50 years (91; 12.18%). For all patients experiencing

TABLE 3.36 Distribution of Payments for All Adverse Outcomes of Nursing Care (N = 747)

Amount of Payments ($)	No. of Cases	% of Cases
20 to 50,000	63	8.43
50,001 to 100,000	51	6.82
100,001 to 400,000	173	23.15
400,001 to 600,000	63	8.43
600,001 to 800,000	46	6.15
800,001 to 1,000,000	64	8.56
1,000,001 to 2,000,000	130	17.40
2,000,001 to 4,000,000	77	10.30
4,000,001 to 6,000,000	32	4.28
6,000,001 to 8,000,000	13	1.74
8,000,001 to 10,000,000	11	1.47
10,000,001 to 12,000,000	9	1.20
12,000,001 to 16,000,000	4	0.53
16,000,001 to 20,000,000	4	0.53
20,000,001 to 26,000,000	2	0.26
26,000,001 to 75,000,000	5	0.66

TABLE 3.37 Distribution of Payments for Injury as an Adverse Outcome of Nursing Care (N = 528)

Amount of Payments ($)	No. of Cases	% of Cases
20 to 50,000	59	11.17
50,001 to 100,000	42	7.95
100,001 to 400,000	103	19.50
400,001 to 600,000	33	6.25
600,001 to 800,000	27	5.11
800,001 to 1,000,000	36	6.81
1,000,001 to 2,000,000	91	17.23
2,000,001 to 4,000,000	60	11.36
4,000,001 to 6,000,000	34	6.43
6,000,001 to 8,000,000	11	2.08
8,000,001 to 10,000,000	10	1.89
10,000,001 to 12,000,000	6	1.13
12,000,001 to 16,000,000	5	0.94
16,000,001 to 20,000,000	4	0.75
20,000,001 to 26,000,000	2	0.37
26,000,001 to 75,000,000	5	0.94

TABLE 3.38 Distribution of Payments for Death as an Adverse Outcome of Nursing Care (*N* = 219)

Amount of Payments ($)	No. of Cases	% of Cases
1,000 to 50,000	5	2.28
50,001 to 100,000	9	4.10
100,001 to 400,000	66	30.13
400,001 to 600,000	34	15.52
600,001 to 800,000	19	8.67
800,001 to 1,000,000	28	12.78
1,000,001 to 2,000,000	39	17.80
2,000,001 to 4,000,000	13	5.93
4,000,001 to 6,000,000	2	0.91
6,000,001 to 8,000,000	2	0.91
8,000,001 to 10,000,000	1	0.45
10,000,001 to 12,000,000	1	0.45
12,000,001 to 16,000,000	0	0.00
16,000,001 to 20,000,000	0	0.00
20,000,001 to 26,000,000	0	0.00
26,000,001 to 75,000,000	0	0.00

TABLE 3.39 Malpractice Payments for All Deaths and Injuries, by Clinical Setting

Clinical Setting	No. (%)	Range ($)	Mean ($)	Median ($)
	Payments for All Deaths and Injuries (*N* = 747)			
Psychiatric	35 (4.68)	17,000 to 12,300,000	1,335,714	650,000
Emergency dept.	70 (9.37)	3,000 to 16,000,000	1,739,457	625,000
Medical	148 (19.81)	1,000 to 11,000,000	769,000	322,500
Surgical	155 (20.74)	2,000 to 25,250,000	1,358,206	525,000
Pediatric	53 (7.09)	1,000 to 10,350,000	1,958,962	1,000,000
Labor room	128 (17.13)	3,000 to 72,650,000	3,812,023	1,715,000
Delivery room	21 (2.81)	50,000 to 49,271,000	4,754,952	1,240,000
Newborn nursery	52 (6.96)	22,000 to 56,000,000	3,342,673	1,000,000
Operating room	44 (5.89)	20 to 3,000,000	498,705	116,000
Recovery room	41 (5.48)	150,000 to 12,000,000	2,133,449	1,500,000

an adverse outcome of nursing care, the largest age distribution group was fetal/newborn through 10 years.

Of the 747 patients, 38.01% were male, and 61.98% were female. However, if one excludes the labor and delivery settings, where the entire population is female, then males make up 47.49% (284) of the patients experiencing a nursing care adverse outcome, and females account for 52.50% (314). For the total population, the largest percentage of male deaths (31.57%) and female deaths (28.08%) respectively occurred in the medical setting and surgical setting. In terms of injury, it was just the opposite. The largest percentage of male injuries (37.42%) occurred in the surgical setting, whereas for females (30.43%) it occurred in the medical setting.

The most common diagnosis or presenting problem associated with hospital admission was that of pregnancy and childbirth (178; 23.82%). Other frequent presenting problems of patients experiencing a nursing care adverse outcome were musculoskeletal problems (99; 13.25%) and gastrointestinal problems (90; 12.04%).

Adverse outcomes due to nursing negligence were notably severe. Death or brain damage occurred in 59.43% (444 of 747) of the patients. A communication problem was responsible for the majority of the negative outcomes (27.17%; 203). Thus the most common mechanism of injury was failure to inform the physician of a change in the patient's condition or of abnormal assessment data.

The majority of adverse events in the emergency department, surgical setting, labor room, and delivery room were in fact due to inadequate communication of nursing assessment data to the physician. However, inadequate nursing assessment was the most frequent cause of nursing-care-related adverse outcomes in the psychiatric setting and recovery room. Medication administration negligence was responsible for the majority of the negative incidents in the medical and pediatric setting, and problems associated with a nursing intervention caused most of the adverse events in the nursery and operating room.

Nursing negligence in the hospital setting was very costly. Payments for nursing-care-related adverse events ranged from $20 to $72,650,000. The mean payment was $2,170,313, and the median was $825,000. Mean payments for injury were greater than those for death. The large number of injuries involving brain damage with the need for lifelong assistance related to activities of daily living was the major reason for the difference in payments.

The largest mean payment associated with a nursing care problem area involved equipment and products. In terms of clinical setting, the labor room was responsible for the largest mean payment.

4

Nursing Malpractice
in the Emergency Department

The emergency department nurse is an integral and a vital member of the health care team. The nurse in this setting is uniquely positioned to assume an active role in patient care by providing immediate emergency health care intervention. Patients with complex problems, and the increasing complexities of patient care associated with technological innovations, place many demands on the emergency department nurse. Should the nurse in this setting depart from acceptable standards of nursing care, the effectiveness of the entire team diminishes or fails. This in turn may result in serious injury or death to the patient. Competent care, on the other hand, will save lives and assist in the reduction of hospital costs and the length of hospital stay.

Patients experiencing an adverse nursing care outcome in the emergency department accounted for 9.37% (70 of 747) of the nursing malpractice cases in the database. Nursing negligence caused or contributed to deaths in 44.28% of the emergency department cases. Serious injury occurred in the remaining 55.71% of the cases.

Inadequate communication between the nurse and the physician was the predominant departure from the standard of nursing care that caused both death and serious injury in the emergency department setting. Failure to communicate adequately led to 76.92% of the patient deaths, all of the fetal/newborn deaths, 41.77% of the patient injuries, and 60.00% of the fetal/newborn injuries. The term *fetal/*

56

newborn is used in cases of pregnancy in which there is a childbirth-associated/induced adverse outcome that involves only the fetus or newborn infant. Failure to inform the physician that a patient's condition had not improved prior to executing the emergency department discharge order was the most frequent communication problem. This was associated with readmission of the patient to the emergency department. Serious injury or death was the result of delayed care in this situation. Table 4.1 presents a summary of adverse outcomes due to nursing malpractice and associated departures from standards of care in the emergency department setting.

TABLE 4.1 Nursing Malpractice Adverse Outcomes and Associated Departures From the Standard of Care in the Emergency Department

Adverse Outcome Category	Departure From the Standard of Nursing Care Causing the Adverse Outcome	No. of Cases	% of Category	% of Total
Death (patient)		26	100.00	37.14
	Inadequate communication with the physician regarding nursing assessment data	20	76.92	
	Inadequate care by the physician	2	7.69	
	Medication administration error	2	7.69	
	Inadequate nursing assessment	2	7.69	
Death (fetal/ newborn)		5	100.00	7.14
	Inadequate communication with the physician regarding nursing assessment data	5	100.00	
Injury (patient)		34	100.00	48.57
	Inadequate communication with the physician regarding nursing assessment data	14	41.77	
	Inadequate nursing assessment	3	8.82	
	Medication administration error	5	14.71	
	Unsafe environment	9	26.47	
	Inadequate nursing intervention	2	5.88	
	Inadequate care by the physician	1	2.94	
Injury (fetal/ newborn)		5	100.00	7.14
	Inadequate communication with the physician regarding nursing assessment data	3	60.00	
	Inadequate nursing assessment	2	40.00	

TABLE 4.2 Age of Patients Experiencing a Nursing-Care-Related Adverse
Outcome in the Emergency Department

		Cases of Death		Cases of Injury	
Age	All Cases (N = 70)	Patient (N = 26)	Fetal/ Newborn (N = 5)	Patient (N = 34)	Fetal/ Newborn (N = 5)
Range	Fetal/newborn to 93 yr.	2 mo. to 80 yr.	Fetal/ newborn	3 mo. to 93 yr.	Fetal/ newborn
Mean	33.18 yr.	33.74 yr.	Fetal/ newborn	34.90 yr.	Fetal/ newborn
Median	31.50 yr.	33.00 yr.	Fetal/ newborn	32.50 yr.	Fetal/ newborn

PATIENT CHARACTERISTICS

Patients experiencing an adverse nursing care outcome in the emergency department ranged in age from fetal/newborn to 93 years. The mean age of patients in this group (excluding fetal/newborn cases) was 33.18, and the median age was 31.50 years. Table 4.2 summarizes age data for patients experiencing a nursing care adverse outcome in the emergency department.

The majority of the patients were between 21 and 40 years of age. The fetal/newborn-through-10-year age group constituted the next largest age distribution category (28.57%). Other age groupings were 41 through 50 years, 8.57%; 51 through 60 years, 5.71%; 61 through 70 years, 1.42%; 71 through 80 years, 4.20%; and 81 through 100 years, 2.85%. Figure 4.1 presents age frequency distribution data for patients experiencing adverse outcomes in the emergency department.

Patients experiencing injury or death as an adverse nursing care outcome were predominantly under 41 years of age. Of the patients suffering death (excluding fetal/newborn deaths) in the emergency department, 38.46% were between 31 and 40 years of age, 23.07% were 21 through 30 years, 15.38% were 41 through 50 years, 7.69% were under 1 year through 10 years, 7.69% were 11 through 20 years, 3.84% were 51 through 60 years, and 3.84% were 71 through 80 years. Figure 4.2 contains age distribution data for patients in the emergency department suffering death.

The age distribution of patients experiencing an injury as a result of nursing negligence (excluding fetal/newborn) were as follows: 3

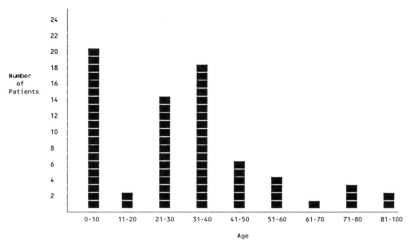

Figure 4.1. Age Distribution of Patients Experiencing a
Nursing-Care-Related Adverse Outcome in the Emergency Department

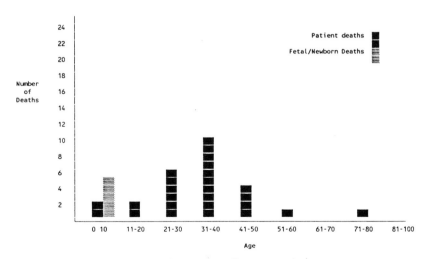

Figure 4.2. Age Distribution of Patients Suffering Death as a
Nursing-Care-Related Adverse Outcome in the Emergency Department

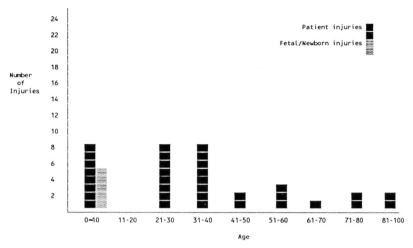

Figure 4.3. Age Distribution of Patients Experiencing Injury as a Nursing-Care-Related Adverse Outcome in the Emergency Department

months through 10 years, 23.52%; 21 through 30 years, 23.52%; 31 through 40 years, 23.52%; 51 through 60 years, 8.82%; 41 through 50 years, 5.88%; 71 through 80 years, 5.88%; 81 through 100 years, 5.88%; and 61 through 70 years, 2.94%. Figure 4.3 summarizes the age distribution of patients experiencing an injury in the emergency department.

In the emergency department setting, 48.57% of those who suffered adverse outcomes were male, and 37.14% were female (excluding fetal/newborn cases). Of those who suffered death, 54.84% were male and 29.03% were female. The remaining 16.13% were cases of fetal/newborn death. Cases of injury due to nursing negligence, on the other hand, were equally divided between male and female patients. Table 4.3 summarizes sex data of patients experiencing a nursing-care-related adverse outcome in the emergency department.

The most common presenting problems of emergency department patients encountering an adverse outcome were those associated with pregnancy (13; 18.57%), the nervous system (12; 17.14%), the gastrointestinal tract (10; 14.29%), and the respiratory system (10; 14.29%). Other presenting problems were those associated with car-

diovascular alterations, infection, wounds, musculoskeletal alterations, multiple trauma, psychosocial alterations, and thermoregulatory alterations. The majority of patients presenting with a respiratory
problem, cardiovascular problem, or multiple trauma suffered death
as a consequence of nursing negligence. Fetal/newborn injury or death
was the most common adverse outcome for patients admitted to the
emergency department with a problem associated with pregnancy.
Table 4.4 summarizes presenting problems of emergency department
patients experiencing a nursing-care-related adverse outcome.

TABLE 4.3 Sex of Patients Experiencing a Nursing-Care-Related Adverse
Outcome in the Emergency Department

Emergency Department Patients	Male		Female		Fetal/Newborn	
	No.	%	No.	%	No.	%
Cases, all (N = 70)	34	48.57	26	37.14	10	14.29
Cases, death (N = 31)	17	54.84	9	29.03	5	16.13
Cases, injury (N = 39)	17	43.59	17	43.59	5	12.82

TABLE 4.4 Diagnoses/Presenting Problems of Patients Experiencing a
Nursing-Care-Related Adverse Outcome in the Emergency
Department

Patient Diagnosis/ Presenting Problem	Adverse Outcome					
	Total (N = 70)		Death (N = 31)		Injury (N = 39)	
	No.	%	No.	%	No.	%
Pregnancy problem, fetal/newborn	10	14.29	5	16.13	5	12.82
Pregnancy problem, maternal	3	4.28	1	3.22	2	5.13
Neurological problem	12	17.14	2	6.45	10	25.64
Gastrointestinal problem	10	14.29	4	12.90	6	15.39
Respiratory problem	10	14.29	8	25.81	2	5.13
Cardiovascular problem	7	10.00	5	16.13	2	5.13
Infection (local, systemic)	6	8.57	3	9.68	3	7.69
Wound and/or orthopedic problem	6	8.57	0	0.00	6	15.39
Multiple trauma	4	5.71	3	9.68	1	2.56
Psychosocial problem	1	1.43	0	0.00	1	2.56
Thermoregulatory problem	1	1.43	0	0.00	1	2.56

ADVERSE NURSING
CARE OUTCOMES

The most common nursing-care-related adverse outcome in the emergency department setting was that of death (44.28%). Other frequent adverse outcomes included severe brain damage (12.86%); fracture, wound, and/or sprain (11.43%); paraplegia or quadriplegia (8.57%); infection (5.71%); psychosocial alteration (4.29%); and amputation (4.29%). All adverse outcomes for the emergency department setting caused by nursing malpractice are summarized in Table 4.5.

Analysis of nursing care in the emergency department revealed that communication between nurse and physician was the predominant problem related to nursing negligence. Failure to inform the physician of abnormal assessment data or failure to inform the physician that a patient's condition did not improve prior to discharge accounted for 60.00% of the nursing care problems. Nursing care problems associated with assessment, environmental safety, and medication administration were responsible for 32.86% of the adverse events in this setting, and nursing intervention problems and nursing negligence associated with inadequate care by the physician caused the remaining 7.15% of the negative outcomes. Table 4.6 summarizes nursing care problems and associated departures from acceptable standards of care.

The most common causes of patient injury in the emergency department were inadequate communication with the physician regarding a patient's condition (41.18%), falls (26.47%), medication administration error (14.70%), and inadequate nursing assessment (8.82%). Mechanisms of injury to the fetal/newborn group included inadequate nursing assessment (40.00%) and inadequate communication of patient status data to the physician (60.00%).

In cases of fetal/newborn death, inadequate communication with the physician caused the adverse events. The predominant mechanism of injury responsible for patient death was inadequate communication to the physician of changes in patient condition (76.92%). Inadequate nursing assessment (7.69%), medication administration error (7.70%), and nursing negligence associated with inadequate care by the physician (7.69%) accounted for the remaining patient deaths. Table 4.7 summarizes data relating to the mechanisms of injury responsible for adverse outcomes in the emergency department.

TABLE 4.5 Type of Adverse Outcome Caused by Nursing Malpractice in the Emergency Department ($N = 70$)

Adverse Outcome Caused by Nursing Malpractice	No. of Cases	% of Cases
Death (patient)	26	37.14
Severe brain damage	9	12.86
Fracture, wound, and/or sprain	8	11.43
Paraplegia/quadriplegia	6	8.57
Death (fetal/newborn)	5	7.14
Infection	4	5.71
Psychosocial alteration	3	4.29
Amputation: limb	3	4.29
Sensory loss: hearing, sight	2	2.85
Myocardial infarction	1	1.43
Neurovascular problem	1	1.43
Thrombophlebitis	1	1.43
Sciatic neuropathy	1	1.43

TABLE 4.6 Nursing Care Problems and Associated Departures From the Standard of Care in the Emergency Department

Problem Area	Departure From the Standard of Care	No. of Adverse Outcomes	% of Adverse Outcomes
Nursing assessment	Failure to assess the patient systematically	7	10.00
Environmental safety	Failure to provide a safe environment	9	12.86
Medication administration	Failure to administer medication(s) properly	7	10.00
Nursing intervention	Failure to perform a nursing treatment or procedure properly	2	2.86
Communication	Failure to inform the physician of abnormal assessment data or lack of patient improvement prior to discharge	42	60.00
Inadequate physician care	Failure to obtain help for a patient not receiving adequate care from a physician	3	4.29

NURSING CARE PROBLEMS

Nursing Assessment Negligence

Problems associated with nursing assessment and observation of the patient were responsible for 10.00% of the adverse events in the emergency

TABLE 4.7 Mechanisms of Injury Responsible for Nursing-Care-Related Adverse Outcomes in the Emergency Department

	Adverse Outcome							
	Patient Injuries (N = 34)		Fetal/Newborn Injuries (N = 5)		Patient Deaths (N = 26)		Fetal/Newborn Deaths (N = 5)	
Mechanism of Injury	No.	%	No.	%	No.	%	No.	%
Inadequate nursing assessment	3	8.82	2	40.00	2	7.69	0	0.00
Wrong medication dose	0	0.00	0	0.00	1	3.85	0	0.00
Wrong medication	1	2.94	0	0.00	0	0.00	0	0.00
Medication allergy ignored	1	2.94	0	0.00	1	3.85	0	0.00
Incorrect injection technique	3	8.82	0	0.00	0	0.00	0	0.00
Inadequate cardiopulmonary resuscitation	1	2.94	0	0.00	0	0.00	0	0.00
Inadequate communication of abnormal assessment findings to the physician	4	11.76	1	20.00	0	0.00	4	80.00
Inadequate communication to the physician of lack of improvement or deterioration in condition prior to discharge	10	29.42	2	40.00	20	76.92	1	20.00
Fall	9	26.47	0	0.00	0	0.00	0	0.00
Inadequate care by the physician	1	2.94	0	0.00	2	7.69	0	0.00
Incorrect nursing procedure	1	2.94	0	0.00	0	0.00	0	0.00

department. Failure to assess the patient systematically caused 40.00% of the fetal/newborn injuries, 8.82% of the patient injuries, and 7.69% of the patient deaths in this setting.

Seventy-one percent of the patients in this subgroup were female, and 29% were male. The mean age of patients was 27.00 years, and the median age was 26.00 years. Presenting problems of patients included pregnancy (57.14%), trauma (14.28%), respiratory system alteration (14.28%), and gastrointestinal system alteration (14.28%).

Adverse outcomes due to inadequate nursing assessment were those of fetal/newborn brain damage (28.57%), patient death (28.57%), emotional distress (28.57%), and infection (14.28%). The mechanism of injury responsible for all negative outcomes in this subgroup was either omission of patient observation and assessment or infrequent patient observation and assessment.

Case 4-1: Nursing Assessment Negligence

A 26-year-old, unemployed, steroid-dependent asthmatic presented to the emergency department in acute respiratory distress with severe bronchospasm. Treatment was instituted promptly. Vital signs were taken on admission, but systematic nursing assessment after this point was ignored. An x-ray ordered by the physician to verify the placement of the subclavian catheter was ignored. In addition, there were no observations relevant to the subclavian catheter, and complaints of chest discomfort were not reported.

Five hours later, before a bed was available in the intensive care unit, the patient suffered a cardiopulmonary arrest and was pronounced dead in the emergency department. A lacerated right subclavian artery from placement of a subclavian catheter went unrecognized.

The failure to assess the patient systematically while he was in the emergency department contributed to the patient's death. Legal action resulted in a payment of $1,010,000 to the estate of the patient.

Communication Negligence

Problems associated with communication between the nurse and the physician were responsible for the majority (60.00%) of the emergency department adverse events. Failure to inform the physician of abnormal assessment data or lack of patient improvement prior to discharge caused 76.92% of the patient deaths, 100.00% of the fetal/newborn deaths, 41.77% of the patient injuries, and 60.00% of the fetal/newborn injuries in this setting.

Patients in this subgroup were equally divided between the sexes. Only 1 patient out of 42 was over 65 years of age. The mean and median ages respectively were 28.35 and 31.50 years. Over half of the patients experiencing an adverse outcome associated with inadequate communication presented to the emergency department with pregnancy (21.42%), a neurological alteration (16.66%), or a cardiovascular alteration (14.28%). Other conditions bringing the patient to the emergency department were gastrointestinal problems (11.90%), symptoms of infection (11.90%), respiratory problems (9.52%), wounds or musculoskeletal problems (4.76%), multiple trauma (4.76%), psychosocial problems (2.38%), and thermoregulatory problems (2.38%).

Death, including that of both patients and fetal/newborns, occurred in 59.52% of the cases in this subgroup. Other adverse outcomes related to communication negligence were paraplegia/quadriplegia, 11.90%; amputation, 7.14%; newborn brain damage, 7.14%; infection, 4.76%; murder/wounds to others, 2.38%; peripheral nerve damage 2.38%, patient brain damage, 2.38%; and hearing loss, 2.38%. Mechanisms of injury in the emergency department included (a) failure to inform the physician that the patient's condition had not improved prior to discharge (59.52%); (b) failure to inform the physician that the patient's condition had deteriorated prior to discharge (16.66%); (c) failure to inform the physician of abnormal nursing assessment or laboratory data (11.90%); and (d) failure to inform the physician that the medical evaluation of a patient was incomplete or absent prior to discharge (11.90%).

An overwhelming 90.47% of the patients in the subgroup of those experiencing an adverse outcome due to inadequate nurse-physician communication were readmitted to the emergency department after discharge. Of the patients readmitted to the emergency department, 60.52% suffered death as an adverse outcome, and 39.47% experienced a serious injury. Patients who were readmitted presented with pregnancy problems (21.05%), respiratory problems (21.05%), cardiovascular problems (15.78%), neurological problems (15.78%), infection (10.52%), wound or orthopedic problems (5.26%), trauma (5.26%), psychosocial problems (2.60%), and thermoregulatory problems (2.60%). All patients readmitted for respiratory problems died. One patient that was negligently discharged from the emergency department with a psychosocial problem (even after the staff was warned of the patient's violent and assaultive behavior) was later readmitted after killing his father and seriously wounding his mother.

In this instance, not only was the patient harmed by nursing negligence, but family members suffered adverse consequences.

Case 4-2: Communication Negligence

A 35-year-old owner of a mattress manufacturing company presented to an emergency department with tachycardia, dyspnea, and an elevated temperature. Mr. D. was examined by a physician, and a "viral syndrome" was suspected. At this time, the physician wrote an order for the patient to be discharged home after treatment. The treatment consisted of medication administration and observation for a short period of time.

Mr. D. became apprehensive about his condition and reported to the nurse that he had ingested cocaine several times over the previous week. In addition, documented nursing observations indicated that the patient's condition had failed to improve. This information was not communicated to the physician.

At the time of discharge, "chest pain on inspiration, shortness of breath, fever, and sweating" were noted. The nursing staff failed to apprise the physician of the patient's condition prior to executing the discharge order. Mr. D. was discharged home.

Several hours later, Mr. D.'s wife found him on the floor of a walk-in closet clutching his chest. An ambulance was summoned to take Mr. D. back to the hospital; however, en route, the patient suffered a massive pulmonary embolism. Upon arrival at the hospital, the patient suffered a complete cardiopulmonary arrest. Resuscitation efforts were unsuccessful.

Failure to inform the physician that the patient's condition had not improved prior to discharge contributed to Mr. D.'s death. Legal action resulted in a payment of over $300,000 to the estate of the patient.

Medication Administration Negligence

Problems associated with medication administration were responsible for 10.00% of the emergency department adverse events. Failure to administer medications in accordance with prevailing professional standards of nursing care caused 7.69% of the patient deaths and 14.71% of the patient injuries in this setting.

Seventy percent of the patients in this subgroup were male, and 30% were female. Patients were relatively young, with a mean age of 40.57

years and a median age of 37.00 years. Patients experiencing a medication error presented to the emergency department with respiratory problems (42.85%), gastrointestinal problems (42.85%), and orthopedic problems (14.28%).

Twenty-nine percent of the patients in this subgroup died. Death was due to administering the wrong dose of medication or medication allergy. Seventy-one percent of the patients experienced an injury because of medication administration negligence. Injuries included brain damage (40.00%), peripheral nerve injury (40.00%), and thrombophlebitis (20.00%). These injuries were caused by the wrong medication, medication allergy, and incorrect injection technique (intramuscular, intravenous). Thus mechanisms of injury included administering the wrong dose of medication (14.28%), ignoring patient allergy status (28.57%), administering the wrong medication (14.28%), and incorrect parenteral administration technique (42.85%).

Case 4-3: Medication Administration Negligence

On December 26, Ms. R. presented to the emergency department with an acute asthma attack. She was a 41-year-old, unemployed, unmarried mother with eight children aged 2, 4 (twins), 13, 16, 19, 22, and 23 years. Four of her children lived at home, and four were living independently or with a relative. Her only sources of income were Social Security disability payments (for a mental problem) and food stamps.

Oxygen via nasal cannula at 5 liters per minute was administered along with albuterol via nebulizer, corticosteroids, and aminophylline. Intubation was eventually indicated. The first attempt was unsuccessful, and Ms. R. became combative because of hypoxia and anxiety. Prior to another intubation attempt, Versed 2.5 milligrams was ordered for conscious sedation. Because this drug is a highly potent intravenous sedative, a warning about it had recently appeared in the hospital's pharmacy newsletter. The nurse administered 25 milligrams rather than 2.5 milligrams. Following this, the patient was not assessed by the nurse. Ms. R. suffered a cardiopulmonary arrest shortly after the Versed overdose. Resuscitation was unsuccessful.

Failure by the nurse to administer the correct dosage of medication and to assess cardiorespiratory status systematically caused the patient's death. Legal action resulted in a $2,740,000 payment to the estate of the patient.

Environmental Safety Negligence

Problems associated with environmental safety were responsible for 12.86% of the adverse events in the emergency department. The failure to provide a safe environment and to protect the patient from foreseeable harm caused 26.47% of the patient injuries in this setting.

The mean age of patients was 57 years, and the median age was 59 years. Fifty-six percent of the patients in this subgroup were between 59 and 93 years of age. The majority of the patients were female (77.77%). The most common presenting problem was that of a neurological alteration (44.44%). Other reasons for admission included infection (11.11%), gastrointestinal tract problems (11.11%), musculoskeletal problems (11.11%), cardiovascular problems (11.11%), and wounds (11.11%).

Adverse outcomes experienced by patients in this subgroup included fractures (55.55%), sprains (22.22%), unilateral loss of sight (11.11%), and lacerations (11.11%). A fall was the mechanism of injury in all cases of environmental safety negligence. Safety problems causing falls included failure to assist the patient, particularly after the patient requested help or complained of dizziness (22.22%); failure to use side rails on stretchers, especially with the elderly, disoriented, or sedated patient (11.11%); and failure to apply restraints when indicated (66.66%).

Case 4-4: Environmental Safety Negligence

Ms. S., a 79-year-old woman, developed bradycardia and was taken to an emergency department by ambulance. It was noted in the medical record that the day before she had experienced cataract extraction surgery with implantation of an intraocular lens.

She was evaluated by a cardiologist, and hospitalization was indicated. Because a bed in the coronary care unit was not ready, the patient was placed in a holding area in the emergency department.

Nursing assessment indicated that Ms. S. was in "a confused and agitated state." In addition, it was noted that she had made several attempts to "climb off the stretcher." The patient was not restrained in any manner and was not attended by a nurse or any other member of the health care team.

While the patient was waiting to be admitted, she fell from the stretcher and landed on her face. The resident on duty in the emergency department was told of the fall, but the nurse did not inform her of the patient's recent eye surgery. When Ms. S. was finally admitted to the coronary care unit, neither attending cardiologist nor coronary care unit staff had been apprised of the fall. After 4 days of treatment, the bradycardia was resolved, and Ms. S. was discharged to her home from the hospital.

Two days after discharge, Ms. S. made her first postoperative visit to the ophthalmologist. He noted that the surgical wound had "traumatically dehised" and that there was a large hemorrhage into the anterior chamber of the eye. These findings were consistent with a fall. Surgical repair of the eye was unsuccessful. It was determined that if the surgical repair had been attempted shortly after the fall, Ms. S. would not have lost vision in the eye.

Failure by the nursing staff to prevent the foreseeable fall and failure to inform the attending physician of the fall in light of the patient's recent eye surgery caused the loss of vision. Legal action resulted in a payment of $510,000 to the patient.

Nursing Negligence Associated
With Inadequate Care by the Physician

Nursing negligence associated with inadequate care by the physician was responsible for 4.29% of the emergency department adverse events. Failure to obtain help for the patient not receiving adequate care by the physician resulted in 7.69% of the patient deaths and 2.94% of the patient injuries in this setting.

Patients in this subgroup were young, with a mean age of 35.00 years and a median age of 27.00 years. All of the patients were male. They presented to the emergency department with neurological problems (33.33%), trauma (33.33%), and respiratory problems (33.33%).

Adverse outcomes due to failure by the nurse to obtain adequate care for the patient included death (66.66%) and neurological injury (33.33%). Mechanisms of injury were inadequate or incomplete medical evaluation of the patient (66.66%) and the inability by the physician to perform a medical procedure (33.33%).

Case 4-5: Inadequate Care by the Physician

A 27-year-old man was invited by a friend to attend a meeting of a secret society. At the meeting, Mr. J. was told that he could become a member of the organization by going through an initiation ceremony. Mr. J. agreed to the terms of the membership, and the initiation ritual took place. He was blindfolded, pushed onto a canvas blanket, and repeatedly bounced in the air. The bouncing was violent, and Mr. J. struck the back of his head on the concrete floor.

Mr. J. was transported by ambulance to the emergency department. The physician did not perform a neurological evaluation and concluded that the patient was suffering from a "psychological disorder." The patient was to remain in the emergency department for "observation."

Various nurses noted that the patient's limb movements were becoming progressively weaker. The physician was informed of the neurological changes, but he did not examine the patient or modify the treatment plan.

As the night progressed, motor and sensory function in all four limbs deteriorated. The physician was again apprised of the patient's condition, and "observation" was to be continued. A neurological evaluation by a specialist was not ordered until the next morning. The examination was performed at noon. By this time, permanent and irreversible spinal cord damage had occurred. The patient was rendered quadriplegic.

Failure by the nursing staff to follow established hospital policy in obtaining adequate medical care for the patient in all probability caused Mr. J. to become quadriplegic. Legal action resulted in an $8 million payment to the patient.

Nursing Intervention Negligence

Problems associated with nursing interventions were responsible for 2.86% of the adverse outcomes in the emergency department. Failure to perform a nursing treatment or procedure according to accepted standards of care caused 5.88% of the total injuries in this setting. All of the patients in this subgroup were of pediatric age. Both mean and median age was 4.00 years. Patients were male and presented with a respiratory problem (50.00%) or wound (50.00%).

Nursing intervention negligence resulted in brain damage (50.00%) and nosocomial infection (50.00%). The mechanism of injury in all cases was inability to perform a nursing procedure properly because of inadequate knowledge.

Case 4-6: Nursing
Intervention Negligence

A 2-year-old child was taken to the emergency department after a "minor" motor vehicle accident. E. T. had not been restrained in an automobile safety seat.

X-ray examination revealed multiple rib fractures and a bilateral pneumothorax. Shortly after admission to the emergency department, the child suffered a respiratory arrest. The nurse caring for E. T. was new and inexperienced. He did not know how to establish an airway, how to use the ambu bag, or how to administer mouth-to-mouth resuscitation. In addition, the nurse was not familiar with the procedure for calling a cardiopulmonary resuscitation ("Code Blue"). Resuscitation was delayed, and the child sustained hypoxic brain damage. E. T. is in a chronic vegetative state.

The nurse's lack of adequate knowledge and the skills of basic resuscitation technique, along with inadequate knowledge of hospital procedure for calling a code, contributed to the development of hypoxic encephalopathy. Legal action resulted in an $8,640,000 payment to the patient for lifelong care.

MALPRACTICE PAYMENTS

Nursing negligence in the emergency department resulted in an overall mean payment of $1,739,457. Payments ranged from $3,000 to $16,000,000. The median payment was $625,000. The mean payments in cases of patient death and fetal/newborn death respectively were $1,016,115 and $718,000. In cases of injury in the emergency department, the mean payment to patients was $2,264,206, and the mean payment in fetal/newborn cases was $2,954,000. Table 4.8 summarizes malpractice payments by adverse outcome.

The largest mean malpractice payments were for nursing negligence associated with inadequate care by the physician ($4,733,333) and nursing intervention negligence ($4,318,366). Table 4.9 presents data regarding emergency department malpractice payments by nursing care problems.

The majority (55.69%) of the payments for adverse nursing care outcomes in the emergency department were distributed between

TABLE 4.8 Malpractice Payments in the Emergency Department, by Adverse Outcome

Adverse Outcome	Malpractice Payments			
	No.	Range ($)	Mean ($)	Median ($)
Death (patient)	26	4,000 to 4,500,000	1,016,115	725,500
Death (fetal/newborn)	5	160,000 to 2,610,000	718,000	300,000
Injury (patient)	34	3,000 to 16,000,000	2,264,206	471,000
Injury (fetal/newborn)	5	500,000 to 5,820,000	2,954,000	2,000,000
All deaths and injuries	70	3,000 to 16,000,000	1,739,457	625,000

TABLE 4.9 Malpractice Payments in the Emergency Department, by Nursing Care Problem

Problem Area	Malpractice Payments (N = 70)			
	No.	Range ($)	Mean ($)	Median ($)
Nursing assessment	7	40,000 to 2,000,000	806,571	475,035
Environmental safety	9	3,000 to 510,000	111,333	26,000
Nursing intervention	2	15,000 to 8,636,733	4,318,366	4,318,366
Medication administration	7	3,000 to 11,150,000	2,594,143	740,000
Inadequate physician care	3	1,200,000 to 8,000,000	4,733,333	5,000,000
Communication	42	4,000 to 16,500,000	1,764,286	862,500

$1,000 and $800,000. However, 34.38% were between $800,001 and $4,000,000, and 9.96% were $4,000,001 or larger. Figure 4.4 contains data regarding the distribution of payments for all nursing care adverse outcomes in the emergency department.

In cases of death, 61.26% of the malpractice payments were between $1,000 and $1,000,000, and 38.69% of the payments were greater than $1,000,000. Figure 4.5 presents the distribution of malpractice payments in cases of death.

Sixty-one and one-half percent of the payments for injury as an adverse outcome of nursing care in the emergency department were between $1,000 and $1,000,000, whereas 38.41% were greater $1,000,000. Figure 4.6 displays the distribution of malpractice payments in cases of injury.

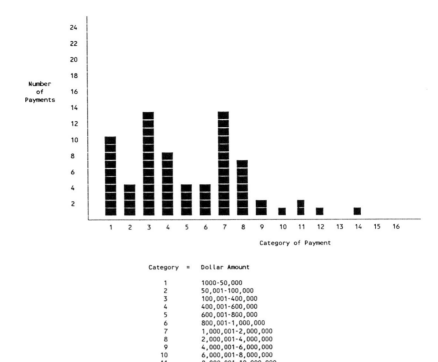

Figure 4.4. Distribution of Payments to Patients Experiencing a
Nursing-Care-Related Adverse Outcome in the Emergency Department

RISK PREVENTION STRATEGIES
IN THE EMERGENCY DEPARTMENT

Risk management strategies applicable to all clinical settings as well
as those common to selected nursing care problem areas will be found
in Chapter 14.

Death was the most frequent adverse outcome of nursing negligence
in the emergency department setting. Inadequate communication
between the nurse and the physician accounted for the majority of the

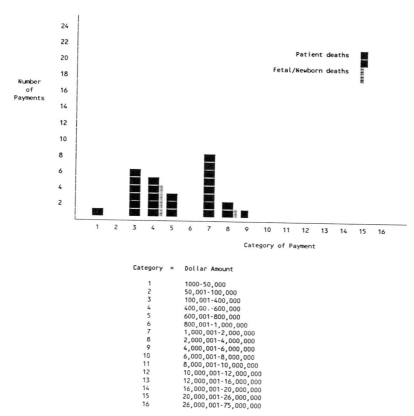

Figure 4.5. Distribution of Payments to Patients Suffering Death as a Nursing-Care-Related Adverse Outcome in the Emergency Department

emergency department adverse events. Prevention of nursing-care-related deaths and injuries unique to the emergency department patient requires the nurse to ask the following questions:

- Has the physician been apprised of the patient's condition prior to executing a discharge order if a significant amount of time has elapsed between the time the order was written and the time of discharge?
- Has the physician been informed of the patient's condition if it has not improved prior to discharge?

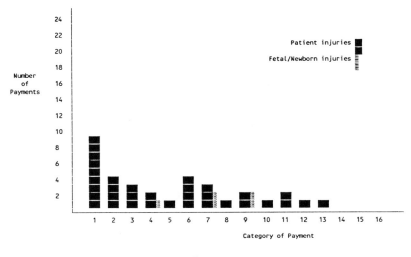

Category = Dollar Amount

Category	Dollar Amount
1	1000-50,000
2	50,001-100,000
3	100,001-400,000
4	400,001-600,000
5	600,001-800,000
6	800,001-1,000,000
7	1,000,001-2,000,000
8	2,000,001-4,000,000
9	4,000,001-6,000,000
10	6,000,001-8,000,000
11	8,000,001-10,000,000
12	10,000,001-12,000,000
13	12,000,001-16,000,000
14	16,000,001-20,000,000
15	20,000,001-26,000,000
16	26,000,001-75,000,000

Figure 4.6. Distribution of Payments to Patients Experiencing Injury as a Nursing-Care-Related Adverse Outcome in the Emergency Department

- Has the physician been informed of the patient's condition if it has deteriorated prior to discharge?
- Has the physician been informed of any abnormal nursing assessment data prior to patient discharge?
- Has the physician been informed of any abnormal laboratory data prior to patient discharge?
- Has the patient been evaluated by a physician prior to discharge?
- Has the physician completed the evaluation of the patient prior to discharge?

SUMMARY

Of the adverse events in the emergency department, 44.28% were deaths. Frequent injuries caused by nursing malpractice included severe brain damage (12.86%); fracture, wound, and/or sprain (11.43%); and paraplegia or quadriplegia (8.57%). The mean age of patients experiencing a negative nursing care outcome was 33.18 years, and 48.57% of the patients were male.

Predominant presenting problems of patients were associated with pregnancy and neurological function. Sixty percent of the nursing care problems in the emergency department involved communication negligence. Failure to inform the physician that a patient's condition had not improved or had deteriorated prior to executing the discharge order was the major departure from the standard of nursing care causing a negative outcome. Inadequate nursing assessment, an unsafe environment, medication administration error, inadequate nursing intervention, and inadequate nursing action related to negligent care by the physician constituted the other mechanisms of injury associated with adverse events in the emergency department.

Adverse outcomes resulted in a mean payment to the patient of $1,739,457.

5

Nursing Malpractice in
the Psychiatric Unit Setting

The nurse in the psychiatric setting plays a crucial role in providing care to patients exhibiting serious psychosocial problems. Nursing care is focused on behavior, which consists of one's perceptions, thoughts, feelings, and actions. The nursing process is utilized in assisting the patient toward a mode of behavior that contributes to a cohesive and integrated personality. The nurse skillfully employs the interpersonal process to assist the patient in the attainment of therapeutic goals. The goal of the interpersonal process is to restore psychosocial equilibrium and promote optimum mental health.

Patients experiencing an adverse nursing care outcome in the psychiatric setting accounted for 4.68% (35 of 747) of the nursing malpractice cases in the database. Forty percent of the psychiatric patients suffered death because of nursing negligence, and 60.00% experienced serious injury.

Inadequate nursing assessment resulting in suicide was the most common departure from acceptable standards of nursing care associated with cases of death. The majority of the injuries were related to incorrect restraint application, which created an unsafe environment. Table 5.1 summarizes adverse outcomes and associated departures from the standard of care in the psychiatric setting.

PATIENT CHARACTERISTICS

Patients in the psychiatric setting ranged in age from 15 to 79 years. The mean age was 40.31, and the median was 37.00 years. Table 5.2 summarizes age data for the psychiatric patients.

The greatest number of psychiatric patients experiencing an adverse event were between 31 and 40 years of age. Figure 5.1 presents age distribution data for psychiatric patients experiencing an adverse nursing care outcome.

Patients suffering death due to negligent nursing care were clustered in the 41-through-50-year age category, and those experiencing injury were in the 31-through-40-year age category. Figures 5.2 and 5.3 summarize age distribution data for psychiatric patients experiencing death and injury, respectively.

TABLE 5.1 Nursing Malpractice Adverse Outcomes and Associated Departures From the Standard of Care in the Psychiatric Setting

Adverse Outcome Category	Departure From the Standard of Nursing Care Causing the Adverse Outcome	No. of Cases	% of Category	% of Total
Death		14	100.00	40.00
	Inadequate nursing assessment	8	57.14	
	Medication administration error	5	35.71	
	Inadequate communication	1	7.14	
Injury		21	100.00	60.00
	Unsafe environment	7	33.33	
	Inadequate nursing assessment	5	23.80	
	Inadequate nursing intervention	2	9.52	
	Medication administration error	3	14.28	
	Inadequate communication	4	19.04	

TABLE 5.2 Age of Patients Experiencing a Nursing-Care-Related Adverse Outcome in the Psychiatric Setting

Age	All Cases (N = 35)	Cases of Death (N = 14)	Cases of Injury (N = 21)
Range	15 to 79 yr.	16 to 79 yr.	15 to 70 yr.
Mean	40.31 yr.	31.70 yr.	36.52 yr.
Median	37.00 yr.	44.50 yr.	34.00 yr.

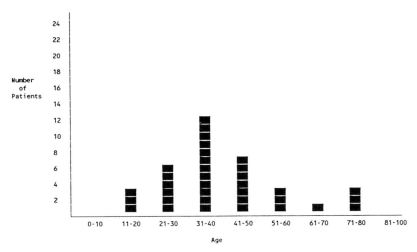

Figure 5.1. Age Distribution of Patients Experiencing a
Nursing-Care-Related Adverse Outcome in the Psychiatric Setting

Sixty percent of the patients in the psychiatric setting were male,
and 40.00% were female. The majority of the psychiatric patients
presented to the hospital for treatment related to acute psychosis
(82.85%). The remaining patients (17.14%) were admitted for treatment of substance abuse. Tables 5.3 and 5.4 summarize data regarding
patient sex and diagnosis.

ADVERSE NURSING CARE OUTCOMES

A wide variety of adverse nursing care outcomes occurred in the
psychiatric setting. Death and brain damage accounted for 60.00% of
the adverse outcomes; this underscores the seriousness of nursing
negligence in this setting. Table 5.5 summarizes all of the adverse
outcomes in the psychiatric setting caused by nursing malpractice.

Approximately four fifths of the adverse outcomes in the psychiatric
setting involved problems associated with nursing assessment, medication administration, and environmental safety. The remaining fifth
of the incidents were related to problems of communication and
nursing intervention. Table 5.6 summarizes nursing care problem areas

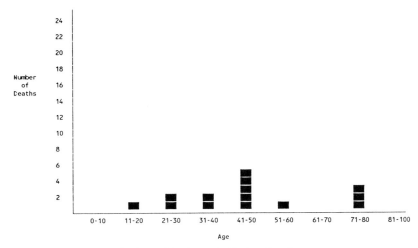

Figure 5.2. Age Distribution of Patients Suffering Death as a
Nursing-Care-Related Adverse Outcome in the Psychiatric Setting

in the psychiatric setting, along with associated departures from
standards of care.

The most common mechanism of injury in the psychiatric setting
was inadequate psychosocial status assessment; this was followed by
medication administration error. Adverse outcomes caused by failure
to administer medication properly involved the wrong dose of medication, the wrong medication, and neglect of toxicity assessment.
Other mechanisms of injury are summarized in Table 5.7.

NURSING CARE PROBLEMS

Nursing Assessment Negligence

Nursing assessment negligence was responsible for 37.14% (13 of
35) of the adverse events in the psychiatric setting. Failure to assess
psychosocial status systematically with the appropriate frequency (as
determined by the patient's condition) caused or contributed to 57.14%
of the deaths and 23.80% of the injuries in this setting.

The age of patients in this subgroup ranged from 16 to 79 years
with mean and median ages of 39 and 33 years, respectively. Sixty-two

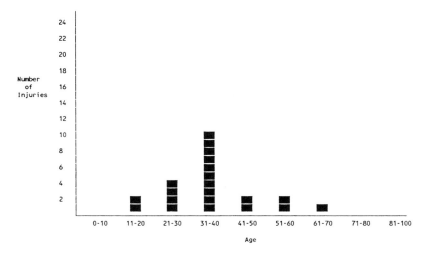

Figure 5.3. Age Distribution of Patients Experiencing Injury as a Nursing-Care-Related Adverse Outcome in the Psychiatric Setting

percent of the patients experiencing a nursing assessment related negative outcome were male, and 38.00% were female.

Substandard psychosocial nursing assessment produced devastating outcomes. The most frequent adverse event caused by inadequate assessment was that of suicide (53.84%). Means of suicide included (a) hanging by an electrical cord, (b) elopement and jumping in front of a moving motor vehicle, (c) jumping out of a window, (d) hanging by a shower curtain, (e) hanging by a sheet tied to a ceiling fire sprinkler head, (f) hanging by a baggage strap, (g) hanging by the nurse's call cord, and (h) hanging from an extension cord supplied by the nurse for a hair dryer. In fact, all of the deaths in this subgroup were classified as suicide.

Patient injuries in this subgroup related to nursing assessment negligence resulted from attempted suicide, either by elopement (23.07%) or by a jump from a window, platform, or atrium (23.07%). All of the patients sustained multiple trauma. Injuries occurring on the psychiatric unit were the result of (a) jumping from a multistoried atrium, (b) jumping from a balcony, and (c) jumping from a window. Injury to the psychiatric patient by elopement was the result of

TABLE 5.3 Sex of Patients Experiencing a Nursing-Care-Related Adverse Outcome in the Psychiatric Setting

Psychiatric Patients	Male		Female	
	No.	%	No.	%
Cases, all (N = 35)	21	60.00	14	40.00
Cases, death (N = 14)	10	71.42	4	28.57
Cases, injury (N = 21)	11	52.38	10	47.61

TABLE 5.4 Presenting Problems of Patients Experiencing a Nursing-Care-Related Adverse Outcome in the Psychiatric Setting

Psychiatric Patients	Acute Psychosis		Substance Abuse	
	No.	%	No.	%
All patients (N = 35)	29	82.85	6	17.14
Cases of death (N = 14)	10	71.42	4	28.57
Cases of injury (N = 21)	19	90.47	2	9.52
Male patients (N = 21)	18	85.71	3	14.28
Female patients (N = 14)	11	78.57	3	21.42

TABLE 5.5 Type of Adverse Outcome Caused by Nursing Malpractice in the Psychiatric Setting (N = 35)

Adverse Outcome Caused by Nursing Malpractice	No. of Cases	% of Cases
Death	14	40.00
Severe brain damage	7	20.00
Multiple trauma	5	14.28
Fracture	2	5.71
Rape	2	5.71
False imprisonment	1	2.85
Subdural hematoma	1	2.85
Paraplegia	1	2.85
Burns	1	2.85
Limb amputation	1	2.85

jumping in front of a train or jumping from a subway platform. The injuries included multiple fractures, brain damage, paraplegia, internal organ damage, and limb amputation.

TABLE 5.6 Nursing Care Problems and Associated Departures From the Standard of Care in the Psychiatric Setting

Problem Area	Departure From the Standard of Care	No. of Cases	% of Cases
Nursing assessment	Failure to assess the patient systematically	13	37.14
Environmental safety	Failure to provide a safe environment	7	20.00
Medication administration	Failure to administer medication(s) properly	8	22.85
Nursing intervention	Failure to perform a nursing treatment or procedure properly	2	5.71
Communication	Failure to inform the physician of a change in the patient's condition	5	14.28

TABLE 5.7 Mechanisms of Injury Responsible for Nursing-Care-Related Adverse Outcomes in the Psychiatric Setting

	Adverse Outcome			
	Patient Injury (N = 21)		Patient Death (N = 14)	
Mechanism of Injury	No.	%	No.	%
Inadequate psychosocial status assessment	5	23.80	8	57.14
Wrong medication dose	1	4.76	2	14.28
Wrong medication	0	0.00	3	21.42
Medication toxicity	2	9.52	0	0.00
Medical consultation not executed	1	4.76	0	0.00
False imprisonment	1	4.76	0	0.00
Inadequate restraint application	4	19.04	0	0.00
Unsafe physical environment	3	14.28	0	0.00
Inadequate communication with the physician	4	19.04	1	7.14

Case 5-1: Nursing Assessment Negligence

Mr. T., a 42-year-old "creative and sensitive" architect, experienced an employment-related transfer from Denver to Los Angeles. Not only was the new job more stressful, but the transfer created family problems. First, it was decided that Mr. T.'s three children ages 8, 11, and 14 would finish the school year in Denver. Thus Mr. T. had to live alone in Los Angeles in a rented apartment for a period of time. In addition, Mr. T.'s wife was not enthusiastic about the move, and the family experienced difficulty in procuring affordable housing.

Mr. T. was in good general physical health, and his past medical history was negative for psychosocial disorder. However, as time progressed, Mr. T. became increasingly depressed and ultimately began to harbor thoughts of suicide.

One morning, Mr. T. experienced delusions about killing himself as well as his wife, children, and parents. He presented to the emergency department and agreed to be admitted to the locked psychiatric unit of the hospital.

Evaluation by a psychiatrist revealed that the patient was suffering from homicidal and suicidal ideation. Mr. T. expressed a special concern to members of the health care team that he was unsure of his ability to control himself. The nursing staff assessed the patient and then removed the following potentially harmful objects: a cologne bottle, a small mirror, nail clippers, and a safety razor. Written hospital procedure dictated that other conceivable injurious objects (e.g., belts, straps) not be removed unless the patient was "imminently" suicidal. A 30-inch detachable leather shoulder strap on the patient's briefcase was therefore not removed.

As the day progressed, Mr. T. was variously described in the nurses' notes as "pacing in the room," "clenching his fists," "wringing his hands," and "hunched over, rigid, with a fearful look." According to the medical record, his condition continued to deteriorate during the afternoon and evening. However, nursing assessments were infrequent and incomplete. At 10:10 p.m., Mr. T. was discovered dead, hanging by the strap of his briefcase.

Failure by the nursing staff to assess the patient systematically with appropriate frequency caused Mr. T.'s death. By late afternoon, based on the patient's condition, constant nursing observation was warranted to protect him from harm associated with the psychopathology. Legal action resulted in a payment of $940,000 to the estate of the patient.

Medication Administration Negligence

Medication administration negligence was responsible for 22.85% of the adverse events in the psychiatric setting. Failure to administer medication(s) properly resulted in 35.71% of the deaths and 14.28% of the injuries on the psychiatric unit.

Patients in this subgroup ranged in age from 25 to 71 years. Both mean and median age was 50.00 years. Patients were evenly divided by sex.

Nursing negligence associated with medication administration resulted in either death (62.50%) or brain damage (37.50%). Two mechanisms of injury were responsible for almost three quarters of the devastating outcomes. These were administration of the wrong dosage of medication (37.50%) and administration of the wrong medication (37.50%). The remaining 25.00% of the incidents associated with medication administration were the result of medication toxicity. Failure by the nurse to execute the physician's order for monitoring serum lithium levels caused all cases of medication toxicity.

Case 5-2: Medication Administration Negligence

A 51-year-old woman with a history of bipolar disorder was admitted to the psychiatric unit suffering from episodes of depression. When Ms. K. was a young adult, she first began experiencing mood swings, ranging from depression to mania. Hospitalization was necessary when medication was not effective in controlling her symptoms.

Upon admission, Ms. K. was placed on lithium carbonate for the bipolar condition. At this time, it was noted that Ms. K.'s blood pressure was elevated, and Maxzide, a diuretic anti-hypertensive drug, was also prescribed. Because of the two medications, serum lithium assays were ordered and were to be performed weekly.

Approximately 10 days after admission, a nursing note indicated that Ms. K. had developed slurred speech and tremors of both hands. The next day, the nurses noted that Ms. K. was short of breath, experiencing anxiety, and hardly able to get out of bed and that she refused to dress herself.

Signs of lithium carbonate toxicity were ignored by the nursing staff. Furthermore, execution of the physician's order for weekly lithium levels was neglected.

Ms. K.'s condition continued to deteriorate, and several days later she was described as "unresponsive and incontinent of urine and stool." At this time she was transferred to the emergency department for evaluation. An emergency serum lithium level was performed, and it indicated gross lithium intoxication. Ms. K. was transferred to the intensive care unit for treatment. The extreme lithium toxicity, however, caused permanent central nervous system damage.

Failure to execute the physician's order for serum lithium assays and failure to intervene when the patient exhibited signs and symptoms of medication toxicity resulted in brain damage with loss of motor function. The patient's speech is garbled, and she has difficulty with nutrition because of swallowing problems. Ms. K. has been confined to a nursing home for the remainder of her life. Legal action resulted in a $4 million payment to the patient for lifelong care.

Environmental Safety Negligence

Environmental safety negligence was responsible for 20.00% of the adverse incidents suffered by psychiatric patients. Failure to provide a safe environment accounted for 33.33% of the injuries in the psychiatric setting.

The mean age of patients in this subgroup was 40.00 years, and the median was 35.00 years. Ages ranged from 27 to 70 years. Fifty-seven percent of these patients were male.

The most common mechanism of injury was related to the use of restraints. Failure to apply restraints when indicated (28.57%) and failure to apply restraints properly (28.57%) caused 57.14% of these adverse incidents. Other mechanisms of injury in this subgroup were failure to protect the patient from foreseeable attack by another patient (28.57%) and failure to supervise adequately a patient with hot liquids (14.28%). Injuries because of failure to protect the patient from foreseeable and avoidable harm associated with the physical environment were varied. The resulting injuries included (a) multiple trauma (28.57%), (b) rape (28.57%), (c) hip fracture (14.28%), (d) brain damage (14.28%), and (e) thermal burns (14.28%).

Case 5-3: Environmental Safety Negligence

One evening, Mr. G., a 34-year-old automobile mechanic, went to three police stations and stated that people were attempting to kill him. He was transported to an emergency department and later admitted to a psychiatric unit. The patient was evaluated, and Haldol was administered.

Several hours after admission, Mr. G. went into the bathroom and attempted suicide by placing a plastic garbage bag over his head. The physician was informed of this action, and restraints were ordered.

Mr. G. was placed in restraints but was able to free himself from them. He turned the steel frame bed on its end and proceeded to hang himself with the linens. He did not succeed in committing suicide because he was found by another patient. But the hanging action compromised circulation, causing cerebral hypoxia.

Failure to apply the restraints properly and failure to monitor the restrained patient adequately resulted in severe brain damage. Mr. G. remains in an extended care facility. He is completely paralyzed except for the ability to blink and move his eyes. The patient's mother believes that he recognizes her. Legal action resulted in a $1.85 million payment to the patient for lifelong care.

Communication Negligence

Nursing negligence associated with communication resulted in 14.28% of the nursing-care-related adverse events in the psychiatric setting. Failure to apprise the physician adequately of the patient's condition caused 7.14% of the deaths and 19.04% of the injuries in this setting.

Sixty percent of the patients in this subgroup were male and 40.00% were female. The mean age was 30.00 years, and the median was 34.00 years. All patients presented with an acute psychosis.

Two mechanisms of injury were responsible for adverse outcomes in this subgroup. Sixty percent of the incidents were due to failure by the nurse to apprise the physician of a significant change in a patient's condition. Release of a patient without informing the physician that the patient's condition had not improved caused the remaining 40.00% of the negative events.

In terms of adverse outcome, the failure to inform the physician of persistent complaints of chest pain resulted in the death of one patient (20.00%) in this subgroup. Autopsy revealed that the patient had suffered a myocardial infarction. However, the most common adverse outcome in this subgroup was that of neurological damage (80.00%). One patient suffered hemiparesis and brain damage because signs of increased intracranial pressure were not reported. In another case, the physician was not apprised of signs of severe mental decompensation, and brain damage was caused by an attempted suicide. Jumping from a building after being released without improvement in condition led to multiple neurological injuries in one patient and a closed head injury requiring the evacuation of a subdural hematoma in another patient.

Case 5-4: Communication Negligence

Mr. W., a 31-year-old coal miner, was experiencing severe emotional and domestic problems. A psychiatrist arranged for admission to a psychiatric unit.

It was noted in the initial nursing assessment and each day thereafter that the patient was complaining of chest pain. On the fifth day, the patient's insistent complaints of chest pain prompted the nursing staff to call the psychiatrist. The physician was informed that the patient was becoming increasingly "combative, agitated, and uncooperative." The complaints of chest pain were not reported. The physician, on the basis of the information provided by the nurse, had the patient transferred to a locked unit. Mr. W. died in less than 1 hour after the transfer.

Failure to report complaints of chest pain and the consequent lack of treatment in all probability caused the patient's death. An autopsy revealed a myocardial infarction. Legal action resulted in a payment of $278,000 to the estate of the patient.

Nursing Intervention Negligence

Nursing intervention negligence resulted in 5.71% of the adverse outcomes in the psychiatric setting. Failure to perform a nursing procedure properly caused 9.52% of the injuries experienced by psychiatric patients.

All patients in this subgroup were male, and the mean as well as the median age was 36.00 years. One mechanism of injury in this subgroup was failure by the nurse to obtain medical consultation for a patient manifesting physiological problems along with psychosocial problems. Hospital policy was ignored, and the physician's order for consultation was not executed. This resulted in a delay of treatment, with the consequent development of subdural empyema and severe brain damage. Another mechanism of injury involved false imprisonment. Contrary to the patient's wishes, the physician's order, and hospital policy, a patient was sedated and isolated for 6 days. The patient suffered additional emotional injury as a result of the incident.

Case 5-5: Nursing Intervention Negligence

Mr. S., a 42-year-old unskilled laborer, presented to the emergency room with an altered mental status. He had a long history of paranoid schizophrenia. He was evaluated and admitted to the psychiatric unit in a "catatonic state."

An immediate medical consultation was ordered by the psychiatrist because the patient's pupils did not properly react to light. Extrapyramidal symptoms had been ruled out. The physician's order for the medical evaluation was not executed by the nurse.

Approximately 8 hours after admission, the nurse's notes read "patient comatose, pupils fixed and dilated." An emergency CT scan revealed a large area of subdural empyema. The accumulation of purulent material was evacuated, but not before Mr. S. was rendered cortically blind.

Failure by the nursing staff to obtain the ordered "stat medical consultation" resulted in a delay of treatment that caused brain damage. Legal action resulted in a $2,000,000 payment to the patient.

MALPRACTICE PAYMENTS

Malpractice payments in the psychiatric setting ranged from $17,000 to $12,300,000. The mean award was $1,335,714, and the median was $650,000. In terms of adverse outcome, neurological damage necessitating lifelong assistance with the activities of daily living was not uncommon in the psychiatric setting. Thus, reflecting this need, the mean malpractice payment for injury was $1,728,095, and that for death was $747,143. Table 5.8 presents malpractice payment data by adverse outcome.

The largest number of malpractice payments in this setting was made because of nursing assessment negligence. However, the largest mean payment of $2,880,625 was related to medication administration negligence. Table 5.9 contains malpractice payment data by nursing care problem area.

The distribution of payments in the psychiatric setting, when categorized by dollar amount, was quite varied. Figures 5.4 through 5.6 present the frequency distribution data for malpractice payments by adverse outcome in the psychiatric setting.

RISK PREVENTION STRATEGIES
IN THE PSYCHIATRIC SETTING

Risk management strategies applicable to all clinical settings as well as those common to selected nursing care problem areas are contained in Chapter 14.

Suicide, attempted suicide, and the failure to recognize life-threatening physiological alterations are calamitous adverse outcomes due

TABLE 5.8 Malpractice Payments in the Psychiatric Setting, by Adverse Outcome

Adverse Outcome	Malpractice Payments			
	No.	Range ($)	Mean ($)	Median ($)
All patients	35	17,000 to 12,300,000	1,335,714	650,000
Death	14	17,000 to 4,000,000	747,143	486,500
Injury	21	20,000 to 12,300,000	1,728,095	755,000

TABLE 5.9 Malpractice Payments in the Psychiatric Setting, by Nursing Care Problem

Problem Area	Malpractice Payments (N = 35)			
	No.	Range ($)	Mean ($)	Median ($)
Nursing assessment	13	17,000 to 3,000,000	892,462	540,000
Environmental safety	7	20,000 to 1,850,000	472,143	300,000
Nursing intervention	2	35,000 to 2,000,000	1,017,500	1,017,500
Medication administration	8	412,000 to 12,300,000	2,880,625	675,000
Communication	5	755,000 to 3,610,000	1,352,600	900,000

to negligent nursing care in the psychiatric setting. Prevention of nursing-care-related injuries unique to the patient with a psychosocial disorder requires the nurse to ask the following questions:

- Are the frequency and content of nursing assessment determined by an accurate and up-to-date evaluation of the patient's condition?
- Is the patient protected from foreseeable attack by another patient?
- Is the patient adequately supervised when using potentially harmful agents such as hot liquids, matches, and cigarettes?
- Are physiological complaints or alterations carefully assessed and reported to the physician?
- Prior to releasing a patient, is the physician informed if the patient's condition has not improved or has deteriorated?
- Are orders for medical or other specialty consultations executed promptly?
- Are false imprisonment situations avoided?

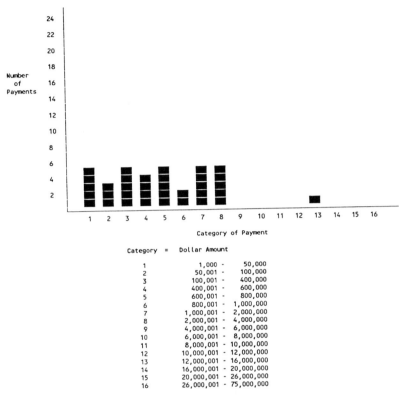

Figure 5.4. Distribution of Payments to Patients Experiencing a Nursing-Care-Related Adverse Outcome in the Psychiatric Setting

If suicidal behavior is a possibility or suspected, the nurse must ask:

- Does the nursing care plan incorporate measures to identify suicidal behavior?
- Are windows secured to prevent patients from jumping?
- Are windows, doors, or other means of exit secured to prevent elopement?
- Is patient access to balconies, atriums, or elevated platforms blocked?
- Is the patient's environment free of objects that can cause harm, such as sharps, linens, electrical cords, shower curtain, belts and straps, and nurse's call cord?

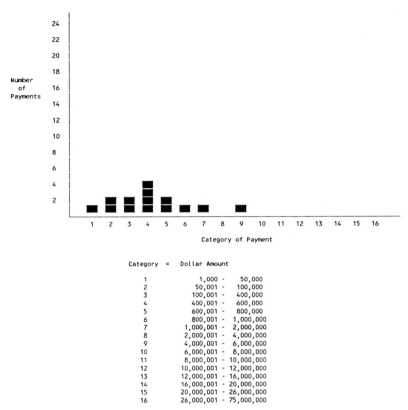

Figure 5.5. Distribution of Payments to Patients Suffering Death as a Nursing-Care-Related Adverse Outcome in the Psychiatric Setting

- Are restraints used when indicated? Are they properly applied, and is the patient assessed with the appropriate frequency?

SUMMARY

Sixty percent of the patients in the psychiatric setting experiencing an adverse nursing care outcome either died or suffered brain damage. The majority of the deaths were suicides because of inadequate nursing assessment. Patient injury on the other hand was primarily due to lack of adequate nursing assessment or an unsafe environment.

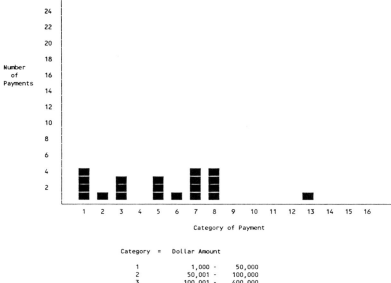

Figure 5.6. Distribution of Payments to Patients Experiencing Injury as a Nursing-Care-Related Adverse Outcome in the Psychiatric Setting

The age range of patients was 15 through 79 years. The mean age was 40.31 years, and 60.00% of the patients were male. The majority of the patients were admitted to the hospital because of an acute psychosis.

Failure to assess the patient systematically was the most common departure from the standard of care. The predominant mechanism of injury was inadequate psychosocial assessment.

Malpractice payments in the psychiatric setting were substantial, with an overall mean of $1,335,714. Mean payments for injury and death respectively were $1,728,095 and $747,143.

6

Nursing Malpractice in the Medical Unit Setting

The nurse in the medical setting is concerned with the delivery of nursing care to the adult patient at risk for or experiencing pathophysiological alteration requiring nonsurgical intervention. Nursing practice in this setting involves, among other things, health promotion, health maintenance, health restoration, and care of the dying.

The medical patient is a biopsychosocial being in dynamic interaction with the environment. The patient may present with a wide variety of pathophysiological alterations, requiring the application of expert knowledge and skills to meet actual or potential nursing care needs. Thus the role of the nurse is to meet physiological, psychosocial, spiritual, and educational needs of the medical patient.

Shorter hospital admissions, the increasing incidence of chronic disease regardless of age, and increased human longevity are placing additional demands on the nurse in meeting needs of medical patients. These factors, coupled with the increasing frequency of complex medical needs of patients, create the potential for adverse nursing care events.

Patients experiencing an adverse outcome in the medical setting accounted for 19.81% or 148 of the 747 nursing malpractice cases in the database. Nursing negligence caused or contributed to the death of 35.81% of the medical patients. The remaining 64.19% of the medical patients suffered serious injury as a consequence of nursing malpractice.

Over half (58.49%) of the deaths in this setting were due to either a medication administration error or inadequate communication of nursing assessment data to the physician. A little over three quarters (77.89%) of the injuries were due to either an unsafe environment or a medication administration error. Adverse outcomes due to nursing malpractice in the medical setting are summarized in Table 6.1.

PATIENT CHARACTERISTICS

Medical patients experiencing a nursing care adverse outcome ranged in age from 18 to 95 years. The overall mean age was 54.62 years. Mean ages of patients suffering death and injury as the result of nursing malpractice were 50.53 and 56.89 years, respectively. The median age for all patients in the medical setting was 54.50. Patients suffering death had a median age of 50.00 years, and those experiencing an injury had a median of 58.00 years. Table 6.2 summarizes the age data of medical patients experiencing a nursing care adverse outcome.

Medical patients were grouped by age, and the distribution of ages was diverse. The least number of patients were aged 18 through 20 years (0.67%), 81 through 90 years (8.78%), and 91 through 100 years (1.35%). The majority of the medical patients were 21 through 30 years (13.51%), 31 through 40 years (12.83%), 41 through 50 years (17.56%), 51 through 60 years (16.89%), 61 through 70 years (13.51%), or 71 through 80 years (14.86%). Figure 6.1 presents the age distribution of all medical patients experiencing an adverse outcome of nursing care.

Medical patients suffering death as an adverse outcome of nursing care were clustered in the following age groups: 31 through 40 (20.75%), 41 through 50 (18.86%), and 51 through 60 (20.75%). On the other hand, most medical patients experiencing an injury were more widely distributed by age. Figures 6.2 and 6.3 contain age distribution data for medical patients experiencing death and injury respectively.

Over fifty percent (58.11%) of the medical patients were female and 41.89% were male. One third of the patients experiencing injury as an adverse outcome of nursing care were male, and two thirds were female. Of those suffering death as an adverse outcome, 56.60% were male and 43.40% were female. Table 6.3 summarizes

TABLE 6.1 Nursing Malpractice Adverse Outcomes and Associated Departures From the Standard of Care in the Medical Setting

Adverse Outcome Category	Departure From the Standard of Nursing Care Causing the Adverse Outcome	No. of Cases	% of Category	% of Total
Death		53	100.00	35.81
	Medication administration error	18	33.96	
	Inadequate communication with the physician regarding nursing assessment data	13	24.53	
	Unsafe environment	5	9.43	
	Inadequate nursing intervention	5	9.43	
	Inadequate nursing assessment	5	9.43	
	Inadequate care by the physician	4	7.56	
	Inadequate infection control	2	3.77	
	Improper use of equipment	1	1.89	
Injury		95	100.00	64.19
	Unsafe environment	42	44.21	
	Medication administration error	32	33.68	
	Inadequate communication with the physician regarding nursing assessment data	10	10.53	
	Inadequate nursing intervention	6	6.32	
	Inadequate infection control	2	2.11	
	Inadequate nursing assessment	2	2.11	
	Inadequate care by the physician	1	1.05	

TABLE 6.2 Age of Patients Experiencing a Nursing-Care-Related Adverse Outcome in the Medical Setting

Age	All Cases (N = 148)	Cases of Death (N = 53)	Cases of Injury (N = 95)
Range	18 to 95 yr.	24 to 81 yr.	18 to 95 yr.
Mean	54.62 yr.	50.53 yr.	56.89 yr.
Median	54.50 yr.	50.00 yr.	58.00 yr.

data regarding the sex of medical patients experiencing a nursing care adverse outcome.

The most common presenting problem of medical patients was associated with altered neurological functioning (23.65%). Neurological problems included cerebrovascular accident (31.42%), transient ischemic attack (22.85%), closed head injury (14.28%), neuromuscular

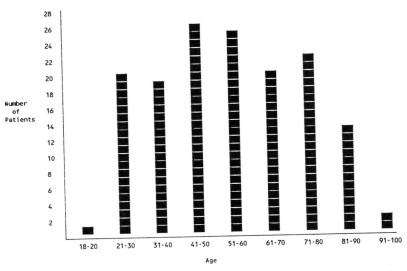

Figure 6.1. Age Distribution of Patients Experiencing a Nursing-Care-Related Adverse Outcome in the Medical Setting

dysfunction (11.42%), seizure disorder (8.57%), cerebral aneurysm (5.71%), and general neurological alteration (5.71%).

Presenting problems associated with the cardiovascular and respiratory systems occurred in 16.22% and 9.46% of the medical patients, respectively. Cardiovascular problems consisted of congestive heart failure (45.83%), myocardial infarction (25.00%), possible myocardial infarction (16.66%), and arrhythmias (12.50%). Respiratory problems included asthma (42.85%), pulmonary embolism (28.57%), chronic obstructive pulmonary disease (21.42%), and pleural effusion (7.14%).

Slightly less than one fifth (19.59%) of these patients presented with a gastrointestinal problem, such as abdominal pain (44.82%), gastroenteritis (17.24%), bowel obstruction (10.34%), chronic inflammatory bowel disease (10.34%), gastrointestinal bleeding (10.34%), liver abscess (3.44%), or esophageal pathology (3.44%). Infection, both systemic and local, accounted for 11.49% of the presenting problems. Cases of infection involved the respiratory system (52.94%), bone and/or soft tissue (23.52%), the central nervous system (17.64%), and the liver (5.88%).

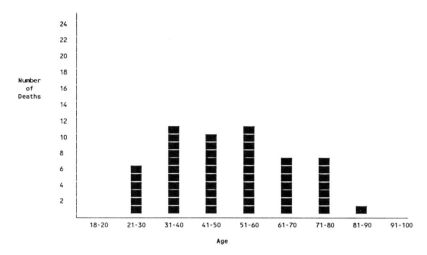

Figure 6.2. Age Distribution of Patients Suffering Death as a Nursing-Care-Related Adverse Outcome in the Medical Setting

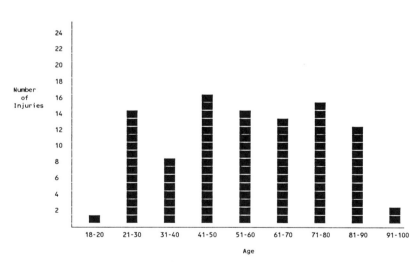

Figure 6.3. Age Distribution of Patients Experiencing Injury as a Nursing-Care-Related Adverse Outcome in the Medical Setting

Eighty-eight percent of the patients presenting with neoplasia were admitted for chemotherapy, and the remaining 12.00% were admitted for treatment associated with metastatic lesions. Musculoskeletal presenting problems consisted of back pain (54.54%) and fracture (45.45%). Other presenting problems included endocrine-metabolic alterations (diabetes, 100.00%), trauma (multiple injuries due to motor vehicle accidents, not requiring surgical intervention, 100.00%), genitourinary dysfunction (end-stage renal disease, 100.00%), and psychiatric alterations (eating disorder, 100.00%). The presenting problems of medical patients experiencing a nursing care adverse outcome are summarized in Table 6.4.

TABLE 6.3 Sex of Patients Experiencing a Nursing-Care-Related Adverse Outcome in the Medical Setting

Medical Patients	Male		Female	
	No.	%	No.	%
Cases, all (N = 148)	62	41.89	86	58.11
Cases, death (N = 53)	30	56.60	23	43.40
Cases, injury (N = 95)	32	33.68	63	66.32

TABLE 6.4 Diagnoses/Presenting Problems of Patients Experiencing a Nursing-Care-Related Adverse Outcome in the Medical Setting

Patient Diagnosis/ Presenting Problem	Adverse Outcome					
	Total (N = 148)		Death (N = 53)		Injury (N = 95)	
	No.	%	No.	%	No.	%
Neurological	35	23.65	11	20.75	24	25.26
Gastrointestinal	29	19.59	11	20.75	18	18.95
Cardiovascular	24	16.22	9	16.98	15	15.79
Infection (local, systemic)	17	11.49	7	13.21	10	10.53
Respiratory	14	9.46	7	13.21	7	7.37
Musculoskeletal	11	7.43	3	5.66	8	8.42
Neoplasm	8	5.41	2	3.77	6	6.32
Trauma (no surgical intervention)	5	3.38	0	0.00	5	5.26
Endocrine-metabolic	3	2.03	1	1.89	2	2.11
Genitourinary	1	0.68	1	1.89	0	0.00
Psychiatric	1	0.68	1	1.89	0	0.00

ADVERSE NURSING CARE OUTCOMES

The most frequent adverse outcome associated with nursing negligence in the medical setting was death (35.81%; 53 of 148). Injuries caused by substandard nursing care included fracture, dislocation, and/or sprain (24.32%); brain damage (10.14%); chemical or thermal burn (8.11%); peripheral nerve damage (7.43%); amputation of a limb or digits (4.73%); sensory or motor loss (4.06%); and other injury (5.41%). Table 6.5 summarizes adverse outcomes experienced by the medical patient.

Nearly two thirds (65.54%) of the adverse nursing care outcomes in this setting were due to problems associated with either medication administration (33.78%) or environmental safety (31.76%). Communication problems in which the nurse failed to inform the physician of abnormal assessment data and/or a change in the patient's condition led to 15.54% of the adverse outcomes. The remainder of the negative nursing care outcomes due to nursing negligence were the result of problems associated with nursing intervention (7.43%), nursing assessment (4.73%), inadequate care by the physician (3.38%), nosocomial infection (2.70%), and equipment/products (0.68%). Table 6.6 presents data regarding nursing care problems and associated depar-

TABLE 6.5 Type of Adverse Outcome Caused by Nursing Malpractice in the Medical Setting (N = 148)

Adverse Outcome Caused by Nursing Malpractice	No. of Cases	% of Cases
Death	53	35.81
Fracture, dislocation, sprain	36	24.32
Brain damage	15	10.14
Burn, chemical or thermal	12	8.11
Nerve damage, limb	11	7.43
Amputation: limb(s)	4	2.70
Amputation: digit(s)	3	2.03
Sensory loss: hearing, sight	3	2.03
Paraplegia	3	2.03
Back injury	2	1.35
Genitourinary system injury	2	1.35
Infection	2	1.35
Duodenal ulcer hemorrhage	1	0.68
Emotional distress	1	0.68

TABLE 6.6 Nursing Care Problems and Associated Departures From the Standard of Care in the Medical Setting

Problem Area	Departure From the Standard of Care	No. of Cases	% of Cases
Medication administration	Failure to administer medication(s) properly	50	33.78
Environmental safety	Failure to provide a safe environment	47	31.76
Communication	Failure to inform the physician of abnormal assessment data and/or a change in the patient's condition	23	15.54
Nursing intervention	Failure to perform a nursing procedure or treatment properly	11	7.43
Nursing assessment	Failure to assess the patient systematically	7	4.73
Inadequate physician care	Failure to obtain help for a patient not receiving adequate care from a physician	5	3.38
Nosocomial infection	Failure to prevent infection	4	2.70
Equipment and products	Failure to use equipment/products properly	1	0.68

tures from the standard of care causing adverse outcomes in the medical setting.

Mechanisms of injury related to medication errors were diverse. However, the most common deviations from acceptable standards of nursing care associated with medication administration included failure to administer the correct dose of a drug, failure to administer the correct intravenous infusion solution, failure to administer a medication, failure to administer the correct medication, failure to use correct parenteral injection technique, failure to care for and/or maintain an intravenous infusion properly, failure to utilize a correct and/or complete physician's order for medication administration, failure to observe for signs of medication toxicity, and failure to note or respect the allergy status of a patient.

Falls were the predominant mechanism of injury in terms of environmental safety negligence. Departures from the standard of nursing care related to environmental safety problems were associated with failure to use safety devices properly to restrain the patient or failure to assist or supervise the patient properly.

Other mechanisms of injury in the medical setting included the improper use of equipment, inadequate execution of a nursing treatment or procedure, omission of a nursing treatment or procedure, inadequate nursing assessment, and inadequate communication with the physician. Mechanisms of injury responsible for adverse outcomes in the medical setting are summarized in Table 6.7.

TABLE 6.7 Mechanisms of Injury Responsible for Nursing-Care-Related Adverse Outcomes in the Medical Setting

| | Adverse Outcome | | | |
| | Patient Injury (N = 95) | | Patient Death (N = 53) | |
Mechanism of Injury	No.	%	No.	%
Wrong medication or intravenous infusion dose	6	6.32	10	18.87
Failure to administer a medication	5	5.26	1	1.89
Wrong medication	1	1.53	7	13.21
Incorrect parenteral medication administration technique (IM, IV, SQ)	17	17.89	0	0.00
Incorrect medication order	1	1.53	0	0.00
Medication toxicity or allergy ignored	2	2.11	0	0.00
Fall: patient unattended	6	6.32	0	0.00
Fall: improper use of restraints	11	11.57	2	3.78
Fall: improper use of side rails	7	7.37	0	0.00
Fall: patient not assisted with ambulation	6	6.32	0	0.00
Fall: improper patient transfer technique	7	7.37	0	0.00
Fall: patient heavily sedated	2	2.11	0	0.00
Inadequate supervision with cigarette smoking or consuming hot liquids	2	2.11	1	1.89
Inadequate supervision: elopement	0	0.00	1	1.89
Improper use of equipment	0	0.00	1	1.89
Nursing treatment or procedure not executed properly	9	9.47	8	15.09
No physician response to telephone calls regarding patient condition change	0	0.00	3	5.66
Physician failed to alter treatment plan as patient's condition changed	1	1.05	1	1.89
Inadequate nursing assessment	2	2.11	5	9.43
Failure to inform the physician of abnormal nursing assessments	8	8.42	4	7.55
Failure to inform the physician of a patient's deteriorating condition	2	2.11	9	16.98

NURSING CARE PROBLEMS

Medication Administration Negligence

Slightly over one third (33.78%) of the nursing-care-related adverse events experienced by the medical patient were due to the failure to administer medications properly. Medication administration errors accounted for 33.96% of the deaths and 33.68% of the injuries in the medical setting.

Medical patients in this subgroup were evenly divided between the sexes. The mean age was 51.00 years, and the median age was 50.00 years. Presenting problems of patients were varied and included gastrointestinal alterations (22.00%); cardiovascular alterations (18.00%); neurological alterations (16.00%); neoplasia (12.00%); respiratory alterations (10.00%); musculoskeletal alterations (10.00%); wound, infection, or trauma (10.00%); and endocrine alterations (2.00%).

The most common adverse patient care outcomes due to medication errors in this subgroup were death (36.00%) and brain damage (18.00%). These catastrophic nursing-care-related outcome categories were followed by the categories of peripheral nerve damage (16.00%), thermal or chemical burn (14.00%), cerebrovascular accident (2.00%), hearing loss (2.00%), emotional distress (2.00%), infection (2.00%), renal failure (2.00%), and gastrointestinal hemorrhage (2.00%). Mechanisms of injury included improper technique for parenteral medication administration (34.00%), administration of the wrong dose of medication or intravenous infusion solution (30.00%), omission of medication (14.00%), administration of the wrong medication (12.00%), and administration of medication to a patient manifesting symptoms of toxicity or with known allergy (10.00%).

Administration of the wrong dose of a medication or the wrong dose of an intravenous infusion solution was associated with nearly one third of all adverse events experienced by patients in this subgroup. When the wrong dose of a medication was given to patients, it was not uncommon to find that an extremely large dose had been administered. For example, there were several cases in which 10 times the ordered dose of a chemotherapeutic agent or 20 times the ordered dose of lidocaine was administered. All cases of administration of intravenous infusion solution in excess of that ordered by the physician were associated with fluid overload and death. Heparin was frequently involved when a medication was administered in less than the prescribed dosage. The consequences of such administration were often associated with a stroke or fatal pulmonary emboli.

Administering the wrong medication was another common medication error and was responsible for 12% of the adverse outcomes in this subgroup. The most common drug category associated with administration of the wrong medication was that of the antihypertensive. Eighty percent of the patients receiving antihypertensive medication in error died.

Incorrect parenteral medication administration technique accounted for 34.00% of the nursing-care-related injuries in this subgroup. The majority of the injuries were caused by infiltration of intravenous infusion fluids (especially chemotherapeutic and vasopressor agents), intra-arterial injection of medication rather than intramuscular injection, and inaccurate site location for intramuscular injection.

Other medication errors in this subgroup included the administration of narcotics when the patient exhibited signs of toxicity such as depressed respiration, omission of ordered medications, execution of an incomplete or incorrect medication order, and ignoring of the patient's allergy status. These errors combined were responsible for the remaining 24.00% of the adverse outcomes in this subgroup.

Case 6-1: Medication Administration Negligence

Mr. N., a 53-year-old factory manager, had recently been diagnosed with cancer of the larynx. He was hospitalized for intensive radiation therapy and chemotherapy. Near the end of the chemotherapy protocol, Vincristine 1.5 milligrams was prescribed. The nurse administered 12 to 15 milligrams of Vincristine.

Failure to administer the proper dosage of the medication prolonged the patient's hospitalization by 3 weeks and caused a permanent disability. Mr. N. developed neuropathies and suffers from incontinence of the bowel and bladder as well as impotence. Legal action resulted in a $450,000 payment to the patient.

Environmental Safety Negligence

Problems associated with environmental safety were responsible for 31.76% of the adverse events in the medical setting. Failure to provide a safe environment caused 9.43% of the deaths and 44.21% of the injuries in this setting.

Seventy-seven percent of the medical patients experiencing an adverse outcome associated with environmental safety were 65 years of age or older. Only 11 patients (23.40%) were under 65 years of age. The mean age was 69.00 years, and the median age was 75.00 years. Neurological (34.04%) and cardiovascular (21.27%) problems were the most common reasons for hospital admission in this sub-group. Other reasons for hospitalization included gastrointestinal problems (19.14%), infectious diseases (10.63%), respiratory problems (6.38%), musculoskeletal problems (4.25%), trauma (2.12%), and neoplasia (2.12%). Sixty-eight percent of the medical patients in this subgroup were female, and 32.00% were male.

The most common nursing-care-related injury in this subgroup was that of a fracture (70.21%). The majority of the fractures involved the hip (69.69%), but others included the arm (21.21%), the ankle (6.06%), and the coccyx (3.03%). Additional adverse outcomes in the form of nonfatal injuries included thermal burns (4.25%), sprain (4.25%), limb amputation (2.12%), digit amputation (2.12%), peripheral nerve damage (2.12%), hearing loss (2.12%), and paraplegia (2.12%).

Almost 11% (10.63%) of the medical patients subjected to environmental safety negligence experienced death as an adverse nursing care outcome. Deaths were the result of elopement, jumping from a window, smoking a cigarette without supervision, and discontinuing oxygen administration during a room transfer.

A fall was the most common mechanism of injury (87.23%) to medical patients suffering a negative outcome related to environmental safety negligence. Falls were due to failure to apply restraints properly (19.51%), failure to apply restraints when ordered and indicated (12.19%), failure to provide assistance with ambulation (17.07%), failure to use side rails when indicated (14.63%), failure to lock side rails properly when in the up position (12.19%), failure to use proper patient transfer technique (12.19%), and failure to remain with the patient when needed (i.e., leaving the patient unattended; 12.19%). Of note is that 6.38% of the falls involved a patient jumping out of a window.

Other mechanisms of injury to medical patients in this subgroup included contact with hot liquids (spills; 4.25%), lack of supplemental oxygen during a room transfer (2.12%), lack of supervision for a patient smoking a cigarette (2.12%), elopement (2.12%), and a patient's sitting on a bedpan washer bar of a toilet that was carelessly left in the down position (2.12%).

Case 6-2: Environmental Safety Negligence

A 72-year-old retired man was admitted to the hospital with the diagnosis of syncope and altered mental status. Mr. K. was not oriented to time and place. Occasionally he was disoriented as to person.

One evening after dinner, at approximately 6:00 p.m., Mr. K. told the nurse that he wanted to take a walk in the snow. The weather was bad, with near-blizzard conditions and severe cold temperatures. The nurse did not pay attention to the patient's request because he was "confused."

According to the medical record, the nursing staff did not attempt to assess Mr. K. again until around 9:00 p.m. that night, when it was noted that he was missing from the medical unit. The nurse caring for the patient assumed that he was "wandering around the hospital," and a search was not instituted for several hours. The police were called later in the evening, and Mr. K. was found 3 days later frozen in the snow.

The patient's altered mental status warranted close observation to protect him from harm. Failure to provide a safe environment caused the death of Mr. K. Legal action resulted in a payment of $1,000,000 to the estate of the patient.

Communication Negligence

Problems associated with communication were responsible for 15.54% of the adverse outcomes in the medical setting. Failure to apprise the physician of abnormal assessment data and/or a change in the patient's condition resulted in 24.53% of the deaths and 10.53% of the injuries in this setting.

Medical patients experiencing a nursing-care-related adverse outcome due to inadequate communication were relatively young. Eighty-three percent of the patients were under 65 years of age. The mean age of patients was 44.00 years, and the median age was 40.00 years. Over 65% (65.22%) of the patients were female, and 34.78% were male.

The majority of the patients in this subgroup (34.77%) presented with respiratory system problems (infection, asthma, pleural effusion) or cardiovascular system problems (myocardial infarction). Neurological alterations (seizure disorder, transient ischemic attack, meningitis) and musculoskeletal alterations (low-back syndrome and fractures) were responsible for 26.08% and 21.73% of the hospital admissions, respectively. The remaining 17.37% of the patients in this subgroup presented with endocrine-metabolic problems (diabetes), gastrointestinal problems (bowel perforation), and local infection (cellulitis, foot).

Adverse nursing care outcomes due to communication negligence included death (56.52%), brain damage (13.04%), neurovascular damage to a limb (13.04%), amputation (8.69%), and hemiparesis (8.69%). Failure by the nurse to communicate nursing assessment data adequately to the physician was the mechanism of injury common to all negative outcomes in this subgroup. More specifically, all deaths as well as all injuries were related to inadequate communication of neurological changes (26.08%), respiratory changes (30.43%), cardiovascular changes (21.73%), and/or neurovascular changes (21.73%).

Case 6-3: Communication Negligence

A 24-year-old unmarried nursing student presented to the emergency department with a 2-day history of nausea, vomiting, and diarrhea. A diagnosis of gastroenteritis was made, and she was admitted to the hospital.

By 8:00 p.m. on the day of admission, Ms. L. complained of "a headache and severe stiff neck." Her temperature, 99 degrees Fahrenheit at admission, was now 103 degrees. Tylenol with one half a grain of codeine was administered for "discomfort." In addition, it was noted by a nurse that she "appeared lethargic and sleepy."

According to the nurse's notes, as the night progressed, her level of consciousness deteriorated. By 4:00 a.m., Ms. L. was described as "comatose with occasional spasticlike movements." The change in level of consciousness was attributed to the "narcotic pain medication," and the physician was not consulted.

At 7:00 a.m., Ms. L. was found in full cardiopulmonary arrest. She was resuscitated, and further diagnostic studies revealed pneumococcal meningitis. The patient received antimicrobial therapy along with supportive therapy but died several days later.

Failure to inform the physician promptly of significant neurological status changes contributed to the death of Ms. L. Legal action resulted in a payment of $425,000 to the estate of the patient.

Nursing Intervention Negligence

Problems associated with nursing intervention were responsible for 7.43% of the adverse events in the medical setting. Failure to perform a nursing procedure or treatment properly caused 9.43% of the deaths and 6.32% of the injuries in this setting.

Of the patients experiencing nursing intervention negligence, 55.55% were female, and 45.45% were male. Only one patient in this subgroup was over 65 years of age. Patients ranged in age from 29 years to 74 years, with median and mean ages of 52.00 and 50.00, respectively. Patients in this subgroup presented with gastrointestinal problems (27.27%), neurological problems (18.18%), cardiovascular problems (18.18%), infectious diseases (18.18%), genitourinary problems (9.09%), and musculoskeletal problems (9.09%).

Adverse nursing care outcomes due to a nursing treatment or procedure included death (45.45%), peripheral nerve damage (18.18%), fracture and/or dislocation (18.18%), brain damage (9.09%), and a torn urethra (9.09%). Mechanisms of injury in this subgroup were varied. Adverse events were caused by failure to prevent extubation by the patient; application of four-point restraints to a patient experiencing multiple seizures; severing an arterial catheter during removal, causing retention and migration of the catheter; failure to apply pressure after an arterial stick; failure to deflate the balloon of a Foley catheter before removal; forcing a bedpan under a patient; failure to attach a patient's endotracheal tube properly to a mechanical ventilator; ignoring an obstructed nasogastric tube; initiating hemodialysis in a markedly hypotensive patient; and permitting a patient in hematogenic shock to get out of bed.

Case 6-4: Nursing Intervention Negligence

Mr. D., a 58-year-old retiree, was found in a state of unconsciousness in the bedroom of his home by his wife. He was admitted to the hospital, and a cerebrovascular accident was diagnosed. Past medical history revealed hypertension and episodes of transient ischemic attacks, along with reversible neurological deficit.

The patient regained consciousness 48 hours after admission, and his neurological functioning was greatly improved. Two days later, an order was written for the removal of the Foley catheter. The nurse experienced difficulty in removing the Foley catheter, and it was forcefully removed. This action resulted in a torn urethra, requiring surgical repair.

The nurse did not perform the procedure according to acceptable standards and failed to deflate the balloon on the catheter prior to its removal. Legal action resulted in a payment of $75,000 to the patient.

Nursing Assessment Negligence

Problems associated with nursing assessment were responsible for 4.73% of the adverse outcomes in the medical setting. Failure to assess the patient systematically resulted in 9.43% of the deaths and 2.11% of the injuries in this setting.

Of the patients in this subgroup, 71.43% were male, and 28.57% were female. Patients ranged in age from 26 to 50 years, with 39.00 and 37.00 years of age being the mean and median ages, respectively. Presenting problems were related to gastrointestinal alterations (28.57%), infection (14.28%), musculoskeletal alterations (14.28%), respiratory alterations (14.28%), neurological alterations (14.28%), and trauma (14.28%).

Adverse nursing care outcomes in this subgroup due to assessment negligence were death (71.42%) and serious neurological injury (28.57%). The mechanism of injury common to all patients was inadequate assessment by the nurse of cardiorespiratory status (71.42%) or neurological status (28.57%).

Case 6-5: Nursing Assessment Negligence

A 48-year-old certified public accountant suffering from chronic headaches became increasingly drowsy one afternoon and was taken to the emergency department of a hospital. Mr. H. presented with a history of being hit in the head with a baseball 3 months prior to the development of the headaches. He was admitted to the hospital for observation and evaluation for a possible subdural hematoma.

On arrival to the medical unit at 2:00 p.m., Mr. H. was alert but drowsy, and he was oriented to person, place, and time. Vital signs were within normal limits (blood pressure 120/76, pulse 68, respiration 16), and it was noted that both pupils were equal and reactive to light and accommodation.

At 11:00 p.m., only the patient's blood pressure and pulse were assessed. The blood pressure was 180/110, and the pulse rate was 168. These findings were significantly different from the 2:00 p.m. set of vital signs. However, there were no further nursing assessments noted in the medical record until Mr. H. was found in full cardiopulmonary arrest at approximately 1:00 a.m. Resuscitation efforts were unsuccessful.

Increased intracranial pressure went unrecognized because of the failure to assess vital signs and neurological status systematically. The brain stem ultimately herniated due to the increased intracranial pressure and caused the death of Mr. H. Legal action resulted in a payment of $1,200,000 to the estate of the patient.

Nursing Negligence Associated
With Inadequate Care by the Physician

Problems associated with inadequate care by the physician were responsible for 3.38% of the adverse events in the medical setting. Failure by the nurse to obtain help for the medical patient receiving inadequate care from a physician caused 7.56% of the deaths and 1.05% of the injuries in this setting.

Within this subgroup, patients ranged in age from 24 to 52 years. The mean age was 42.00 years, and the median age was 50.00 years. Sixty percent of the patients were female, and 40.00% were male. Patients presented with possible bowel obstruction (40.00%), status asthmaticus (20.00%), chest pain (20.00%), and head injury (20.00%).

Two catastrophic adverse nursing care outcomes occurred in this subgroup. Eighty percent of the patients died, and 20.00% experienced brain damage. The mechanism of injury in all of the cases except one was failure by the physician to alter a patient's treatment plan after being apprised by the nurse of the patient's deteriorating condition. The nurse was aware of the decline in the patient's condition and had documented it in the medical record. However, the nurse did not seek any additional medical intervention for the patient. In only one case, the mechanism of injury was failure by the physician to return promptly the nurse's call about a change in the condition of a patient.

Case 6-6: Inadequate Care by the Physician

Mr. B., a 52-year-old divorced single parent, presented to the emergency department at approximately 2:00 p.m., complaining of severe chest pains. He was evaluated and admitted to the medical unit.

By 6:00 p.m., the patient began complaining of severe abdominal pain along with intermittent chest pain. He was medicated for the pain and shortly thereafter had a "seizure."

An emergency call was placed to the physician. The physician did not return the telephone call because he "forgot his beeper." The nurse waited an hour before attempting to summon another physician.

Failure to obtain prompt medical care for the patient in acute distress caused a delay in treatment that resulted in the patient's death. Autopsy revealed that the patient was suffering from a ruptured ascending dissecting aortic aneurysm. Mr. B. is survived by two sons, ages 16 and 14. One son is mentally handicapped. Legal action resulted in a payment of $1,050,000 to the estate of the patient.

Nosocomial Infection

Problems associated with nosocomial infection were responsible for 2.70% of the negative outcomes in the medical setting. Failure to prevent or control infection caused 3.77% of the deaths and 2.11% of the injuries in this setting.

Patients in this subgroup were equally divided by gender. The mean age was 47.00, and the median age was 51.00. Patients presented with neurological problems (50.00%), neoplasia (25.00%), and psychosocial problems (25.00%).

Half of the patients suffered death as an adverse nursing care outcome, and the other 50.00% experienced injury as a result of a metastatic infection to a distant site. The mechanism of injury in all cases was inadequate care of the intravenous infusion site, as well as faulty maintenance of the catheter. Half of the adverse outcomes were due to failure by the nurse to change the peripheral intravenous infusion catheter within the maximum of 72 hours. The other half of the negative outcomes in this subgroup were related to failure to care properly for a central venous catheter.

Case 6-7: Nosocomial Infection

A 58-year-old man with a history of cancer received routine chemotherapy via a Groshong catheter as an outpatient. Mr. C. later required intensive chemotherapy and was admitted to the hospital.

During a treatment, the hub separated from the Groshong catheter. A nurse hurriedly repaired the catheter. Twenty-four hours later, Mr. C. experienced an elevated temperature and pain in the hip region.

It was determined that the nurse failed to use sterile technique in the repair of the Groshong catheter. A Methicillin-resistant *Staphylococcus aureus* bacteremia was diagnosed, and there was hematogenous spread of the infection to the area of the right hip. The infected hip area required surgical intervention. Eventually a total hip replacement was necessary. Legal action resulted in a payment of $600,000 to the patient.

Equipment Negligence

Problems associated with equipment were responsible for 0.68% of the adverse events in the medical setting. Failure to use equipment properly caused 1.89% of the deaths in this setting.

The patient in this subgroup was a 57-year-old female. She presented with a respiratory problem and suffered death as an adverse outcome of nursing care. The mechanism of injury was related to the improper use of a mechanical ventilator.

Case 6-8: Equipment Negligence

A 57-year-old woman was admitted to the hospital with the diagnosis of an acute asthma attack. Mechanical ventilation became necessary, and the nurse caring for Ms. S. reversed a one-way check valve on the mechanical ventilator.

Failure by the nurse to know how to operate the mechanical ventilator resulted in inadequate oxygenation. Ms. S. suffered "moderate brain damage." Legal action resulted in a payment of $760,000 to the patient.

MALPRACTICE PAYMENTS

Malpractice payments in the medical setting ranged from $1,000 to $11,000,000, with an overall mean of $769,000 and a median of $322,500. For nursing-care-related injuries (64.19%; 95), the mean malpractice payment was $639,232, and the median was $200,000. Patients in the medical setting suffering death as an adverse outcome of nursing care (35.81%; 53) received a mean payment of $988,302. Table 6.8 summarizes malpractice payment data by adverse outcome.

Problems associated with medication administration and environmental safety accounted for the majority (65.54%; 97) of the malpractice payments made in the medical setting. Table 6.9 presents malpractice payment data by nursing care problems.

The largest number of patients (42; 28.40%) experiencing a nursing-care-related adverse outcome in the medical setting received payments

TABLE 6.8 Malpractice Payments in the Medical Setting, by Adverse Outcome

Adverse Outcome	Malpractice Payments			
	No.	Range ($)	Mean ($)	Median ($)
Death	53	75,000 to 11,000,000	988,302	690,000
Injury	95	1,000 to 10,000,000	639,232	200,000
All deaths and injuries	148	1,000 to 11,000,000	769,000	322,500

TABLE 6.9 Malpractice Payments in the Medical Setting, by Nursing Care Problem

Problem Area	Malpractice Payments (N = 148)			
	No.	Range ($)	Mean ($)	Median ($)
Nursing assessment	7	100,000 to 3,000,000	1,151,714	1,200,000
Environmental safety	47	1,000 to 1,600,000	183,553	68,000
Nursing intervention	11	75,000 to 1,250,000	536,000	360,000
Medication administration	50	12,000 to 11,000,000	831,780	399,000
Inadequate physician care	5	460,000 to 2,930,000	1,210,800	1,050,000
Communication	23	75,000 to 10,000,000	1,498,260	900,000
Infection	4	600,000 to 3,500,000	1,845,000	1,640,000
Equipment and products	1	760,000	760,000	760,000

between $100,001 and $400,000; 16.20% received payments between $1,000,001 and 120,000,000; and 15.20% received $1,000 to $50,000. Figure 6.4 summarizes the distribution of all malpractice payments in the medical setting.

The majority of the malpractice payments (50.93%) in cases of death were clustered in two groups: 16 (30.18%) were between $100,001 and $400,000, and 11 (20.75%) were between $1,000,001 and $2,000,000. Figure 6.5 presents the distribution of malpractice payments in cases of death.

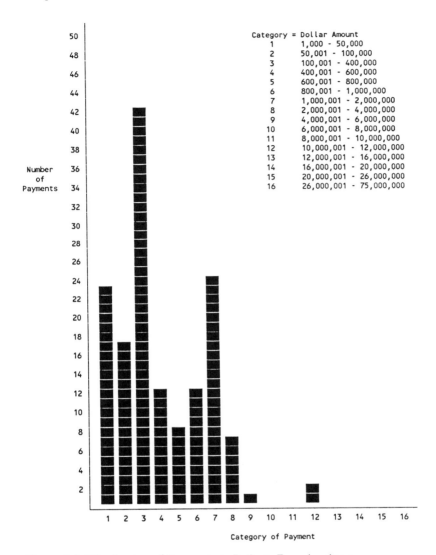

Figure 6.4. Distribution of Payments to Patients Experiencing a
Nursing-Care-Related Adverse Outcome in the Medical Setting

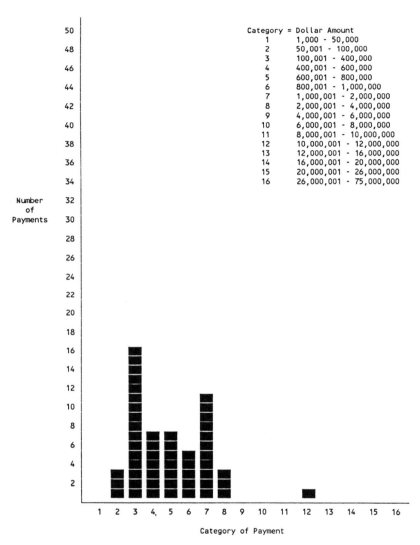

Figure 6.5. Distribution of Payments to Patients Suffering Death as a Nursing-Care-Related Adverse Outcome in the Medical Setting

Over half (66.30%) of the payments to medical patients experiencing an injury as an adverse outcome of nursing care were between $1,000 and $400,000. Nineteen (20.00%) of the malpractice payments were $1,000,001 to $12,000,000, and 13 (13.68%) were between $400,001 and $1,000,000. Figure 6.6 presents the distribution of malpractice payments for cases of nursing-care-related injury.

RISK PREVENTION STRATEGIES
IN THE MEDICAL SETTING

Risk management strategies applicable to all clinical settings as well as those common to selected nursing care problem areas will be found in Chapter 14.

Medication errors and an unsafe environment were the two problems responsible for the majority of the adverse incidents in the medical setting. Prevention of nursing-care-related negative outcomes unique to the patient in the medical setting requires the nurse to ask the following questions:

- Have I respected the "five rights" of medication administration? (See Chapter 14, section "Prevention of Medication Administration Problems.")
- Is the intravenous infusion catheter properly maintained?
- Is the intravenous infusion catheter changed at the first sign of a problem?
- Is the intravenous infusion catheter changed after a maximum of 72 hours?
- Are signs of medication toxicity recognized and reported?
- Is medication withheld when there are signs of toxicity until further direction is received?
- Is the patient's allergy status noted and respected?
- Are restraints promptly applied when the patient's condition warrants such protection?
- Is the restraint properly applied?
- Is the patient systematically assessed while in restraints? (See Chapter 14, section "Prevention of Environmental Safety Problems.")
- Is someone assigned to remain with a patient when indicated?
- Is the patient assisted with ambulation when indicated?
- Is assistance with ambulation promptly provided when requested by the patient?

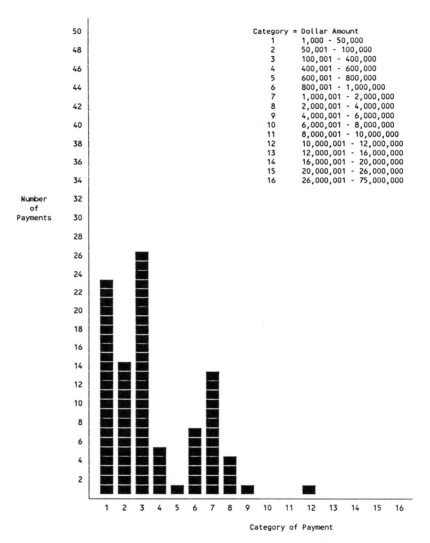

Figure 6.6. Distribution of Payments to Patients Experiencing Injury as a Nursing-Care-Related Adverse Outcome in the Medical Setting

- Is proper transfer technique used when assisting the patient with ambulation?
- Are side rails used when indicated?
- Are side rails properly secured when used?

SUMMARY

Nursing negligence resulted in death to 35.81% of the patients in the medical setting. Medication errors and inadequate communication between the nurse and the physician were the nursing care problems responsible for the majority of the deaths. The remaining patients (64.19%) experienced a nursing-care-related injury. Over three quarters of the injuries were due to an unsafe environment or medication administration error.

Patients ranged in age from 18 to 95 years. The mean age was 54.62 years, and the median age was 54.50 years. Over half (58.11%) of the patients in the medical setting were female. The majority of the patients presented with neurological, gastrointestinal, or cardiovascular problems.

Death was the most common adverse outcome in this setting. The predominant mechanisms of injury were associated with nursing care problems related to medication administration and environmental safety.

Malpractice payments ranged from $1,000 through $11,000,000. The mean payment for all adverse outcomes (148) in the medical setting was $769,000, and the median payment was $322,500.

7

Nursing Malpractice in the Operating Room

The nurse in the operating room setting has the responsibility to apply the nursing process to the delivery of intraoperative nursing care. The operative procedure is not an isolated event, and its outcome depends on many factors related not only to the patient but to the environment in which the process occurs. Safe patient care is the overall goal, and to accomplish this, the nurse must, among other things, ensure freedom from contamination and infection; provide for accurate patient identification; protect the patient from injury due to explosions, burns, improper positioning, and defective equipment; prevent falls and other possible patient injury; and ensure accurate counts and records of foreign bodies such as sponges, needles, and instruments.

Patients experiencing adverse nursing care outcomes in the operating room accounted for 5.89% (44 of 747) of the nursing malpractice cases in the database. Nursing negligence caused or contributed to four deaths (9.09%) and 40 injuries (90.90%) in this setting.

The majority of the injuries were due to inadequate nursing intervention, and half of the deaths were due to inadequate nursing action related to negligent care by the physician. That is, the nurse failed to obtain adequate care for the patient. Table 7.1 summarizes adverse nursing care outcomes due to negligence in the operating room.

120

PATIENT CHARACTERISTICS

Operating room patients experiencing an adverse outcome ranged in age from 1.5 to 75 years. The overall mean age of patients was 46.22 years, and the median age was 47.00 years. In cases of death, the mean age was 37.37 years, in comparison to 47.11 years in cases of injury. Table 7.2 presents age data for operating room patients experiencing a nursing care adverse outcome.

Fifty percent of the patients in the operating room setting were between 41 and 60 years of age. Patients under 41 years of age made up 31.81% of the group, and patients over 60 years of age constituted 18.18% of the group. Figure 7.1 presents age distribution data for operating room patients.

Fifty percent of the patients suffering death in the operating room as an adverse outcome of nursing care were 41 through 50 years of

TABLE 7.1 Nursing Malpractice Adverse Outcomes and Associated Departures From the Standard of Care in the Operating Room

Adverse Outcome Category	Departure From the Standard of Nursing Care Causing the Adverse Outcome	No. of Cases	% of Category	% of Total
Injury		40	100.00	90.90
	Inadequate nursing intervention	23	57.50	
	Improper use of equipment	8	20.00	
	Inadequate care by the physician	4	10.00	
	Inadequate nursing assessment	4	10.00	
	Medication administration error	1	2.50	
Death		4	100.00	9.09
	Inadequate nursing intervention	1	25.00	
	Improper use of equipment	1	25.00	
	Inadequate care by the physician	2	50.00	

TABLE 7.2 Age of Patients Experiencing a Nursing-Care-Related Adverse Outcome in the Operating Room

Age	All Cases (N = 44)	Cases of Death (N = 4)	Cases of Injury (N = 40)
Range	1.5 to 75 yr.	1.5 to 58 yr.	3.5 to 75 yr.
Mean	46.22 yr.	37.37 yr.	47.11 yr.
Median	47.00 yr.	45.00 yr.	47.00 yr.

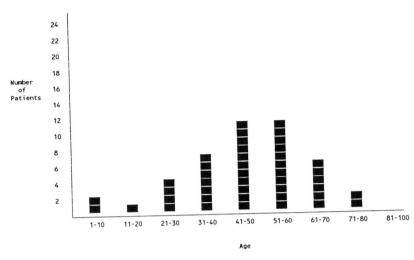

Figure 7.1. Age Distribution of Patients Experiencing a
Nursing-Care-Related Adverse Outcome in the Operating Room

age. The remaining patients were distributed in two age categories:
0 through 10 years (25.00%) and 51 through 60 years (25.00%).
Figure 7.2 presents age distribution data for operating room patients
suffering death.

The majority (65.00%) of the operating room patients experiencing
an injury were clustered in three age groups: 31 through 40 years,
17.50%; 41 through 50 years, 22.50%; and 51 through 60 years,
25.00%. Fifteen percent of the patients were from 1.5 through 30
years, and 20.00% were from 61 through 80 years. Figure 7.3 presents
age distribution data for patients experiencing an injury in the operating room setting.

Of the patients experiencing an adverse outcome in the operating
room, 31.81% were male, and 68.18% were female. Table 7.3 presents
gender data for operating room patients experiencing a nursing care
adverse outcome.

Slightly over one third (34.09%) of the patients presented to the
operating room for an orthopedic procedure. The procedures included joint, ligament, and/or muscle surgery (53.00%); laminectomy
(27.00%); and open reduction with internal fixation of a fracture

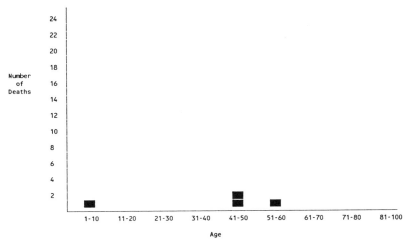

Figure 7.2. Age Distribution of Patients Suffering Death as a
Nursing-Care-Related Adverse Outcome in the Operating Room

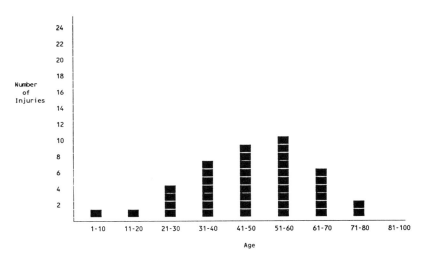

Figure 7.3. Age Distribution of Patients Experiencing Injury as a
Nursing-Care-Related Adverse Outcome in the Operating Room

(20.00%). Genitourinary surgery was performed in 25.00% of the cases and included procedures related to gynecological intervention (91.00%) or kidney, ureter, or bladder surgery (9.00%). Surgery on the gastrointestinal tract accounted for 22.72% of the procedures: 80.00% of these cases involved a laparotomy, and 20.00% involved colorectal surgery. Cardiovascular procedures made up 11.36% of the cases. Sixty percent of the cardiovascular surgical procedures were coronary artery bypass grafts, and 40.00% were femoral artery bypass grafts. Neurological surgery was performed on 4.54% of the patients (carotid endarterectomy, 50.00%; aneurysm clipping, 50.00%), and the remaining 2.27% of the cases involved ear, nose, and throat surgery (tonsillectomy-adenoidectomy, 100.00%). Table 7.4 summarizes the presenting problems of operating room patients experiencing a nursing care adverse outcome.

TABLE 7.3 Sex of Patients Experiencing a Nursing-Care-Related Adverse
            Outcome in the Operating Room

Operating Room	Male		Female	
Patients	No.	%	No.	%
Cases, all (N = 44)	14	31.81	30	68.18
Cases, death (N = 4)	1	25.00	3	75.00
Cases, injury (N = 40)	13	32.50	27	67.50

TABLE 7.4 Types of Surgery/Presenting Problems of Patients Experiencing
            a Nursing-Care-Related Adverse Outcome in the Operating
            Room

Type of Surgery/	Adverse Outcome					
Presenting	Total (N = 44)		Death (N = 4)		Injury (N = 40)	
Problem	No.	%	No.	%	No.	%
Orthopedic	15	34.09	0	0.00	15	37.50
Genitourinary	11	25.00	1	25.00	10	25.00
Gastrointestinal	10	22.72	1	25.00	9	22.50
Cardiovascular	5	11.36	1	25.00	4	10.00
Ear, nose, throat	1	2.27	1	25.00	0	0.00
Neurological	2	4.54	0	0.00	2	5.00

ADVERSE NURSING
CARE OUTCOMES

The most common adverse outcome related to nursing malpractice in the operating room setting was the need for additional surgery due to retained sponges, instruments, or other foreign bodies introduced during surgery (52.27%). This negative outcome category was followed by the categories of surgery on the wrong limb (9.09%) and death (9.09%). Other nursing-care-related injuries in the operating room included thermal or electrical burn (6.81%), corneal burn (4.54%), lumbar disc injury (4.54%), emotional distress (2.27%), chemical burn (2.27%), infection (2.27%), perforation of a hollow viscus (2.27%), brain damage (2.27%), and stroke (2.27%). Table 7.5 summarizes operating room adverse outcomes.

The majority of the nursing-care-related adverse events were associated with nursing intervention problems. Failure to perform a nursing treatment or procedure properly was the departure from the standard of nursing care responsible for 54.54% of the negative outcomes in the operating room setting. Other nursing care problems in the operating room were those associated with equipment and products (20.45%), inadequate care by the physician (13.69%), nursing assessment (9.09%), and medication administration (2.27%). Nursing

TABLE 7.5 Type of Adverse Outcome Caused by Nursing Malpractice in the Operating Room

Adverse Outcome Caused by Nursing Malpractice	No. of Cases	% of Cases
Additional surgery for retained sponge(s), instrument, or other foreign body introduced at surgery	23	52.27
Wrong limb operated upon	4	9.09
Death	4	9.09
Thermal or electrical burn	3	6.81
Corneal burn	2	4.54
Lumbar disc injury	2	4.54
Emotional distress	1	2.27
Chemical burn	1	2.27
Infection	1	2.27
Perforated uterine wall	1	2.27
Brain damage	1	2.27
Cerebrovascular accident	1	2.27

TABLE 7.6 Nursing Care Problems and Associated Departures From the Standard of Care in the Operating Room

Problem Area	Departure From the Standard of Care	No. of Cases	% of Cases
Nursing intervention	Failure to perform a nursing treatment or procedure properly	24	54.54
Equipment and products	Failure to use equipment/products properly	9	20.45
Inadequate physician care	Failure to obtain help for a patient not receiving adequate care from a physician	6	13.69
Nursing assessment	Failure to assess the patient properly	4	9.09
Medication administration	Failure to administer medication(s) properly	1	2.27

care problems and the associated departures from the standard of care are summarized in Table 7.6.

The most frequent mechanisms of injury causing harm to the patient in the operating room setting were those of a retained sponge due to an absent or negligent sponge count (32.50%) or a retained instrument or instrument part/fragment due to negligent inspection or count (17.50%). Mechanisms of injury related to cases of death included improper cleansing of a cardiac catheter (25.00%); supplying an incorrect laser tip (25.00%); abandonment of the patient by the anesthesiologist, with failure to obtain help for the patient (25.00%); and patient hemorrhage in the presence of the surgeon, with failure to obtain help for the patient (25.00%). All mechanisms of injury in the operating room setting are presented in Table 7.7.

NURSING CARE PROBLEMS

Nursing Intervention Negligence

Nursing intervention problems were responsible for 54.54% of the adverse events in the operating room setting. Failure to perform a nursing procedure or treatment properly caused 57.50% of the injuries and 25.00% of the deaths in this setting.

Seventy-five percent of the patients in this subgroup were female, and only 25.00% were male. The mean and median ages were 45.12

TABLE 7.7   Mechanisms of Injury Responsible for Nursing-Care-Related
Adverse Outcomes in the Operating Room

	Adverse Outcome			
	Patient Injury (N = 40)		Patient Death (N = 4)	
Mechanism of Injury	No.	%	No.	%
Retained sponge due to absent or negligent count	13	32.50	0	0.00
Retained instrument or instrument part/fragment due to negligent inspection or count	7	17.50	0	0.00
Wrong limb operated upon	4	10.00	0	0.00
Retained sponge, surgeon closed when sponge reported missing	4	10.00	0	0.00
Eye not shielded	2	5.00	0	0.00
Suture packet dropped in operative site but not removed	1	2.50	0	0.00
Surgical consent signed after patient premedicated	1	2.50	0	0.00
Patient not immobilized properly	1	2.50	0	0.00
Cardiac catheter not properly cleansed	0	0.00	1	25.00
Nurse supplied incorrect laser tip	0	0.00	1	25.00
Improper placement of grounding pads	1	2.50	0	0.00
Cautery unit not functioning properly but used	1	2.50	0	0.00
Improper heat application to a limb	1	2.50	0	0.00
Supply or equipment not available	1	2.50	0	0.00
Poor operating room lighting	1	2.50	0	0.00
Instrument failure due to accumulation of biological material	1	2.50	0	0.00
Anesthesiologist abandoned patient, and no help was obtained for the patient	0	0.00	1	25.00
Surgeon permitted patient to hemorrhage, and no help was obtained for the patient	0	0.00	1	25.00
Wrong solution supplied to the surgeon	1	2.50	0	0.00

and 47.00 years, respectively. In addition, 88% of the patients in this subgroup were under 65 years of age. Patients presented for the following types of surgery: genitourinary (33.33%), gastrointestinal (33.33%), orthopedic (16.66%), and cardiovascular (16.66%).

The most common nursing-care-related adverse outcome was that of the need for additional surgery (83.33%). Other negative outcomes due to nursing negligence included death (4.16%), perforated hollow viscus (4.16%), infection (4.16%), and emotional distress (4.16%).

The mechanism of injury common to 54.16% of the adverse incidents in this subgroup was a retained sponge or sponges due to a negligent or absent sponge count. Retained instruments or instrument parts/fragments were the mechanism of injury to 29.16% of the patients. A negligent instrument count or inspection was the basis of the injury. Other mechanisms of injury were dropping a suture packet into the operative site without removing it (4.16%), inadequate surgical consent because of signing after premedication (4.16%), inadequate patient immobilization (4.16%), and inadequate cleansing of a cardiac catheter (4.16%).

Case 7-1: Nursing Intervention Negligence

A 42-year-old woman was taken to the operating room for a total abdominal hysterectomy and bilateral salpingoophorectomy. Prior to closing the abdomen, the scrub nurse was concerned about a possible missing sponge. However, she failed to alert the surgeon to the potential problem because "he closed so fast." The sponge count in the medical record was recorded as "correct."

Postoperatively, the patient experienced abdominal pain, and an exploratory laparotomy was performed. An 18-inch by 18-inch laparotomy sponge was found in the abdominal cavity, where it had caused a fecal fistula. A temporary colostomy was created for a period of 9 months to permit healing of the fecal fistula.

Failure to execute the sponge count properly caused a serious injury to the patient. Legal action resulted in a payment of $207,000 to the patient.

Equipment and Product Negligence

Problems associated with equipment and products caused 20.45% of the adverse incidents in the operating room setting. Failure to use equipment and/or products properly was responsible for 20.00% of the injuries and 25.00% of the deaths in this setting.

Of the patients in this subgroup, 55.56% were female, and 44.44% were male. Mean and median ages were 50.66 and 50.00 years, respectively. Seventy-eight percent of the patients were under 65 years of age. Patients in this subgroup presented to the operating room for four types of surgery: orthopedic (66.66%), cardiovascular (11.11%), neurological (11.11%), and genitourinary (11.11%).

Adverse nursing care outcomes in this subgroup included electrical and thermal burns (33.33%), corneal burns (22.22%), lumbar disc injury (22.22%), cerebrovascular accident (11.11%), and death (11.11%). Mechanisms of injury were varied. The most common was improper shielding of the eye (22.22%). Other mechanisms of injury included improper placement of grounding pads (11.11%), improper functioning of the cautery unit (11.11%), improper heat application to a limb (11.11%), unavailability of a required supply or type of equipment (11.11%), provision of an incorrect laser tip (11.11%), poor lighting (11.11%), and accumulation of biological material on an instrument, causing it to fail (11.11%).

Case 7-2: Product Negligence

J. K., a 57-year-old tool-and-die business owner, had a history of chronic sinusitis. He developed a third episode of frontal sinusitis in a 1-year period that failed to respond to antibiotics and medical management. The patient was admitted to the hospital for nasal surgery and was taken to the operating room for surgical obliteration of the right frontal sinus.

Hibiclens (chlorhexidine gluconate) was accidentally splashed in the patient's right eye. The surgical nurse who was cleansing the skin was "rushed" because of a "heavy operating room schedule."

Failure to protect the patient's eyes when preparing the skin at the surgical site caused a corneal burn. Vision to the affected eye is 20/400. Legal action resulted in a payment of $1,100,000 to the patient.

Nursing Negligence Associated With Inadequate Care by the Physician

Nursing negligence associated with inadequate care by the physician was responsible for 13.69% of the adverse events in the operating room setting. Failure to obtain help for a patient not receiving adequate care from a physician caused 10.00% of the injuries and 50.00% of the deaths in this setting.

Patients in this subgroup were evenly divided by sex. The mean age was 42.58 years, and the median was 50.00. All patients were less than 65 years of age. Patients experienced the following types of surgery:

gastrointestinal (33.33%); orthopedic (16.66%); ear, nose, throat (16.66%); genitourinary (16.66%); and neurological (16.66%).

Nursing negligence in this subgroup was associated with devastating outcomes. Fifty percent of the patients suffered either severe brain damage (16.66%) or death (33.33%). The remaining 50.00% of the adverse nursing care outcomes were related to a need for additional surgery.

The mechanism of injury in 66.66% of the cases was a retained sponge. In all of these cases, a surgeon closed the surgical wound even though a sponge was reported missing. Furthermore, the nurse involved failed to report the incident to the operating room supervisor. Other mechanisms of injury included abandonment of the patient by the anesthesiologist (16.66%) and a patient hemorrhaging in the presence of the surgeon (16.66%). In both situations, the nurse failed to obtain professional care for the patient.

Case 7-3: Inadequate Care by the Physician

P. Z., a 52-year-old maintenance worker, presented to the hospital with a severe headache after losing consciousness at work. She was examined, and the diagnosis of a subarachnoid hemorrhage secondary to a ruptured berry aneurysm was established.

The bleeding stopped without surgical intervention, but CT scans and an arteriogram indicated three aneurysms. The patient was hospitalized for 9 days to stabilize her condition. On the 10th day, she was taken to the operating room for repair of the aneurysms.

The aneurysms were clipped without incident, but the circulating nurse and scrub nurse reported to the surgeon that eight one-quarter-inch by one-quarter-inch gauze paddies were missing on the final count. The surgeon was in a "hurry" to finish the operation, and he elected to close the wound without taking an x-ray in the operating room. A Jackson Pratt drain was inserted in the subdural space. The eight missing gauze paddies were never found, and the incident was not reported to the operating room nursing supervisor.

The patient recovered from the anesthesia and responded well to her family. Neurological assessments were within normal limits.

Twenty-four hours later, neurological changes began to occur. P. Z. became lethargic and experienced motor weakness in all four extremities. The observations were reported to the surgeon, but the treatment plan was not altered. The patient's neurological condition continued to deteriorate.

Forty-eight hours into the postoperative period, the patient's temperature was 102 degrees Fahrenheit and a foul odor was emanating from the surgical site. These observations were reported to the surgeon, but again the surgeon did not alter the treatment plan.

On the third postoperative day, P. Z. suffered a cardiopulmonary arrest. Resuscitation was successful, but the patient sustained severe brain damage. P. Z. was taken back to the operating room, and an extensive intracranial infection was found along with the eight missing gauze paddies.

When the scrub nurse and circulating nurse involved in the first surgical procedure learned of P. Z.'s problem, they reported the missing gauze paddies to hospital authorities; however, by this time it was too late to help the patient. In addition, it was noted that the entire surgical procedure had been videotaped. However, when the videotape was reviewed, experts determined that a significant portion of the videotape had been either erased or mechanically edited out.

Failure to report immediately the eight missing gauze paddies as well as the actions by the surgeon caused P. Z. to suffer severe brain damage. Legal action resulted in a payment of $2,700,000 for the continuing care of P. Z.

Nursing Assessment Negligence

Problems associated with nursing assessment were responsible for 9.09% of the adverse events in the operating room setting. Failure to assess the patient systematically caused 10.00% of the injuries in this setting.

Seventy-five percent of the patients in this subgroup were female, and 25.00% were male. The mean age was 34.50 years, and the median age was 30.50 years. Seventy-five percent of the patients were under 65 years old. All patients presented to the operating room for orthopedic procedures.

All patients in this subgroup experienced surgery on the wrong limb as an adverse outcome of nursing negligence. The mechanism of injury was incorrect identification of the limb for a surgical procedure. In 50.00% of the cases, the surgical consent signed by the patient specified the incorrect limb. In 25.00% of the cases, the operating room schedule was incorrect in that it indicated the wrong limb, and preparing and draping the wrong limb accounted for the remaining 25.00% of the incidents. The nursing staff in all instances failed to use assessment skills to identify and verify the correct limb for surgery.

Case 7-4: Assessment Negligence

A 3-year-old child who suffered cerebral palsy at birth was admitted to the hospital for release of contractures in the right hip and hamstring. During the admission nursing assessment, the child's mother noted that various consent forms specified the wrong limb for the surgical procedure. The mother corrected the forms in the presence of the nurse. However, the corrected information was not communicated to the operating room. When the child was taken to the operating room, surgery was performed on the wrong limb.

The nursing staff failed to communicate that the information on the initial operative permit and operating room schedule was incorrect. In addition, the nursing staff failed to identify properly the correct extremity for the contracture release. Legal action resulted in a payment of $230,000 to the child's parents.

Medication Administration Negligence

Problems associated with medication administration were responsible for 2.27% of the adverse events in the operating room setting. Failure to administer a medication properly caused 2.50% of the operating room injuries.

The patient in this subgroup was a 37-year-old female who presented for gynecological surgery. Severe chemical burns occurred when a solution 40 times the concentration ordered was applied to the patient's skin.

Case 7-5: Medication Administration Negligence

A 27-year-old homemaker was admitted to the hospital for a laser colposcopy and a hysterectomy. M. G. had a long history of genital warts and severe endometriosis.

On the day of the patient's surgery, the nursing staff in the operating room was unable to locate the surgeon's procedure cards. An acetic acid solution was to be applied to make the genital warts visible. In the absence of the procedure cards, the nurse proceeded to apply acetic acid. A 30% acetic acid solution was used rather than the 3% solution specified on the procedure card.

Shortly after the surgery, M. G. complained of burning in the areas of the vagina, vulva, and buttocks. Ten days later, full-thickness, third-degree burns were observed in all areas where the patient had complained of burning.

Failure to establish the correct strength of the acetic acid solution to be used caused severe burns that required skin grafting. In addition, a vaginal stricture eventually developed that required surgical removal to restore a functional vagina. Legal action resulted in a payment of $1,930,000 to the patient.

MALPRACTICE PAYMENTS

Malpractice payments in the operating room setting ranged from $20 to $3,000,000. The mean payment for all adverse outcomes was $498,705, and the median was $116,000. In cases of death, the mean payment was $1,633,750, and in cases of injury it was $385,200. Table 7.8 summarizes payment data by adverse outcome.

Nursing care problems in the operating room setting associated with the largest mean payments were medication administration errors and inadequate care by the physician. The greatest number of malpractice payments, on the other hand, were made for problems related to nursing intervention. Table 7.9 presents malpractice payment data by nursing care problem.

Approximately 73% of the total malpractice payments in the operating room setting were distributed in the following three categories: $20 through $50,000 (22.72%), $50,001 through $100,000 (20.45%), and $100,001 through $400,000 (29.54%). Figure 7.4 presents data regarding the distribution of malpractice payments in the operating room setting.

Patients experiencing a nursing-care-related injury in the operating room setting received smaller payments than those suffering death. Eighty-one percent of the injured patients were compensated $20 to $400,000, whereas all of the payments in cases of death were between $800,001 and $4,000,000. Figures 7.5 and 7.6 present malpractice payment distribution data respectively for cases of death and injury.

TABLE 7.8 Malpractice Payments in the Operating Room, by Adverse Outcome

| Adverse Outcome | No. | Malpractice Payments | | |
		Range ($)	Mean ($)	Median ($)
Death	4	935,000 to 3,000,000	1,633,750	1,300,000
Injury	40	20 to 2,890,000	385,200	110,000
All deaths and injuries	44	20 to 3,000,000	498,705	116,000

TABLE 7.9 Malpractice Payments in the Operating Room, by Nursing Care Problem

| Problem Area | No. | Malpractice Payments (N = 44) | | |
		Range ($)	Mean ($)	Median ($)
Nursing intervention	24	20 to 935,000	187,583	105,000
Equipment and products	9	45,000 to 2,890,000	870,666	701,000
Inadequate physician care	6	55,000 to 3,000,000	1,202,500	680,000
Nursing assessment	4	25,000 to 230,000	115,000	102,500
Medication administration	1	1,930,000	1,930,000	1,930,000

RISK PREVENTION STRATEGIES IN THE OPERATING ROOM SETTING

Risk management strategies applicable to all clinical settings as well as those common to selected nursing care problem areas will be found in Chapter 14.

The most common adverse outcome in the operating room setting was the need for additional surgery because of a retained foreign body introduced during surgery or because of operation on the wrong limb. The majority of these nursing-care-related negative outcomes were due to nursing intervention negligence. Prevention of nursing-care-related injuries unique to the patient in the operating room setting requires the nurse to ask the following questions:

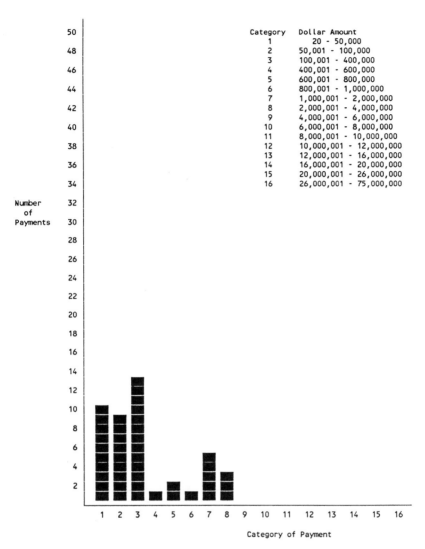

Figure 7.4. Distribution of Payments to Patients Experiencing a Nursing-Care-Related Adverse Outcome in the Operating Room

- Is the surgical consent valid and correct?
- Has the patient been identified properly?

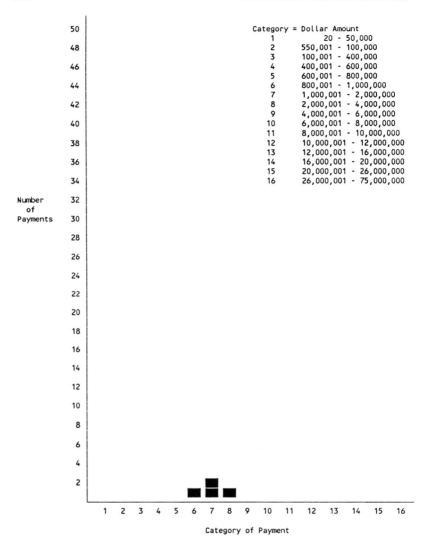

Figure 7.5. Distribution of Payments to Patients Suffering Death as a Nursing-Care-Related Adverse Outcome in the Operating Room

- Has the type of surgery and the body part to be operated on been verified?
- Have sponges been counted?

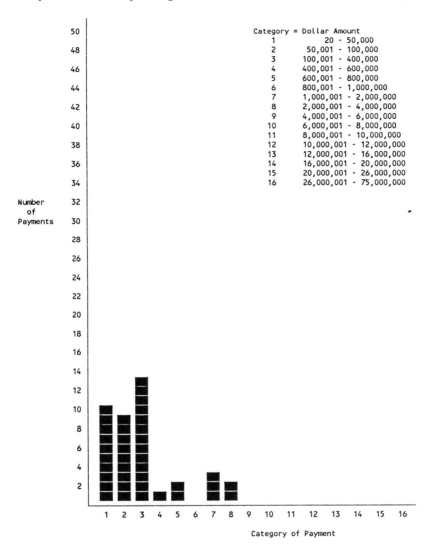

Figure 7.6. Distribution of Payments to Patients Experiencing Injury as a
Nursing-Care-Related Adverse Outcome in the Operating Room

- Has the sponge count been verified?
- Are all instruments accounted for?

- Are all instruments intact?
- Are all instrument components and other materials accounted for?
- Is equipment functioning properly?
- Are required equipment and supplies available?
- Have measures been instituted to protect the patient from injury while he or she is sedated or unconscious?

SUMMARY

Injuries accounted for 90.90% of the adverse outcomes in the operating room setting. A retained foreign body introduced into the patient during surgery or operation on the wrong limb caused 72.50% of the injuries.

Death as an adverse nursing care outcome occurred in 9.09% of the cases. Inadequate nursing action related to negligent care by the physician caused 50.00% of these deaths.

Operating room patients ranged in age from 1.5 to 75 years. The mean age was 46.22, and the median was 47.00 years. Over two thirds of the patients in this group were female. The most common type of surgery consisted of an orthopedic procedure (34.09%).

The need for additional surgery was the most frequent adverse outcome in the operating room setting. Problems associated with nursing intervention were responsible for the majority of the negative outcomes.

Malpractice payments in the operating room setting were not as large as those in other clinical areas of the hospital. The mean payment for all adverse incidents in the operating room was $498,705. Most of the injuries in this group did not cause permanent damage or disability.

8

Nursing Malpractice in the Recovery Room

Nursing care in the recovery room is concerned with optimizing the biopsychosocial status of the patient immediately after a surgical intervention. It demands the integration of specialized knowledge and skills to develop a plan of nursing care for patients of all ages with a wide variety of problems. Patient care priorities must be established, and the plan of nursing care must be implemented. The ability to make informed and rapid decisions in this setting is a necessity. To provide optimal nursing care for the postanesthetic patient, the interventions must be evaluated in terms of outcomes achieved by the postsurgical patient. Nursing-care-related postanesthesia adverse events occurring to both the surgical patient and the postdelivery obstetrical patient are included in this chapter.

Patients experiencing a nursing care adverse outcome in the recovery room accounted for 5.48% (41 of 747) of the nursing malpractice cases in the database. Of these 41 cases, 20 (48.78%) were deaths, and 21 (51.21%) were injuries.

Nursing malpractice in the recovery room caused devastating adverse outcomes. Nursing care that failed to conform to acceptable standards resulted in either brain damage or death to 85.36% of the patients. Failure to assess the patient systematically was the departure from the standard of care responsible for the majority (60.00%) of the deaths. Injuries were caused predominantly by inadequate nursing assessment (33.33%), improper use of equipment (19.04%), and inadequate nursing intervention (19.04%). Table 8.1 summarizes nursing malpractice adverse outcomes and associated departures from the standard of care.

PATIENT CHARACTERISTICS

The age of recovery room patients experiencing a nursing care adverse outcome ranged from 5 months to 77 years. The mean and median ages respectively for all patients were 36.35 and 38.00 years. The mean age of patients experiencing an injury as an adverse outcome was 32.12 years, whereas in cases of death it was 40.80 years. The median age for both death and injury cases was 38.00 years. Table 8.2 summarizes age data for patients experiencing a negative outcome in the recovery room.

The age distribution of recovery room patients was quite varied: 0.4 through 20 years, 21.95%; 21 through 40, 31.70%; 41 through 60, 31.70%; and 61 through 80, 14.63%. Figure 8.1 presents the age distribution of recovery room patients experiencing an adverse outcome.

In cases of death, 80.00% of the patients were between 21 and 50 years of age. The remaining 20.00% of the patients were 51 through 70 years. Figure 8.2 presents age distribution data for patients experiencing death.

Patients experiencing an injury as an adverse nursing care outcome in the recovery room were almost evenly divided between 0.4 through 40 years (52.38%) and 41 through 80 years (47.61%). Figure 8.3 presents the age distribution of recovery room patients experiencing an injury.

Almost three fifths (58.53%) of the recovery room patients were female, and 41.46% were male. Table 8.3 summarizes data regarding gender for this group of patients.

The majority of the recovery room patients presented following obstetrical delivery (24.39%), orthopedic surgery (24.39%), gastrointestinal surgery (24.39%), and genitourinary surgery (12.19%). Obstetrical patients were admitted after cesarean section delivery (60.00%), vaginal delivery (30.00%), and ectopic pregnancy (10.00%). All gastrointestinal surgery cases involved a laparotomy; orthopedic procedures consisted of joint repair/replacement (50.00%), open reduction with

TABLE 8.1 Nursing Malpractice Adverse Outcomes and Associated
           Departures From the Standard of Care in the Recovery Room

Adverse Outcome Category	Departure From the Standard of Nursing Care	No. of Cases	% of Category	% of Total
Injury		21	100.00	51.21
	Inadequate nursing assessment	7	33.33	
	Improper use of equipment	4	19.04	
	Inadequate nursing intervention	4	19.04	
	Medication administration error	3	14.28	
	Inadequate communication with the physician regarding nursing assessment data	2	9.52	
	Inadequate care by the physician	1	4.76	
Death		20	100.00	48.78
	Inadequate nursing assessment	12	60.00	
	Medication administration error	3	15.00	
	Inadequate communication with the physician regarding nursing assessment data	3	15.00	
	Inadequate care by the physician	1	5.00	
	Inadequate nursing intervention	1	5.00	

TABLE 8.2 Age of Patients Experiencing a Nursing-Care-Related Adverse
           Outcome in the Recovery Room

Age	All Cases (N = 41)	Cases of Death (N = 20)	Cases of Injury (N = 21)
Range	5 mo. to 77 yr.	23 to 67 yr.	5 mo. to 77 yr.
Mean	36.35 yr.	40.80 yr.	32.12 yr.
Median	38.00 yr.	38.00 yr.	38.00 yr.

internal fixation of a fracture (40.00%), and laminectomy (10.00%).
Sixty percent of the genitourinary surgery cases involved the kidney(s),
ureter(s), and/or bladder, and 40.00% were gynecological. Presenting
problems of recovery room patients experiencing an adverse outcome
are summarized in Table 8.4.

ADVERSE NURSING CARE OUTCOMES

The most frequent nursing-care-related adverse outcomes in the
recovery room were death (48.78%) and brain damage (36.58%).

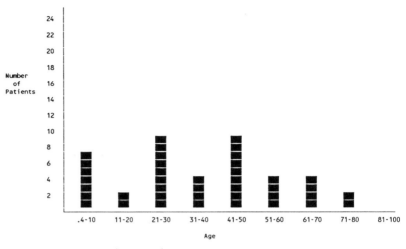

Figure 8.1. Age Distribution of Patients Experiencing a
Nursing-Care-Related Adverse Outcome in the Recovery Room

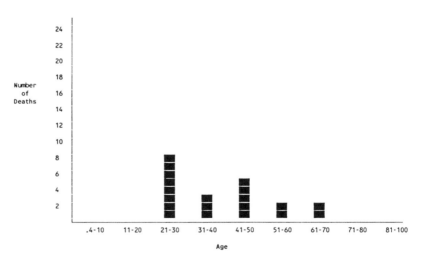

Figure 8.2. Age Distribution of Patients Suffering Death as a
Nursing-Care-Related Adverse Outcome in the Recovery Room

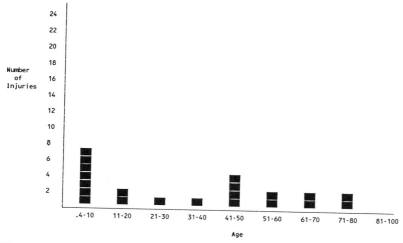

Figure 8.3. Age Distribution of Patients Experiencing Injury as a Nursing-Care-Related Adverse Outcome in the Recovery Room

Other negative outcomes due to nursing negligence included thermal burn, inadvertent T-tube removal, perforated bladder, quadriplegia, amputation, and dislocation of teeth. Table 8.5 summarizes adverse outcomes in the recovery room.

Most of the nursing care problems in the recovery room were related to nursing assessment. Failure to assess the patient systematically caused 46.34% of the negative outcomes. Other nursing care problems were associated with medication administration (14.63%), communication (12.19%), nursing intervention (12.19%), equipment and products (9.75%), and inadequate care by the physician (4.87%).

TABLE 8.3 Sex of Patients Experiencing a Nursing-Care-Related Adverse Outcome in the Recovery Room

Recovery Room Patients	Male		Female	
	No.	%	No.	%
Cases, all (N = 41)	17	41.46	24	58.53
Cases, death (N = 20)	8	40.00	12	60.00
Cases, injury (N = 21)	9	42.85	12	57.14

TABLE 8.4 Types of Surgery/Presenting Problems of Patients Experiencing a Nursing-Care-Related Adverse Outcome in the Recovery Room

Type of Surgery/ Presenting Problem	Adverse Outcome					
	Total (N = 41)		Death (N =20)		Injury (N = 21)	
	No.	%	No.	%	No.	%
Pregnancy	10	24.39	7	35.00	3	14.28
Genitourinary	5	12.19	2	10.00	3	14.28
Orthopedic	10	24.39	6	30.00	4	19.04
Gastrointestinal	10	24.39	2	10.00	8	38.09
Infection	1	2.43	1	5.00	0	0.00
Ear, nose, throat	1	2.43	0	0.00	1	4.76
Plastic repair	2	4.87	1	5.00	1	4.76
Eye	2	4.87	1	5.00	1	4.76

TABLE 8.5 Type of Adverse Outcome Caused by Nursing Malpractice in the Recovery Room (N = 41)

Adverse Outcome Caused by Nursing Malpractice	No. of Cases	% of Cases
Brain damage	15	36.58
Death	20	48.78
Thermal burn	1	2.43
Inadvertent T-tube removal	1	2.43
Perforated bladder	1	2.43
Quadriplegia	1	2.43
Amputation: foot	1	2.43
Dislocation of teeth	1	2.43

Nursing care problems and associated departures from the standard of care in the recovery room are presented in Table 8.6.

The mechanism of injury responsible for 50.00% of the deaths and 28.57% of the injuries was inadequate assessment of vital signs. Other frequent mechanisms of injury in the recovery room were inadequate communication with the physician, medication administration error, and improper execution of nursing treatments and/or procedures. Table 8.7 summarizes all of the mechanisms of injury responsible for adverse nursing care outcomes in the recovery room setting.

TABLE 8.6 Nursing Care Problems and Associated Departures From the Standard of Care in the Recovery Room

Problem Area	Departure From the Standard of Care	No. of Cases	% of Cases
Nursing assessment	Failure to assess the patient systematically	19	46.34
Medication administration	Failure to administer medications properly	6	14.63
Communication	Failure to inform the physician of abnormal assessment data and/or a change in the patient's condition	5	12.19
Nursing intervention	Failure to perform a nursing treatment or procedure properly	5	12.19
Equipment and products	Failure to use equipment/products properly	4	9.75
Inadequate physician care	Failure to obtain help for a patient not receiving adequate care from a physician	2	4.87

TABLE 8.7 Mechanisms of Injury Responsible for Nursing-Care-Related Adverse Outcomes in the Recovery Room

	Adverse Outcome			
	Patient Injury (N = 21)		Patient Death (N = 20)	
Mechanism of Injury	No.	%	No.	%
Inadequate communication with the physician about nursing assessment data	2	9.52	3	15.00
Cardiac monitor alarm ignored	1	4.76	0	0.00
Cardiac monitor alarm not activated	1	4.76	0	0.00
Heating pad applied to a child	1	4.76	0	0.00
Laryngoscope not functional	1	4.76	0	0.00
Physician failed to respond to calls regarding patient problems	1	4.76	1	5.00
Medication administered when contraindicated	0	0.00	2	10.00
Incorrect parenteral medication administration technique	1	4.76	0	0.00
Wrong medication	1	4.76	1	5.00
Wrong medication dose	1	4.76	0	0.00
Nursing treatment or procedure not executed properly	4	19.04	1	5.00
Inadequate assessment of vital signs	6	28.57	10	50.00
Inadequate assessment of blood sugar	0	0.00	1	5.00
Inadequate assessment of airway	1	4.76	1	5.00

NURSING CARE PROBLEMS

Nursing Assessment Negligence

Nursing assessment problems were responsible for 46.34% of the adverse outcomes in the recovery room. Failure to assess the patient systematically caused 60.00% of the deaths and 33.33% of the injuries in this setting.

Of the patients in this subgroup, 63.16% were female, and 36.84% were male. All of the patients were under 65 years of age except for one. Both mean and median age was 38.00 years. Patients experiencing negligent nursing assessment presented to the recovery room following obstetrical delivery (31.57%), orthopedic surgery (26.31%), genitourinary surgery (21.05%), gastrointestinal surgery (15.78%), and surgery for localized infection (5.26%).

Adverse nursing care outcomes in this subgroup were severe and included primarily death (63.15%) and brain damage (31.57%). Only 5.26% of the negative outcomes were minor and involved dislocated teeth. The mechanism of injury common to all patients was inadequate nursing assessment. Specifically, adverse incidents were caused by inadequate assessment of vital signs (84.21%), the airway (10.52%), and blood glucose level (5.26%).

Case 8-1: Nursing Assessment Negligence

A. P., a 50-year-old woman, was admitted to the hospital for removal of renal calculi. Past medical history was insignificant, and the patient was in good health.

The patient tolerated the surgical procedure well and was admitted to the recovery room in "excellent condition." An admission nursing assessment was performed, but systematic assessments after that were neglected for a period of 1 hour. A. P. was found in a state of respiratory arrest by a surgeon who was in the recovery room to examine another patient. Resuscitation was instituted, but the patient never regained consciousness. A. P. died 6 months later.

Failure to assess the patient systematically with appropriate frequency caused A. P. to suffer hypoxic encephalopathy. Legal action resulted in a payment of $305,000 to the estate of the patient.

Medication Administration Negligence

Medication administration problems were responsible for 14.63% of the adverse outcomes in the recovery room setting. Failure to administer medications properly caused 14.28% of the injuries and 15.00% of the deaths in this setting.

Patients in this subgroup were evenly divided by gender. The mean and median ages were 29 and 30 years, respectively. Eighty-three percent of the patients were under 65 years of age. The types of surgical procedures that patients experienced were quite varied. Patients in this subgroup presented to the recovery room following cesarean section delivery (16.66%); orthopedic surgery (16.66%); gastrointestinal tract surgery (16.66%); ear, nose, and throat surgery (16.66%); plastic surgery (16.66%); and eye surgery (16.66%).

Adverse nursing care outcomes were severe and included death (50.00%), brain damage (33.33%), and amputation of the foot (16.66%). The most common mechanisms of injury involved the administration of a narcotic analgesic when signs of respiratory depression were present (33.33%) and the administration of the wrong medication (33.33%). Other causes of negative outcomes were incorrect parenteral medication technique (16.66%) and the administration of the wrong dosage of a medication (16.66%).

Case 8-2: Medication Administration Negligence

C. B., a 23-year-old pregnant woman, presented to the hospital in active labor at 34 weeks gestation. An emergency cesarean section delivery resulted in the birth of Baby B. The mother was admitted to the recovery room in "good condition."

Thirty minutes after admission, C. B.'s blood pressure dropped from 120/80 to 80/50 mm Hg, and her heart rate increased from 80 to 105 beats per minute. "Heavy vaginal bleeding" was also noted. The patient complained of pain at this time and was given the maximum prescribed dose of morphine sulfate by the intravenous route. Her blood pressure fell to 70/33 mm Hg, and the pulse rate increased to 185 beats per minute.

The surgeon was called, and C. B. was taken back to the operating room. Efforts to control bleeding were unsuccessful and a hysterectomy was performed. Postoperatively, the patient developed disseminated intravascular clotting. Transfusions of nearly twice her blood volume were required. C. B. experienced adult respiratory distress syndrome and expired 21 days later.

Administration of the morphine sulfate to the patient while vital signs were unstable contributed to the problems C. B. suffered. Legal action resulted in a payment of $250,000 to the estate of the patient.

Nursing Intervention Negligence

Nursing intervention problems caused 12.19% of the adverse events in the recovery room. Failure to perform a nursing procedure or treatment properly was responsible for 19.04% of the injuries and 5.00% of the deaths in this setting.

Sixty percent of the patients in this subgroup were male, and 40.00% were female. Both mean and median age of patients was 50.00 years. Sixty percent of those experiencing nursing intervention negligence were under 65 years of age. Patients presented to the recovery room following gastrointestinal tract surgery (40.00%), eye surgery (20.00%), plastic/reconstructive surgery (20.00%), and orthopedic surgery (20.00%).

Nursing-care-related adverse outcomes were varied and included inadvertent T-tube removal (20.00%), brain damage (20.00%), death (20.00%), perforated bladder (20.00%), and quadriplegia (20.00%). Mechanisms of injury corresponding to the negative outcomes were inadequate protection of the T-tube (20.00%), delay in cardiopulmonary resuscitation (20.00%), improper airway management (20.00%), improper urinary catheterization (20.00%), and improper body alignment and positioning (20.00%).

Case 8-3: Nursing Intervention Negligence

D. P., 77-year-old female, was admitted to the recovery room following a cataract extraction and an intraocular lens implantation. D. P. had a history of urinary system problems and experienced difficulty in voiding postoperatively. Urinary catheterization was eventually ordered by the physician.

The nurse who performed the urinary catheterization experienced difficulty in inserting the catheter. After several attempts, the catheter was inserted by applying pressure to it. Failure to perform the procedure properly by using excessive force in inserting the catheter caused a perforation of the bladder. Surgical intervention was necessary. Legal action resulted in a payment of $484,000 to the patient.

Communication Negligence

Communication problems were responsible for 12.19% of the adverse events in the recovery room. Failure to inform the physician of abnormal assessment data and/or a change in the patient's condition caused 9.52% of the injuries and 15.00% of the deaths in this setting.

All patients in this subgroup were female, and all were under 65 years of age. Mean and median ages were 26.00 and 27.00 years, respectively. These patients presented to the recovery room following uncomplicated obstetrical delivery (40.00%), open reduction with internal fixation of a fracture (40.00%), and gastrointestinal surgery (20.00%).

Communication negligence resulted in the tragic outcomes. Sixty percent of the patients in this subgroup suffered death, and 40.00% experienced brain damage. The mechanism of injury responsible for 60.00% of the adverse outcomes was inadequate communication of circulatory status changes. A significant change in vital signs was the most frequent circulatory status assessment that was not reported to the physician. Negligent communication to the physician of neurological status changes accounted for the remaining 40.00% of the adverse events.

Case 8-4: Communication Negligence

A 28-year-old woman was taken to the operating room for a ruptured ectopic pregnancy with bleeding. D. T. tolerated the surgery well and was taken to the recovery room in "good condition."

Thirty minutes after D. T. was admitted to the recovery room, a decrease in blood pressure and an increase in pulse rate were noted. Laboratory reports at this time indicated a markedly decreased hematocrit and hemoglobin. Over the next 3 hours, the patient manifested classical signs and symptoms of hematogenic shock. The physician was not informed of the patient's condition until the patient was found in full cardiopulmonary arrest. Resuscitation was not successful.

Failure to inform the physician of the patient's deteriorating condition caused irreversible hematogenic shock and the death of D. T.

Legal action resulted in a payment of $1,000,000 to the estate of the patient.

Equipment and Product Negligence

Equipment problems caused 9.75% of the adverse events in the recovery room. Failure to use equipment properly resulted in 19.04% of the injuries experienced in this setting.

Seventy-five percent of the patients in this subgroup were male. The mean age was 19.37 years, and the median was 12.50. All patients were under 65 years of age. Patients presented to the recovery room following gastrointestinal tract surgery (75.00%) and vaginal delivery (25.00%).

Nursing-care-related adverse outcomes in this subgroup were brain damage (75.00%) and thermal burns (25.00%). The mechanisms of injury included failure to activate cardiac monitor alarms (25.00%), failure to respond to the cardiac monitor alarm due to the assumption that the alarm was false (25.00%), failure to replace the light bulb in the laryngoscope (25.00%), and application of a heating pad to an infant (25.00%).

Case 8-5: Equipment Negligence

J. P., a 4-year-old child with a history of a congenital heart defect, was admitted to the recovery room after an uneventful herniorrhaphy for correction of a left inguinal hernia. As a "precaution," the physician ordered cardiac monitoring.

Shortly after admission, the alarm on the cardiac monitor sounded. It was ignored for at least 5 minutes. The particular monitor that was used for J. P. was regarded by the nurses as malfunctioning because of numerous false alarms. The alarm this time was not false, and J. P. was found in a full cardiopulmonary arrest.

Failure to respond to the cardiac monitor alarm caused the child to sustain a prolonged period of hypoxia. J. P. suffered profound brain damage. Legal action resulted in a payment of $12,000,000 for the continuing care of J. P.

Nursing Negligence Associated With Inadequate Care by the Physician

Problems related to inadequate care by the physician were responsible for 4.87% of the adverse events in the recovery room. Failure by the nurse to obtain care for a patient not receiving adequate treatment from a physician caused 4.76% of the injuries and 5.00% of the deaths in this setting.

Patients in this subgroup were evenly divided by gender. Mean and median age was 65.50 years. Half of the patients were under 65 years of age. Patients presented following orthopedic surgery (50.00%) and urological surgery (50.00%).

Adverse outcomes due to nursing negligence associated with inadequate care by the physician were brain damage (50.00%) and death (50.00%). The mechanism of injury in all cases was a combination of failure by the physician to respond appropriately to telephone calls regarding the condition of a patient and failure by the nurse to obtain appropriate medical care for the patient.

Case 8-6: Inadequate Care by the Physician

A 67-year-old man was admitted to the recovery room in good condition following a total hip replacement. Forty-five minutes after admission, H. Z.'s blood pressure began to decrease, and it was noted that the dressing on the surgical site was "saturated with blood." Numerous calls were placed to the surgeon, but no one was able to locate him. In the meantime, the patient's blood pressure continued to decrease while his heart rate increased. Bleeding at the surgical site continued, and 2 hours later H. Z. suffered a cardiopulmonary arrest. Resuscitation was not successful. The surgeon was not located until after H. Z. expired.

Failure to obtain adequate care for the patient by calling another surgeon caused the death of H. Z. Legal action resulted in a payment of $250,000 to the estate of the patient.

MALPRACTICE PAYMENTS

Malpractice payments in the recovery room setting ranged from $150,000 to $12,000,000. The mean payment combining all adverse events was $2,133,439. A substantial number of negative outcomes involved brain damage with the consequent need for lifelong care. Thus malpractice payments in general were larger for cases of injury than for death. The mean payment in cases of injury was $3,363,047, compared to the mean of $842,350 in cases of death. Table 8.8 summarizes malpractice payment data by adverse outcome.

The largest number of malpractice payments were made because of nursing assessment problems. However, the nursing care problem associated with the largest mean payment was related to equipment and products. Table 8.9 presents malpractice payment data for the recovery room by nursing care problem.

Fifty-one percent of all the malpractice payments in the recovery room fell into two dollar-amount categories: $100,001 to $400,000 (24.30%) and $1,000,001 to $2,000,000 (26.80%). The remainder of the payments were distributed as follows: $400,001 to $600,000 (12.10%), $600,001 to $800,000 (2.40%), $800,001 to $1,000,000 (7.30%), $2,000,001 to $4,000,000 (14.60%), $6,000,001 to $8,000,000 (2.40%), $8,000,001 to $10,000,000 (7.30%), and $10,000,001 to $12,000,000 (2.40%). The distribution of malpractice payments by adverse outcome is presented in Figure 8.4.

TABLE 8.8 Malpractice Payments in the Recovery Room, by Adverse Outcome

| Adverse Outcome | No. | Malpractice Payments | | |
		Range ($)	Mean ($)	Median ($)
Death	20	180,000 to 2,200,000	842,350	723,000
Injury	21	150,000 to 12,000,000	3,363,047	2,000,000
All deaths and injuries	41	150,000 to 12,000,000	2,133,439	1,150,000

TABLE 8.9 Malpractice Payments in the Recovery Room, by Nursing Care Problem

| Problem Area | No. | Malpractice Payments (N = 41) | | |
		Range ($)	Mean ($)	Median ($)
Nursing assessment	19	150,000 to 4,000,000	1,540,578	1,200,000
Nursing intervention	5	268,000 to 9,130,000	2,200,000	487,000
Medication administration	6	250,000 to 1,860,000	782,666	455,000
Inadequate physician care	2	250,000 to 2,000,000	1,125,000	1,125,000
Communication	5	367,000 to 9,000,000	3,473,400	1,000,000
Equipment and products	4	500,000 to 12,000,000	5,722,500	5,195,000

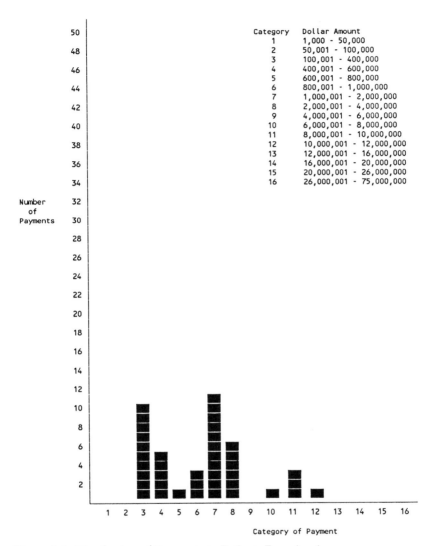

Figure 8.4. Distribution of Payments to Patients Experiencing a Nursing-Care-Related Adverse Outcome in the Recovery Room

Half of the payments in cases of death were between $100,001 and $600,000; the remaining 50.00% were between $800,001 and $4,000,000. Figure 8.5 presents the distribution of malpractice payments for the adverse outcome of death in the recovery room.

Malpractice payments to patients experiencing a nursing-care-related injury fell into three general groups: (a) $100,001 through $800,000 (28.56%), (b) $1,000,000 through $4,000,000 (47.60%), and (c) $6,000,001 through $12,000,000 (23.80%). These payments were substantially larger than those made in cases of death. Figure 8.6 contains the distribution of payments for all recovery room patients experiencing an injury.

RISK PREVENTION STRATEGIES IN THE RECOVERY ROOM SETTING

Risk management strategies applicable to all clinical settings as well as those common to selected nursing care problem areas will be found in Chapter 14.

Eighty-five percent of the patients in the recovery room setting that experienced a nursing-care-related adverse outcome either died or suffered brain damage. The majority of the incidents were related to inadequate patient assessment or medication administration error. Prevention of nursing-care-related injuries unique to the patient in the recovery room setting requires the nurse to ask the following questions:

- Is the content of the nursing assessment appropriate to the patient's condition (especially with regard to vital signs and airway patency)?
- Are nursing assessments performed with appropriate frequency?
- Are the "five rights" of medication administration respected?
- Are respiratory depressants such as narcotics withheld when a patient manifests signs of respiratory depression?
- Are all monitor alarms activated?
- Is there a prompt response to monitor alarms?

SUMMARY

Nursing negligence in the recovery room resulted in devastating outcomes to the patient. The most frequent adverse outcomes were

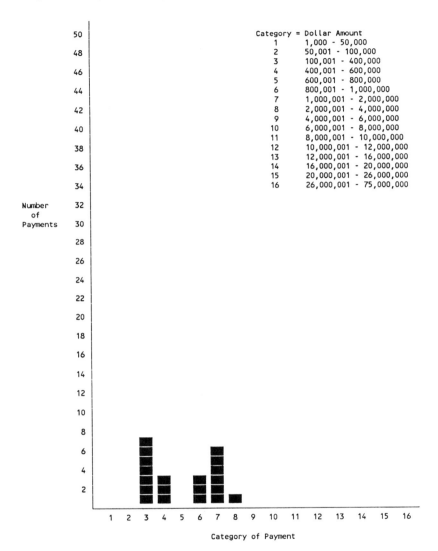

Figure 8.5. Distribution of Payments to Patients Suffering Death as a Nursing-Care-Related Adverse Outcome in the Recovery Room

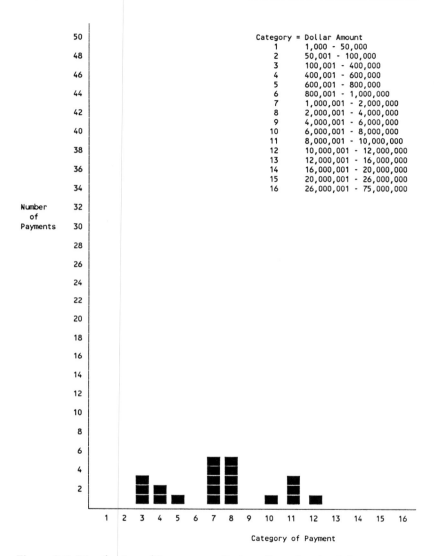

Figure 8.6. Distribution of Payments to Patients Experiencing Injury as a Nursing-Care-Related Adverse Outcome in the Recovery Room

either brain damage or death. The departure from acceptable standards of practice causing the greatest number of nursing-care-related adverse events was failure to assess the patient systematically.

Patients experiencing a negative nursing care outcome in the recovery room ranged in age from 5 months to 77 years. The mean age was 36.35, and the median was 38.00 years. The majority of the patients were female (58.53%). Of the patients experiencing a nursing-care-related injury, 73.17% were admitted to the recovery room following obstetrical delivery (24.39%), orthopedic surgery (24.39%), or gastrointestinal surgery (24.39%).

The most frequent mechanism of injury was inadequate assessment of vital signs. Malpractice payments in the recovery room were substantial because of the large number of patients suffering brain damage. The overall mean payment for recovery room adverse events was $2,133,439. In cases of injury, the mean payment was $3,363,047, compared to the mean of $842,350 for cases of death. The mean payment for injury was thus 3.99 times larger than that for death.

9

Nursing Malpractice in the Surgical Unit Setting

Nursing care of the patient in the surgical setting is centered primarily on the restoration of optimal health after surgical intervention. Postoperative complications may occur after any surgical intervention, regardless of its magnitude. Anticipation and recognition of an early complication are essential nursing responsibilities for safe and effective patient care.

Shortened hospital stays make it more difficult for the nurse to meet the biopsychosocial needs of the postsurgical patient. Patient education and discharge planning take on greater importance with the brief hospital stay and consequently create greater demands on the nursing staff.

The focus of this chapter is on adult patients experiencing nursing care adverse outcomes related to treatment for a pathophysiological disorder requiring surgical intervention. Data for postdelivery obstetrical patients experiencing a negative nursing care outcome are also included in this group because of the small number of cases.

Adverse outcomes in the surgical setting accounted for 20.74% (155 of 747) of the nursing negligence cases examined in the database. Nursing malpractice caused or contributed to 42 deaths (27.10%) and 113 injuries (72.90%) in this setting.

Most of the deaths in the surgical setting were the result of failure to communicate nursing assessment data adequately to the physician

(33.33%) and failure to assess the patient systematically (30.95%). Inadequate communication by the nurse with the physician concerning the condition of the patient and inadequate nursing intervention led to 50.44% of the injuries. Table 9.1 summarizes nursing malpractice adverse outcomes and associated departures from the standard of care in the surgical setting.

PATIENT CHARACTERISTICS

Patients in the surgical setting ranged in age from 18 to 88 years. The mean age was 48.87, and the median age was 47.00. Table 9.2 summarizes age data for patients experiencing a nursing-care-related adverse outcome in the surgical setting.

TABLE 9.1 Nursing Malpractice Adverse Outcomes and Associated Departures From the Standard of Care in the Surgical Setting

Adverse Outcome Category	Departure From the Standard of Care Causing the Adverse Outcome	No. of Cases	% of Category	% of Total
Death		42	100.00	27.10
	Inadequate communication with the physician regarding nursing assessment data	14	33.33	
	Inadequate nursing assessment	13	30.95	
	Inadequate care by the physician	5	11.90	
	Inadequate nursing intervention	3	7.14	
	Medication administration error	3	7.14	
	Unsafe environment	2	4.76	
	Inadequate infection control	1	2.38	
	Improper use of equipment	1	2.38	
Injury		113	100.00	72.90
	Inadequate communication with the physician regarding nursing assessment data	29	25.66	
	Inadequate nursing intervention	28	24.78	
	Unsafe environment	18	15.93	
	Medication administration error	16	14.16	
	Inadequate infection control	8	7.08	
	Inadequate nursing assessment	5	4.42	
	Inadequate care by the physician	5	4.42	
	Improper use of equipment	4	3.54	

TABLE 9.2 Age of Patients Experiencing a Nursing-Care-Related Adverse
Outcome in the Surgical Setting

Age	All Cases (N = 155)	Cases of Death (N = 42)	Cases of Injury (N = 113)
Range	18 to 88 yr.	22 to 82 yr.	18 to 88 yr.
Mean	48.87 yr.	46.11 yr.	49.89 yr.
Median	47.00 yr.	43.00 yr.	48.00 yr.

The age distribution of patients experiencing a nursing-care-related adverse outcome in the surgical setting was varied. The majority of the patients (85.78%) were between 21 and 70 years of age. Only 1.93% of the patients were 18 to 20 years of age, and 12.25% were 71 years of age or over. Figure 9.1 presents the age distribution of patients experiencing an adverse event in the surgical setting.

In cases of death, 47.61% of the patients were between 21 and 40 years of age, and 30.94% were 41 through 60 years. The remaining 21.42% of the patients were 61 or more years of age. Figure 9.2 presents the age distribution of patients suffering the adverse outcome of death.

The largest number of patients experiencing an injury related to negligent nursing care were between 41 and 50 and between 61 and 70 years of age. Patient ages were widely distributed, as follows: 18 through 20 years, 2.65%; 21 through 40 years, 29.19%; 41 through 60 years, 36.27%; 61 through 80 years, 27.15%; and 81 through 90 years, 4.42%. The age distribution for cases of injury is presented in Figure 9.3.

Surgical patients experiencing a nursing care adverse outcome were almost equally divided by sex. Table 9.3 summarizes data regarding gender by adverse outcome.

The greatest number of patients presented to the surgical unit following musculoskeletal system surgery (50 of 155; 32.25%). Gastrointestinal tract and cardiovascular surgical interventions followed in frequency, making up 18.06% and 13.54% of the cases respectively. Surgical procedures involving the gastrointestinal tract were associated with 30.95% of the deaths in the surgical setting, and musculoskeletal system surgery was associated with 38.05% of the injuries. Presenting problems in the surgical setting are summarized in Table 9.4.

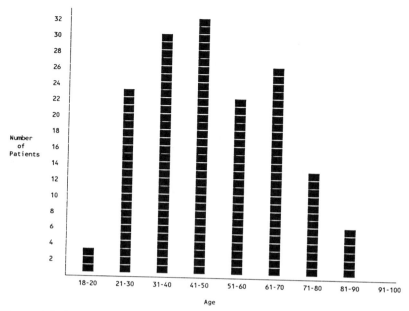

Figure 9.1. Age Distribution of Patients Experiencing a
Nursing-Care-Related Adverse Outcome in the Surgical Setting

ADVERSE NURSING CARE OUTCOMES

Death was the most frequent adverse nursing care outcome in the surgical setting (27.09%). This catastrophic outcome was followed by brain damage (10.32%), infection or wound (10.32%), peripheral nerve damage (9.67%), and paralysis in the form of paraplegia, triplegia, quadriplegia, or hemiplegia (9.03%). All adverse outcomes caused by nursing negligence in the surgical setting are summarized in Table 9.5.

Communication was the most common nursing care problem. Failure to inform the physician of a change in the patient's condition caused 43 of the 155 adverse events (27.74%) in the surgical setting. Nursing intervention problems—namely, those due to failure to perform a nursing treatment or procedure properly—were responsible for 31 of the adverse incidents (20.00%). The remaining adverse

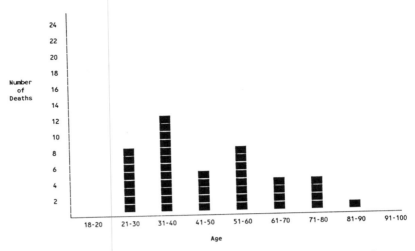

Figure 9.2. Age Distribution of Patients Suffering Death as a Nursing-Care-Related Adverse Outcome in the Surgical Setting

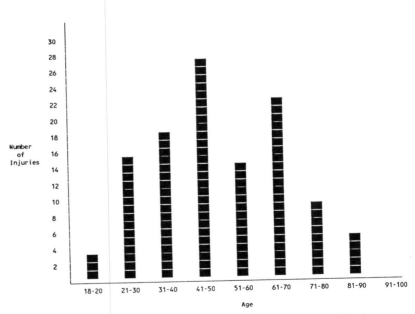

Figure 9.3. Age Distribution of Patients Experiencing Injury as a Nursing-Care-Related Adverse Outcome in the Surgical Setting

TABLE 9.3 Sex of Patients Experiencing a Nursing-Care-Related Adverse Outcome in the Surgical Setting

Surgical Patients	Male		Female	
	No.	%	No.	%
Cases, all (N = 155)	78	50.32	77	49.67
Cases, death (N = 42)	17	40.47	25	59.52
Cases, injury (N = 113)	61	53.98	52	46.01

TABLE 9.4 Types of Surgery/Presenting Problems of Patients Experiencing a Nursing-Care-Related Adverse Outcome in the Surgical Setting

Type of Surgery/ Presenting Problem	Adverse Outcome					
	Total (N = 155)		Death (N = 42)		Injury (N = 113)	
	No.	%	No.	%	No.	%
Musculoskeletal	50	32.25	7	16.66	43	38.05
Gastrointestinal	28	18.06	13	30.95	15	13.27
Cardiovascular	21	13.54	7	16.66	14	12.38
Genitourinary	13	8.38	2	4.76	11	9.73
Trauma	9	5.80	2	4.76	7	6.19
Cesarean section	6	3.87	2	4.76	4	3.53
Central nervous system	6	3.87	2	4.76	4	3.53
Respiratory/thoracic	6	3.87	3	7.14	3	2.65
Ear, nose, and throat	4	2.58	2	4.76	2	1.76
Plastic/reconstructive	4	2.58	0	0.00	4	3.53
Eye	3	1.93	0	0.00	3	2.65
Wound/infection	3	1.93	0	0.00	3	2.65
Endocrine	2	1.29	2	4.76	0	0.00

outcomes were due to problems associated with environmental safety (12.90%), medication administration (12.26%), nursing assessment (11.61%), inadequate care by the physician (6.45%), nosocomial infection (5.81%), and equipment and/or products (3.23%). Nursing care problems encountered in the surgical setting, along with associated departures from the standard of care, are presented in Table 9.6.

The predominant mechanism of injury in the surgical setting associated with adverse nursing care outcomes was inadequate execution of a nursing treatment or procedure (40 of 155; 25.80%). This was

TABLE 9.5 Type of Adverse Outcome Caused by Nursing Malpractice in
             the Surgical Setting ($N = 155$)

Adverse Outcome Caused by Nursing Malpractice	No. of Cases	% of Cases
Death	42	27.09
Brain damage	16	10.32
Infection or wound	16	10.32
Peripheral nerve damage	15	9.67
Paralysis: paraplegia, triplegia, quadriplegia, hemiplegia	14	9.03
Fracture	12	7.74
Amputation: limb or digit	10	6.45
Sprain or dislocation	8	5.16
Respiratory system damage	4	2.58
Tissue necrosis	3	1.93
Cerebrovascular accident	3	1.93
Genitourinary damage	3	1.93
Sensory loss: hearing, sight	2	1.29
Small bowel necrosis	2	1.29
Retained catheter or drain	2	1.29
Emotional distress	1	0.64
Perforated bowel	1	0.64
Thermal or chemical burn	1	0.64

TABLE 9.6 Nursing Care Problems and Associated Departures From the
             Standard of Care in the Surgical Setting

Problem Area	Departure From the Standard of Care	No. of Cases	% of Cases
Communication	Failure to inform the physician of a change in the patient's condition	43	27.74
Nursing intervention	Failure to perform a nursing treatment or procedure properly	31	20.00
Environmental safety	Failure to provide a safe environment	20	12.90
Medication administration	Failure to administer medication(s) properly	19	12.26
Nursing assessment	Failure to assess the patient systematically	18	11.61
Inadequate physician care	Failure to obtain help for a patient not receiving adequate care from the physician	10	6.45
Nosocomial infection	Failure to prevent infection	9	5.81
Equipment and products	Failure to use equipment and/or products properly	5	3.23

followed by inadequate communication to the physician of nursing assessment data (32 of 155; 20.64%). In cases of death, the most frequent mechanism of injury was inadequate nursing assessment (13 of 42; 30.95%). Failure to execute properly a nursing treatment or procedure, on the other hand, was the predominant mechanism causing harm to the patient in cases of injury (36 of 113; 31.85%). All of the mechanisms of injury responsible for adverse outcomes in the surgical setting are found in Table 9.7.

TABLE 9.7 Mechanisms of Injury Responsible for Nursing-Care-Related Adverse Outcomes in the Surgical Setting

| | Adverse Outcome | | | |
| | Patient Injury (N = 113) | | Patient Death (N = 42) | |
Mechanism of Injury	No.	%	No.	%
Inadequate execution of a nursing treatment/procedure	36	31.85	4	9.52
Inadequate communication of assessment data	25	22.12	7	16.66
Absence of communication regarding a patient's deteriorating condition	4	3.53	7	16.66
Inadequate nursing assessment	5	4.42	13	30.95
Physician's treatment plan not altered as patient's condition changed	3	2.65	5	11.90
Physician did not return telephone calls about a change in the patient's condition	2	1.76	0	0.00
Improper use of equipment	5	4.42	1	2.38
Fall: patient not assisted with ambulation	6	5.30	1	2.38
Fall: patient heavily sedated and out of bed	6	5.30	0	0.00
Fall: patient left unattended	1	0.88	1	2.38
Fall: improper use of side rails	2	1.76	0	0.00
Fall: improper use of restraints	2	1.76	0	0.00
Incorrect parenteral administration technique	7	6.19	0	0.00
Wrong dose or drug, or intravenous infusion solution	3	2.65	2	4.76
Medication toxicity or allergy status not monitored	2	1.76	0	0.00
Wrong drug or intravenous infusion solution	1	0.88	1	2.38
Medication(s) not given	2	1.76	0	0.00
Wrong time of medication administration	1	0.88	0	0.00

NURSING CARE PROBLEMS

Communication Negligence

Problems associated with communication were responsible for 27.74% of the adverse events in the surgical setting. Failure to inform the physician of a change in the patient's condition resulted in 25.66% of the injuries and 33.33% of the deaths in this setting.

Of the patients in this subgroup, 53.49% were female, and 46.51% were male. The mean age was 43.00, and the median was 41.00 years. Over 86 (86.05%) of the patients were under 65 years of age, and only 13.95% were 65 or over. Patients presented to the surgical unit following orthopedic surgery, 39.53% (bone/joint, 58.82%; laminectomy/fusion, 41.76%); gastrointestinal tract surgery, 23.26% (laparotomy, 40.00%; cholecystectomy, 20.00%; gastric bypass, 20.00%; esophageal, 20.00%); cesarean section, 9.30%; genitourinary surgery, 6.97% (kidney, ureters, bladder, 100.00%); cardiovascular surgery, 6.97% (open heart, 100.00%); neurological surgery, 4.65% (central nervous system, 100.00%); trauma surgery, 4.65%; endocrine surgery, 2.32%; and ear, nose, and throat surgery, 2.32%.

Adverse outcomes in this subgroup included death (32.56%), paraplegia/quadriplegia (18.60%), amputation (16.28%), brain damage (11.63%), neuromuscular damage (6.98%), stroke (4.65%), small bowel necrosis (4.65%), infection (2.32%), and sensory loss (2.23%). All of the injuries were severe and caused permanent damage to the patient.

The mechanism of injury in all cases was inadequate communication. Failure by the nurse to apprise the physician of a change in the patient's condition caused or contributed to all adverse outcomes. In this subgroup specifically, there was failure by the nurse to report respiratory status changes (30.24%), signs of neurovascular embarrassment (23.26%), neurological status changes (23.26%), gastrointestinal status changes (13.95%), cardiovascular status changes (6.97%), and genitourinary status changes (2.32%).

Case 9-1: Communication Negligence

Mr. R., a 68-year-old semiretired real estate broker, was admitted to the hospital for a partial thyroidectomy. At midnight, 12 hours into the postoperative period, the nurse noted blood on the dressing covering the neck incision. The dressing was reinforced.

At approximately 2:00 a.m., Mr. R. experienced difficulty in breathing. Ecchymosis and edema in the area of the neck were noted at this time. By 2:35 a.m., respiratory distress was marked, and the incisional dressing was soaked with blood.

Around 3:00 a.m., the surgeon was called, and the nurse informed him that the patient was having a "problem with mucus in his throat." The physician ordered suctioning. The surgeon was not told of the respiratory distress or of the bleeding at the wound site.

Failure to communicate complete nursing assessment data resulted in an unrecognized wound hemorrhage. The wound hemorrhage went untreated, and the patient experienced a respiratory arrest. Resuscitation was unsuccessful. Legal action resulted in a payment of $800,000 to the estate of the patient.

Nursing Intervention Negligence

Twenty percent of the adverse events in the surgical setting were related to nursing intervention problems. Failure to perform a nursing treatment and/or procedure properly caused 24.78% of the injuries and 7.14% of the deaths in this setting.

Of the patients in this subgroup, 51.62% were male, and 48.38% were female. The mean age was 53.58 years; the median age was 54.00 years. Over 80% (80.65%) of the patients were under 65 years of age, and 19.35% were 65 or over. Patients presented to the surgical unit following orthopedic surgery, 35.48% (bone/joint, 81.81%; laminectomy/fusion, 18.18%); gastrointestinal tract surgery, 12.90%; genitourinary system surgery, 12.90%; cardiovascular-thoracic surgery, 12.90%; ear, nose, and throat surgery, 9.67%; trauma surgery, 6.45%; plastic surgery, 3.22%; eye surgery, 3.22%; and cesarean section, 3.22%.

Adverse outcomes were varied in this subgroup. Nursing negligence caused or contributed to decubitus ulcer formation and infection (16.12%), hip dislocation (12.90%), genitourinary system damage (9.67%), brain damage (9.67%), death (9.67%), peripheral nerve injury (9.67%), paraplegia/quadriplegia (6.45%), respiratory system damage (6.45%), retained catheter/drain (6.45%), emotional distress (6.45%), perforated bowel (3.22%), and limb amputation (3.22%).

The three mechanisms of injury responsible for over 87% of the adverse outcomes in this subgroup were improper insertion, maintenance, and/or removal of catheters, tubes, or drains (45.16%); improper or inadequate immobilization/positioning (22.58%); and inadequate skin care and turning (19.35%). The remaining 12.90% of the negative outcomes were due to omission of a nursing intervention.

Case 9-2: Nursing Intervention Negligence

Ms. J., a 54-year-old homemaker, was admitted to the hospital for the removal of a mass in the right lung. The surgery was uneventful, and the mass was benign. The progression of Ms. J.'s recovery was within normal limits. However, on the morning of the fourth postoperative day, the patient developed a paralytic ileus. This was treated by the insertion of a nasogastric tube connected to low suction. In the afternoon, the nasogastric tube accidentally became disconnected from the suction. A nurse reattached the nasogastric tube to the suction machine; however, the nurse connected the tube to the exhaust outlet.

Failure to reattach the nasogastric tube to the suction source properly caused air to be pumped into the gastrointestinal tract when the machine was activated. This eventually caused intestinal perforation.

Ms. J. developed a serious abdominal infection. Three additional surgical interventions were required, and her hospitalization was prolonged by 2 months.

The patient continues to suffer from infection. She has been readmitted to the hospital three times since the initial discharge. Legal action resulted in a payment of $925,000 to the patient.

Environmental Safety Negligence

Problems associated with environmental safety were responsible for 12.90% of the adverse events in the surgical setting. Failure to provide a safe environment caused 15.93% of the injuries and 4.76% of the deaths in this setting.

Fifty-five percent of the patients in this subgroup were female, and 45.00% were male. The mean age was 61.35, and the median was 67.00. Fifty-five percent of the patients were 65 years of age or older. Surgical procedures experienced by patients included orthopedic, 35.00% (bone/joint, 42.85%, laminectomy, 57.14%); cardiovascular-thoracic, 30.00%; gastrointestinal, 10.00%; eye, 10.00%; genitourinary, 10.00%; and trauma, 5.00%.

The most frequent adverse outcome due to environmental safety negligence was a fracture (50.00%). Other negative outcomes included soft tissue injury consisting of a sprain and/or dislocation (15.00%), death (10.00%), amputation of a digit (5.00%), loss of sight (5.00%), infection (5.00%), triplegia (5.00%), and peripheral nerve damage (5.00%).

Only one patient in this subgroup was not injured by a fall. The mechanism of injury in this case was that of a door slamming on a finger. A fall was the mechanism of injury responsible for the remaining 95.00% of the adverse outcomes. Falls were a function of failure by the nurse to assist the patient (36.84%), failure by the nurse to protect an ambulatory sedated patient (31.57%), failure by the nurse to remain with a patient when necessary (10.52%), failure by the nurse to raise side rails (10.52%), and failure by the nurse to apply restraints (10.52%).

Case 9-3: Environmental Safety Negligence

Mr. Y., a 68-year-old pedestrian, was struck by a motor vehicle and sustained a left femoral neck fracture. He was taken to the operating room for open reduction and internal fixation of the fracture.

On the first postoperative night, the patient was described as "groggy and confused." He was also incontinent of urine. When the nurse finished with a linen change, she neglected to raise the side rails on the right side of the bed. Shortly thereafter, Mr. Y. was found on the floor.

Failure to provide a safe environment caused Mr. Y. to sustain a fracture of the right femoral neck. This eventually required surgical intervention. Legal action resulted in a payment of $400,000 to the patient.

Medication Administration Negligence

Problems associated with medication administration were responsible for 12.26% of the adverse events in the surgical setting. Failure to administer medications properly caused 14.16% of the injuries and 7.14% of the deaths in this setting.

Sixty-three percent of the patients in this subgroup were female. The mean age was 41.78 years, and the median was 42.00 years. Eighty-nine percent of the patients were under 65 years of age. Patients presented to the surgical unit after orthopedic surgery, 31.57% (laminectomy, 66.66%; bone/joint, 33.33%); gastrointestinal tract surgery, 26.31%; cardiovascular surgery, 15.78%; surgery for wound/infection, 10.52%; plastic/reconstructive surgery, 5.26%; cesarean section delivery, 5.26%; and genitourinary surgery, 5.26%.

Thirty-seven percent of the patients in this subgroup experiencing medication administration negligence suffered either death (15.78%) or severe brain damage (21.52%). Other adverse outcomes included peripheral nerve damage (26.31%), tissue necrosis/chemical burn (15.78%), paraplegia/hemiplegia (10.52%), respiratory system damage (5.26%), and hearing loss (5.26%).

The most common mechanism of injury was the use of incorrect technique for the administration of parenteral medication (36.84%). This was followed by administration of the incorrect dosage of a medication or of an intravenous infusion solution (26.31%), administration of the wrong medication or intravenous infusion solution (10.52%), omission of medication (10.52%), failure to monitor medication toxicity (10.52%), and administration of medication at the wrong time (5.26%).

Case 9-4: Medication Administration Negligence

A 24-year-old mother of two children was admitted to the hospital for a lumbar laminectomy. The surgery was uneventful, and postoperatively, Ms. G. was to receive an intravenous infusion of normal saline solution. When the patient arrived on the surgical unit, a 5% dextrose-in-water intravenous solution was in the process of infusing.

Six hours after surgery, the patient complained of a severe headache. She became lethargic and experienced projectile vomiting. Administration of the 5% dextrose-in-water intravenous infusion solution continued throughout the night.

Ms. G. was very difficult to arouse the next morning, and when she was awakened, she again complained of a severe headache. The 5% dextrose-in-water intravenous solution was still infusing. Ms. G. had a seizure late in the morning, and the physician was notified. By the time the physician arrived at the hospital, the patient had experienced a respiratory arrest. Though she was resuscitated, she remained in a coma. Two weeks later, the patient died.

Failure to administer the correct intravenous infusion solution and failure to detect obvious signs of hyponatremia caused the death of Ms. G. Legal action resulted in a payment of $1,140,000 to the estate of the patient.

Nursing Assessment Negligence

Problems associated with nursing assessment were responsible for 11.61% of the adverse events in the surgical setting. Failure to assess the patient systematically caused 4.42% of the injuries and 30.95% of the deaths in this setting.

Sixty-one percent of the patients experiencing inadequate nursing assessment were female. The mean age was 45.28, and the median was 40.50. Eighty-nine percent of the patients were under 65 years of age.

The most common surgical interventions experienced by patients in this subgroup were cardiovascular, 33.33% (open heart, 83.00%; vascular, 17.00%); orthopedic, 22.22% (laminectomy, 100.00%); gastrointestinal, 11.11%; and neurological, 11.11%. Other surgical procedures involved the genitourinary system (5.55%), sensory system (5.55%), respiratory system (5.55%), and trauma (5.55%).

Negligent patient assessment caused the adverse outcomes of death (72.22%) and permanent neurological damage (27.77%). The mechanism of injury common to all adverse outcomes was inadequate nursing assessment. Nursing negligence specifically involved inadequate respiratory status assessment (38.88%), inadequate cardiovascular status assessment (33.33%), inadequate neurological status assessment (22.22%), and inadequate wound status assessment (5.55%).

Case 9-5: Nursing Assessment Negligence

Ms. B., a 55-year-old homemaker with a history of headache, neck pain, and hand numbness, was diagnosed with advanced degenerative cervical disc disease (C3-C4) with secondary spinal stenosis. She was admitted to the hospital for an anterior cervical diskectomy. The surgery was uneventful.

At 8:00 p.m., 6 hours postoperatively, Ms. B. complained of sensory and motor alterations in her limbs. At this time, a "mild weakness in all extremities" was noted by the nurse in the medical record. No neurological status assessments were made by the nursing staff for the next 10 hours. In the morning, Ms. B. was found to be quadriplegic. Shortly thereafter, she experienced a cardiopulmonary arrest.

Failure to assess systematically the neurological status of the patient and failure to detect significant neurological changes caused the death of Ms. B. Legal action resulted in a payment of $300,000 to the estate of the patient.

Nursing Negligence Associated With Inadequate Care by the Physician

Problems related to inadequate care by the physician were responsible for 6.45% of the adverse events in the surgical setting. Failure to obtain care for a patient not receiving adequate treatment from the physician caused 4.42% of the injuries and 11.90% of the deaths in this setting.

Ninety percent of the patients in this subgroup were male. The mean age was 45.80, and the median age was 48.50. Ninety percent of the patients were under 65 years of age. Patients presented postoperatively following gastrointestinal surgery (30.00%), neurological surgery (20.00%), trauma surgery (20.00%), cardiovascular-thoracic surgery (20.00%), and endocrine surgery (10.00%).

Adverse outcomes suffered by the patients in this subgroup were severe and included death (50.00%), stroke or brain damage (20.00%), infection (20.00%), and amputation (10.00%). The mechanism of injury responsible for 80.00% of the negative outcomes was twofold: first, failure by the physician to institute appropriate treatment when he or she was informed of a patient problem, and then failure by the nurse to secure care for the patient by another physician in accordance with hospital policy/procedure. The remaining 20.00% of the adverse events in this subgroup were caused by the physician's failure to respond to telephone calls about changes in a patient's condition. Again, in this situation, the nurse did not attempt to secure care for the patient by contacting another physician.

Case 9-6: Inadequate Care by the Physician

Mr. Y., a 57-year-old brake form operator, suffered a cerebrovascular accident. He made a complete recovery after several months of rehabilitation and was able to return to his job. However, upon further evaluation, he was advised to have a carotid endarterectomy.

Mr. Y. entered the hospital for the recommended surgery. In the immediate postoperative period, nurses noted that the patient exhibited slurred speech, a facial droop, clonus of the right ankle, and limited eye movement, with a gaze only to the midline. The surgeon was immediately informed of the findings, and medical therapy was prescribed. Mr. Y. became lethargic, and his blood pressure was elevated. The surgeon was called again, and more medications were prescribed.

Neurologically, the patient's condition deteriorated. The surgeon examined Mr. Y. the next morning. At this time, the patient was unable to speak and was unable to move his right arm or leg. The physician noted in the progress record of the chart that he planned to evaluate the patient. No new orders for the patient were written by the physician. Nothing was done for the patient, even though the nursing staff was concerned about his condition.

Failure by the nursing staff to intervene on behalf of the patient contributed to Mr. Y.'s injury. The hospital policy and procedure related to procuring care for a patient receiving inadequate care from a physician was ignored.

Mr. Y. now suffers from a permanent right hemiparesis and a total inability to speak. He can walk only short distances and requires care 24 hours a day. Legal action resulted in a payment of $1,630,000 to the patient.

Nosocomial Infection

Problems associated with nosocomial infection were responsible for 5.81% of the adverse events in the surgical setting. Failure to prevent infection caused 7.08% of the injuries and 2.38% of the deaths in this setting.

Of the patients, 55.56% were male, and 44.44% were female. The mean age of patients in this subgroup was 50.22, and the median was 45.00. Eighty-nine percent of the patients were under 65 years of age.

Patients presented to the surgical unit following orthopedic surgery (33.33%), plastic surgery (22.22%), gastrointestinal tract surgery (22.22%), wound surgery (11.11%), and genitourinary surgery (11.11%).

Adverse outcomes experienced by patients in this subgroup included wound infection (88.88%) and death (11.11%). Three mechanisms of injury were responsible for all of the adverse events. Sixty-seven percent of the negative outcomes were due to failure by the nurse to assess the surgical wound systematically and report signs of infection to the physician. Failure to care properly for the surgical wound (22.22%) and the intravenous infusion site (11.11%) accounted for the remaining mechanisms of injury.

Case 9-7: Nosocomial Infection

Mr. S., a 62-year-old cost analyst, was admitted to the hospital for a total hip arthroplasty. His recovery was uneventful, and he was discharged from the hospital in excellent condition.

Eight days later, while at home, Mr. S. suffered severe shortness of breath and chest pain. He was taken to the hospital by ambulance, and a pulmonary embolism was diagnosed.

An intravenous infusion catheter was inserted, and heparin was administered. Five days later, Mr. S. noted purulent material beneath the skin at the intravenous infusion site. In addition, his arm was red, swollen, and painful. He brought this to the attention of the nurse, and the intravenous infusion site was changed for the first time. The physician was not informed of the signs and symptoms of infection at the intravenous infusion catheter site.

Several days later, Mr. S. developed an elevated temperature and an elevated leukocyte count. In addition, he experienced pain at the site of the recently replaced hip. The orthopedic surgeon performed a needle aspiration in the hip area, and purulent material was recovered. It cultured out as *Staphylococcus aureus*. The hip was opened for drainage and installation of antibiotics. Antibiotics were also administered intravenously.

Failure to change the intravenous infusion catheter and site within an absolute maximum of 72 hours, along with the failure to report the infection, caused serious injury to the patient. Hematogenous migration of the bacteria from the localized infection at the intravenous infusion site caused infection in the prosthetic hip. The infection progressed, and the prosthetic hip was eventually removed. Six months later, a prosthetic hip was reimplanted. Legal action resulted in a payment of $377,000 to the patient.

Equipment and Product Negligence

Problems associated with equipment and/or products were responsible for 3.23% of the adverse events in the surgical setting. Failure to use equipment and/or products properly caused 3.54% of the injuries and 2.38% of the deaths in this setting.

All of the patients in this subgroup were male. The mean age was 49.40; the median age was 47.00. Sixty percent of the patients were under 65 years of age. Patients presented to the surgical unit setting following orthopedic surgery (40.00%), genitourinary surgery (20.00%), cardiovascular surgery (20.00%), and trauma surgery (20.00%).

Adverse outcomes experienced by these patients included peripheral nerve damage (40.00%), thermal burns (20.00%), brain damage (20.00%), and death (20.00%). Three mechanisms of injury were responsible for these unfortunate outcomes. Failure to activate alarms on cardiac monitors or mechanical ventilators was responsible for 40.00% of the incidents; another 40.00% of the incidents involved improper positioning (with sandbags). The remaining 20.00% of the incidents were due to improper use of heat-emitting products.

Case 9-8: Equipment Negligence

Mr. W., a 23-year-old cabinetmaker, was in a single motor vehicle accident. He sustained multiple trauma when his pickup truck left the road. He was transported to the hospital, where treatment was instituted and his condition was stabilized in the intensive care unit. The patient remained on mechanical ventilation and was later transferred to the surgical unit.

Shortly after admission to the surgical unit, the patient experienced an episode of bradycardia. The physician was informed, and Atropine was ordered. However, the medication was not effective, and the physician was called again. This time, the physician came to the unit to examine the patient. A nurse was instructed to draw blood for arterial blood gas analysis. As the arterial blood was drawn, the physician noted its abnormally dark color. He immediately checked the airway and found that the tube connecting the endotracheal tube to the ventilator was disconnected. He also found that the alarms on the ventilator had not been activated.

Failure by the nursing staff to activate the alarms on the mechanical ventilator prevented the alarm from sounding when the ventilator became disconnected from the endotracheal tube. Mr. W. suffered brain damage because of the negligence. Legal action resulted in a payment of $6,500,000 to the patient for lifelong care.

MALPRACTICE PAYMENTS

Malpractice payments made for the 155 adverse events in this setting ranged from $2,000 to $25,250,000. The mean payment was $1,358,206, and the median payment was $525,000. Table 9.8 summarizes malpractice payments by adverse outcome.

The largest number of malpractice payments in this group were made for problems associated with communication (27.74%) and nursing intervention (20.00%). Inadequate care by the physician resulted in the largest mean and median payments for adverse outcomes in the surgical setting. Table 9.9 presents the malpractice payment data by nursing care problem.

The greatest number of malpractice payments in this setting were between $100,001 and $400,000 (31.61%) and between $1,000,001 and $2,000,000 (14.83%). Malpractice payment distribution data are presented in Figure 9.4.

The majority of the payments in cases of death were distributed in the following categories: $100,001 through $400,000 (30.95%), $800,001 through $1,000,000 (19.04%), $1,000,001 through $2,000,000 (16.66%), and $400,001 through $600,000 (11.90%). The distribution of payments for patients suffering death is presented in Figure 9.5.

Most malpractice payments for cases of injury were between $100,001 and $400,000 (31.85%). Payment distribution data for injury are presented in Figure 9.6.

RISK PREVENTION STRATEGIES
IN THE SURGICAL UNIT SETTING

Risk management strategies applicable to all clinical settings as well as those common to selected nursing care problem areas will be found in Chapter 14.

The majority of the adverse events in this setting were due to failure by the nurse to inform the physician of a change in the patient's condition and failure by the nurse to execute a nursing treatment or

TABLE 9.8 Malpractice Payments in the Surgical Setting, by Adverse
           Outcome

| Adverse | | Malpractice Payments | | |
Outcome	No.	Range ($)	Mean ($)	Median ($)
Death	42	20,000 to 10,000,000	1,031,571	750,000
Injury	113	2,000 to 25,250,000	1,453,593	500,000
All deaths and injuries	155	2,000 to 25,250,000	1,358,206	525,000

TABLE 9.9 Malpractice Payments in the Surgical Setting,
           by Nursing Care Problem

| | | Malpractice Payments (N = 155) | | |
Problem Area	No.	Range ($)	Mean ($)	Median ($)
Nursing assessment	18	112,000 to 4,090,000	917,444	826,000
Environmental safety	20	2,000 to 4,700,000	514,700	210,000
Nursing intervention	31	10,000 to 16,500,000	1,315,258	450,000
Medication administration	19	65,000 to 3,580,000	874,105	500,000
Inadequate physician care	10	130,000 to 25,250,000	3,387,900	1,125,000
Communication	43	20,000 to 15,000,000	1,684,721	700,000
Infection	9	130,000 to 6,560,000	1,329,556	377,000
Equipment and products	5	125,000 to 6,500,000	1,621,000	292,000

procedure properly. Prevention of nursing-care-related injuries unique
to the patient with a surgical problem requires the nurse to ask the
following questions:

- Is the physician promptly informed of a change in the patient's condition
  (especially respiratory status changes, neurovascular status changes, and
  neurological changes)?
- Are catheters, drains, and/or tubes properly inserted?
- Are catheters, drains, and/or tubes properly removed?
- Are catheters, drains, and/or tubes properly maintained?
- Are patients properly turned and positioned?

(text continued on page 181)

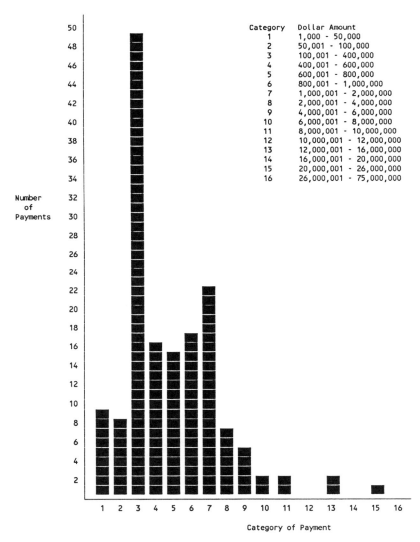

Figure 9.4. Distribution of Payments to Patients Experiencing a Nursing-Care-Related Adverse Outcome in the Surgical Setting

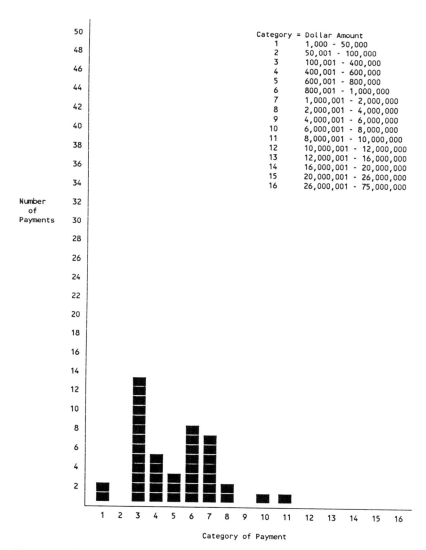

Figure 9.5. Distribution of Payments to Patients Suffering Death as a Nursing-Care-Related Adverse Outcome in the Surgical Setting

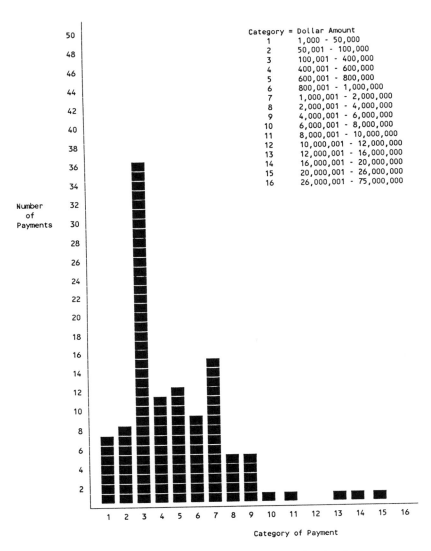

Figure 9.6. Distribution of Payments to Patients Experiencing Injury as a Nursing-Care-Related Adverse Outcome in the Surgical Setting

- Is special attention given to preventing falls
  1. when patients are receiving postoperative sedation or pain medications?
  2. when patients require or request assistance with ambulation?
  3. when patients require constant supervision by a nurse or nursing assistant?
  4. when patients require the use of bed side rails?
  5. when patients require restraint?
- Are parenteral fluids and parenteral medications administered using proper precautions and techniques?
- Is the surgical wound properly assessed?
- Is the surgical wound cared for systematically?
- Are nursing treatments and/or procedures executed promptly and accurately?

SUMMARY

Patients in the surgical setting made up 20.74% of the 747 malpractice cases analyzed in the database. Of the cases in the surgical setting, 27.10% were deaths. The most common departures from the standards of nursing care associated with these deaths were inadequate communication of nursing assessment data to the physician and inadequate nursing assessment.

The other 72.90% of the nursing malpractice cases in this setting were injuries. Inadequate communication with the physician and inadequate nursing intervention caused the majority of injuries.

Patients were almost evenly divided by gender. The mean age of patients experiencing an injury was 49.89 years; the mean age in cases of death was 46.11.

The majority of the patients presented to the surgical setting following musculoskeletal surgery, gastrointestinal tract surgery, or cardiovascular surgery.

Adverse outcomes were varied, but over half included death, brain damage, infection or wound, peripheral nerve damage, and paralysis. The predominant mechanisms of injury in this setting were associated with nursing care problems relating to communication and nursing intervention.

Payments for the 155 adverse outcomes related to nursing negligence in the surgical setting ranged from $2,000 to $25,250,000. The mean payment was $1,358,206, and the median payment was $525,000.

10

Nursing Malpractice
in the Pediatric Unit Setting

The nurse plays an indispensable role in the pediatric setting by providing comprehensive health care to the young patient. The nurse initiates and controls nursing care measures. Through the application of the nursing process to patient care needs, the nurse coordinates the plan of care for the pediatric patient. Due to the limited physiological reserves of the pediatric patient, the nurse must exercise every precaution possible when executing physician orders and providing independent nursing care measures. Hazards that exist in the hospital setting demand special awareness in the pediatric setting to prevent adverse outcomes.

Patients experiencing an adverse outcome in the pediatric setting accounted for 7.09% (53 of 747) of the nursing negligence cases in the database. Of these adverse outcomes, 33 (62.26%) were injuries, and 20 (37.73%) were deaths. A medication error or inadequate communication with the physician caused the majority of the tragic incidents (Table 10.1).

PATIENT CHARACTERISTICS

The mean age of all pediatric patients experiencing a nursing care adverse outcome was 4.97 years, with 2.00 years being the median.

TABLE 10.1 Nursing Malpractice Adverse Outcomes and Associated Departures From the Standard of Care in the Pediatric Setting

Adverse Outcome Category	Departure From the Standard of Care Causing the Adverse Outcome	No. of Cases	% of Category	% of Total
Death		20	100.00	37.73
	Medication administration error	6	30.00	
	Inadequate communication with the physician regarding nursing assessment data	6	30.00	
	Inadequate nursing intervention	3	15.00	
	Improper use of supplies/equipment	3	15.00	
	Inadequate nursing assessment	2	10.00	
Injury		33	100.00	62.26
	Medication administration error	12	36.36	
	Inadequate communication with the physician regarding nursing assessment data	9	27.27	
	Inadequate nursing intervention	5	15.15	
	Inadequate nursing assessment	3	9.09	
	Improper use of equipment/supplies	3	9.09	
	Inadequate care by the physician	1	3.03	

TABLE 10.2 Age of Patients Experiencing a Nursing-Care-Related Adverse Outcome in the Pediatric Setting

Age	All Cases (N = 53)	Cases of Death (N = 20)	Cases of Injury (N = 33)
Range	14 days to 17 yr.	3 mo. to 15 yr.	14 days to 17 yr.
Mean	4.97 yr.	5.42 yr.	4.69 yr.
Median	2.00 yr.	3.50 yr.	1.00 yr.

Ages ranged from 14 days to 17 years. Table 10.2 presents patient age data.

The largest number of pediatric patients experiencing an adverse outcome were distributed in two age groups: 14 days to 11 months (35.84%) and 1 to 3 years (20.75%). Figure 10.1 presents age distribution data for patients experiencing an adverse nursing care outcome in the pediatric setting.

Seventy-five percent of the pediatric patients suffering death as an adverse outcome of nursing care were between 14 days and 6 years of age, and 25.00% were between 11 and 15 years of age. Figure 10.2 presents age distribution data for patients suffering death.

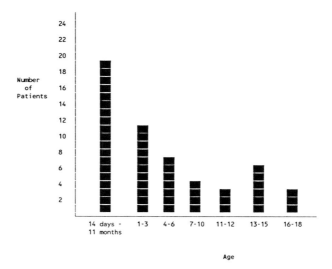

Figure 10.1. Age Distribution of Patients Experiencing a Nursing-Care-Related Adverse Outcome in the Pediatric Setting

The majority of the pediatric patients (62.50%) experiencing an injury as a negative outcome were clustered in the 14-day-through-11-month age group. Figure 10.3 presents age distribution data for patients experiencing a nursing-care-related injury.

Of the patients in the pediatric setting, 60.37% were male, and 39.62% were female. Table 10.3 summarizes gender data in the pediatric setting.

The most common presenting problem of the pediatric patient was that of a systemic or local infection (35.84%). Sixty-three percent of the infections involved the respiratory system or throat. Central nervous system infections (meningitis, encephalitis) were next in frequency (32.00%), followed by joint/soft tissue infections (5.00%).

Orthopedic problems were responsible for 16.98% of the admissions in this setting. Diagnoses were related to correction of congenital musculoskeletal defects (44.00%) and fractures, with or without open reduction with internal fixation (56.00%). Thirteen percent of these patients presented with neurological problems that included head injury (43.00%), corrective surgery for a congenital spinal defect (28.50%), and surgery for hydrocephalic shunting (28.50%). Cardio-

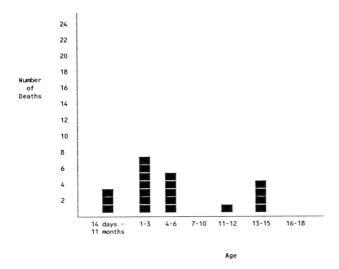

Figure 10.2. Age Distribution of Patients Suffering Death as a Nursing-Care-Related Adverse Outcome in the Pediatric Setting

vascular system alterations made up 9.43% of the presenting problems. Sixty percent of the cardiovascular cases involved open heart surgery, and 40.00% involved treatment for arrhythmias.

Gastrointestinal tract presenting problems (5.66%) were related to bowel obstruction (33.33%), abdominal pain (33.33%), and nausea, vomiting, and diarrhea (33.33%). Wound/integument-system problems accounted for 5.66% of the presenting problems. Thermal burns made up 66.66% of the wound/integument problems, and the remaining 33.33% of these problems involved lacerations. Ear, nose, and throat problems (3.77%) were all related to tonsil and adenoid surgery. Multiple trauma accounted for 3.77% of the presenting problems. All presenting problems are recapitulated in Table 10.4.

ADVERSE NURSING CARE OUTCOMES

Nursing malpractice caused especially severe adverse outcomes in the pediatric setting. Brain damage and death accounted for 79.23% of the nursing-care-related negative outcomes. Other consequences of

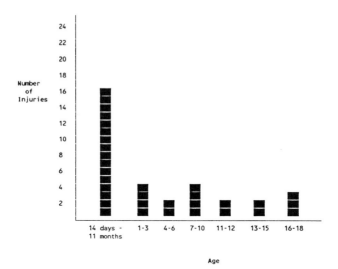

Figure 10.3. Age Distribution of Patients Suffering Injury as a Nursing-Care-Related Adverse Outcome in the Pediatric Setting

nursing negligence included neurovascular/neuromuscular/peripheral nerve damage (7.54%), amputation (3.77%), chemical burns (3.77%), sensory loss (1.88%), paraplegia (1.88%), and laceration (1.88%). Table 10.5 summarizes all adverse outcomes in the pediatric setting.

Nursing care problems associated with medication administration and communication were responsible for 62.26% of the adverse outcomes in the pediatric setting. Failure to administer medications properly accounted for 33.96% of the incidents, and failure to inform the physician of pertinent nursing assessment data was related to

TABLE 10.3 Sex of Patients Experiencing a Nursing-Care-Related Adverse Outcome in the Pediatric Setting

	Male		Female	
Pediatric Patients	No.	%	No.	%
Cases, all (N = 53)	32	60.37	21	39.62
Cases, death (N = 20)	12	60.00	8	40.00
Cases, injury (N = 33)	20	60.60	13	39.39

TABLE 10.4 Diagnoses/Presenting Problems of Patients Experiencing a
Nursing-Care-Related Adverse Outcome in the Pediatric
Setting

Patient Diagnosis/ Presenting Problem	Total (N = 53)		Death (N = 20)		Injury (N = 33)	
	No.	%	No.	%	No.	%
Infection (local or systemic)	19	35.84	7	35.00	12	36.36
Orthopedic	9	16.98	0	0.00	9	27.27
Neurological	7	13.20	4	20.00	3	9.09
Cardiovascular	5	9.43	3	15.00	2	6.06
Gastrointestinal	3	5.66	2	10.00	1	3.03
Wound/integument	3	5.66	1	5.00	2	6.06
Trauma	2	3.77	1	5.00	1	3.03
Ear, nose, throat	2	3.77	2	10.00	0	0.00
Neoplasm	1	1.88	0	0.00	1	3.03
Endocrine-metabolic	1	1.88	0	0.00	1	3.03
Plastic/reconstructive	1	1.88	0	0.00	1	3.03

TABLE 10.5 Type of Adverse Outcome Caused by Nursing Malpractice in
Pediatric Setting (N = 53)

Adverse Outcome Caused by Nursing Malpractice	No. of Cases	% of Cases
Death	20	37.73
Paralysis: paraplegia	1	1.88
Neuromuscular damage	1	1.88
Brain damage	22	41.50
Neurovascular/peripheral nerve damage	3	5.66
Amputation: digits, limb	2	3.77
Chemical burns	2	3.77
Sensory loss: hearing	1	1.88
Laceration	1	1.88

28.30% of the incidents. Other departures from the standard of
practice responsible for nursing-care-related injury included failure to
perform a nursing treatment or procedure properly (15.09%), failure
to use equipment and/or products properly (11.32%), failure to assess
the patient systematically (9.43%), and failure to obtain help for a
patient not receiving adequate care from the physician (1.88%).

Nursing care problems and associated departures from the standard of care are summarized in Table 10.6.

Mechanisms of injury responsible for adverse nursing care outcomes in the pediatric setting were varied. The dominant one, however, was inadequate communication of nursing assessment data to the physician. This was responsible for 27.27% of the injuries and 30.00% of the deaths.

Patient injuries due to medication administration errors involved incorrect parenteral administration technique (12.12%), administration of the wrong medication or intravenous infusion solution (12.12%), administration of the wrong dose of a medication or intravenous infusion solution (6.06%), or failure to monitor medication toxicity (6.06%). Other mechanisms causing injury in the pediatric setting included improper execution of a nursing treatment or procedure (15.15%), inadequate nursing assessment (9.09%), improper use of equipment and/or products (9.09%), and inadequate care by the physician (3.03%).

The dominant mechanism of injury leading to death was inadequate communication of nursing assessment data to the physician (30.00%). Deaths due to medication administration errors involved administration of the wrong dose of a medication or intravenous infusion solution (20.00%), administration of the wrong medication or intravenous infusion solution (5.00%), or failure to monitor medication toxicity (5.00%). Mechanisms of injury responsible for the remaining deaths were inadequate nursing assessment (10.00%), improper execution of a nursing treatment or procedure (15.00%), and improper use of equipment and/or products (15.00%). Table 10.7 addresses mechanisms of injury in the pediatric setting.

NURSING CARE PROBLEMS

Medication Administration Negligence

Medication administration problems were responsible for 33.96% of the adverse events in the pediatric setting. Failure to administer medications properly caused 36.36% of the injuries and 30.00% of the deaths in this setting.

Patients in this subgroup were evenly divided by gender. The mean age of the pediatric patient experiencing a nursing care adverse outcome was 3.33 years; the median age was 1.00 year.

TABLE 10.6 Nursing Care Problems and Associated Departures From the Standard of Care in the Pediatric Setting

Problem Area	Departure From the Standard of Care	No. of Cases	% of Cases
Nursing assessment	Failure to assess the patient systematically	5	9.43
Nursing intervention	Failure to perform a procedure or treatment properly	8	15.09
Medication administration	Failure to administer medications properly	18	33.96
Communication	Failure to inform the physician of a change in the patient's condition or of nursing assessment data	15	28.30
Inadequate physician care	Failure to obtain help for a patient not receiving adequate care from the physician	1	1.88
Equipment and products	Failure to use equipment and/or products properly	6	11.32

TABLE 10.7 Mechanisms of Injury Responsible for Nursing-Care-Related Adverse Outcomes in the Pediatric Setting

	Adverse Outcome			
	Patient Injury (N = 33)		Patient Death (N = 20)	
Mechanism of Injury	No.	%	No.	%
Inadequate nursing assessment	3	9.09	2	10.00
Nursing treatment or procedure not executed properly	5	15.15	3	15.00
Wrong dose of drug or intravenous infusion solution	2	6.06	4	20.00
Incorrect parenteral administration technique	4	12.12	0	0.00
Wrong drug or intravenous infusion solution	4	12.12	1	5.00
Medication toxicity not monitored	2	6.06	1	5.00
Physician not informed of abnormal assessment findings	9	27.27	6	30.00
Inadequate care by the physician	1	3.03	0	0.00
Improper use of equipment and/or products	3	9.09	3	15.00

The predominant presenting problem in this subgroup was that of infection (50.00%). Two thirds of the infections were related to the respiratory system, 22.22% were associated with the central nervous system, and 11.11% were associated with a limb. Other reasons for admission included wound/integument problems (11.11%), cardiovascular problems (11.11%), gastrointestinal tract problems (5.50%), orthopedic problems (5.50%), plastic/reconstructive problems (5.50%), neurological problems (5.50%), and ear, nose, and throat problems (5.50%).

Adverse outcomes due to nursing negligence in this subgroup were severe. Death (33.33%) and brain damage (38.88%) dominated. Other negative outcomes included burn/wound (11.11%), amputation (5.50%), deafness (5.50%), and peripheral nerve damage (5.50%).

The mechanism of injury responsible for 50.00% of the adverse outcomes due to medication negligence was administration of the wrong dose of a medication or intravenous infusion solution. Incorrect parenteral administration technique was the cause of 22.22% of the adverse events, followed by failure to detect medication toxicity (administration of a narcotic to patients exhibiting respiratory depression; 16.66%), and administration of the wrong medication or intravenous infusion solution (11.11%).

Case 10-1: Medication Administration Negligence

A 1-year-old child was admitted to a pediatric unit with the diagnosis of sepsis. Shortly after admission, an intravenous infusion line was placed. It later became "sluggish" and was irrigated with a normal saline solution. Immediately after the procedure, "the child's eyes rolled back, his body shook, and he stopped breathing." A full cardiopulmonary arrest followed.

After the child was resuscitated, routine blood work demonstrated an abnormally high serum potassium. It was determined that potassium chloride had been used mistakenly to irrigate the intravenous infusion line. Both potassium chloride and normal saline solutions were kept in the medication room and on the medication cart. They were stored close to each other, and the vessels were similar in size and shape.

Failure to read the label of the irrigation solution bottle and the use of the wrong solution resulted in the cardiopulmonary arrest with consequent anoxic brain injury. The child suffers from mental retardation, poor memory, and hemiparesis. Legal action resulted in a payment of $1,980,000 to the child's parents for his lifelong care.

Communication Negligence

Communication problems were responsible for 28.30% of the adverse events in the pediatric setting. Failure to inform the physician of essential nursing assessment data caused 27.27% of the injuries and 30.00% of the deaths in this setting.

Of the patients in this subgroup, 53.33% were male, and 46.66% were female. The mean age was 6.80 years, and the median age was 6.00 years.

Neurological problems related to intracranial pathology were responsible for 33.33% of the admissions in this subgroup. Other presenting problems were fractures (20.00%), central nervous system infections (20.00%), gastrointestinal tract alterations (13.33%), endocrine-metabolic alterations (6.66%), and cardiovascular alterations (6.66%).

Adverse outcomes in this subgroup related to nursing negligence were severe and included death (40.00%), brain damage (40.00%), paraplegia (13.30%), and peripheral nerve damage (6.60%). The mechanism of injury common to all negative outcomes was failure by the nurse to apprise the physician of essential nursing assessment data. Specifically, adverse events involved failure to report neurological status changes (66.66%), circulatory status changes (13.30%), signs of infection (13.30%), and neurovascular changes (6.60%).

Case 10-2: Communication Negligence

T. W., a 7-year-old child with a history of hydrocephalus and shunt implantation, struck his head on an open automobile door while playing in the driveway of his grandparents' home. He sustained a brief loss of consciousness and then complained of a headache.

His grandparents took him to the hospital, and a large subdural hematoma was evident on the CT scan. T. W. was taken to the operating room that evening for evacuation of the hematoma. The child tolerated the surgical procedure well, and his initial recovery was within normal limits.

However, on the third postoperative day at 11:30 a.m., his temperature was noted by the nurses to be 103.2 degrees Fahrenheit. Prior to this, his temperature had ranged from 98 degrees to 99 degrees Fahrenheit. At 1:50 p.m., T. W.'s temperature was 103.7 degrees Fahrenheit. The physician was not informed of the elevated temperature.

At 2:15 p.m., it was noted in the medical record by a nurse that the child "appears to be having small seizures." At this point, T. W.'s parents became concerned and suggested that the nurse call the physician. The nurse reassured the child's parents by telling them "it is perfectly normal, kids often have seizures with a temperature."

T. W.'s temperature was taken again at 3:54 p.m., and it was 108 degrees Fahrenheit. The physician was not informed of the elevated temperature until 4:30 p.m. due to the "change of shift activities." Even though the physician went to the hospital immediately, by the time he arrived, the child had suffered extensive brain damage.

Failure to communicate vital nursing observations promptly to the physician caused the severe injury to the patient. Legal action resulted in a payment of $9,000,000 to the child's parents for the lifelong care of T. W.

Nursing Intervention Negligence

Nursing intervention problems accounted for 15.09% of the adverse events in the pediatric setting. Failure to execute a nursing treatment or procedure properly was responsible for 15.15% of the injuries and 15.00% of the deaths in this setting.

The percentage of males (87.50%) in this subgroup was greater than that of females (12.50%). The mean age was 5.84 years, and the median was 3.00 years.

The predominant presenting problems were those of respiratory infection (25.00%) and trauma (25.00%). Remaining reasons for admission included cardiovascular problems (12.50%), neoplasia (12.50%), orthopedic problems (12.50%), and wound/integument problems (12.50%).

The adverse outcomes related to nursing intervention negligence were brain damage (62.50%) and death (37.50%). Mechanisms of injury included inadequate care and maintenance of an artificial airway (tracheotomy, endotracheal tube; 62.50%), omission of procedures to verify the placement of a central venous catheter (12.50%), failure to activate cardiac monitor alarms (12.50%), and feeding liquids to a child restrained on his or her back (12.50%).

Case 10-3: Nursing Intervention Negligence

A 2-year-old child was taken to the office of his physician because of "difficult breathing." Epiglottitis was diagnosed, and the child was immediately sent to the hospital.

D. D. was intubated in the emergency department and admitted to the pediatric unit. The physician's order specified suctioning as needed, as well as routine suctioning every hour. The nurse caring for

D. D. for the first 10-hour period of admission did not suction the child.

Failure to suction as needed caused the endotracheal tube to become obstructed. D. D. suffered a cardiopulmonary arrest and died 2 days later. Legal action resulted in a payment of $300,000 to the parents of the child.

Equipment and Products Negligence

Problems associated with the use of equipment and products caused 11.32% of the adverse events in the pediatric setting. Failure to use equipment or products properly caused 9.09% of the injuries and 15.00% of the deaths in this setting.

Two thirds of the patients were female. The mean age was 2.83 years; the median age was 6 months. Presenting problems of the patients in this subgroup were respiratory system infection (33.33%), orthopedic (33.33%), cardiovascular (16.66%), and neurological (16.66%).

Adverse outcomes related to the negligent use of equipment or products included death (50.00%), brain damage (33.33%), and chemical burns (16.66%). The most common mechanism of injury was improper use of electronic monitoring equipment (50.00%). Other causes of negative outcomes were suffocation by a Chux pad (16.66%), missing items on the crash cart (16.66%), and improper preparation of plaster casting material (16.66%).

Case 10-4: Equipment Negligence

E. C. was born prematurely at a gestational age of approximately 33 weeks on December 18. After an uneventful 3-week hospitalization, E. C. was discharged in good condition. An outpatient examination several weeks later revealed that the child was healthy and developing well.

E. C. had a brief episode of apnea on January 26, and his parents brought him to the hospital. While in the emergency department, the infant experienced a respiratory arrest. Resuscitation was successful, and the child was admitted to the neonatal intensive care unit with the diagnosis of Group B streptococcus sepsis. Antibiotic therapy commenced.

The infant experienced multiple episodes of apnea and bradycardia on January 28 and 29. Medical intervention, however, was not necessary.

On February 3, E. C. was transferred to the pediatric unit because he was no longer experiencing episodes of apnea or bradycardia and because the Group B streptococcal sepsis was resolving. The child was placed on an apnea and cardiac monitor.

On February 5, at 5:25 a.m., the monitor alarm sounded, and vital signs were taken for the first time in 11.5 hours. The nurse readjusted one of the monitor leads, and the heart rate reading was 150 beats per minute (the child's baseline rate). Several minutes later, the alarm sounded again and was ignored. When the nurse finally responded, E. C. was apneic, and his heart rate was 50 beats per minute. A physician was not informed of E. C.'s grave condition until 5:50 a.m. When he arrived on the unit at 5:52 a.m., the child was in full cardiopulmonary arrest. The physician noted that the heart rate alarm on the cardiac monitor was incorrectly set at 70 beats per minute rather than 120.

The failure to set the monitor alarm properly and the failure to respond promptly to the monitor alarm caused a hypoxic insult to the child that resulted in severe brain damage. E. C. suffers from spastic quadriplegia and pseudobulbar cerebral palsy. He requires 24-hour-a-day care and will probably survive to age 35. Legal action resulted in a payment of $8,100,000 to provide for lifelong care.

Nursing Assessment Negligence

Problems associated with nursing assessment were responsible for 9.43% of the adverse events in the pediatric setting. Failure to assess the patient systematically resulted in 9.09% of the injuries and 10.00% of the deaths in this setting.

All of the patients in this subgroup were male. The mean age was 1.50 years, and the median was 1.00 year. Sixty percent of the patients presented with infection (respiratory, 66.66%; meningitis, 33.33%). The remaining reasons for admission included orthopedic problems (20.00%) and ear, nose, and throat problems (20.00%).

Adverse events in this subgroup were severe and included death (40.00%), brain damage (40.00%), and amputation (20.00%). The mechanism of injury common to all negative outcomes was inadequate patient assessment. Specifically, there was failure to assess respiratory status (60.00%), neurological status (20.00%), and neurovascular status (20.00%).

Case 10-5: Nursing Assessment Negligence

B. F., a 4-year-old child, was admitted to the hospital for an elective tonsillectomy and adenoidectomy. The child tolerated the surgical procedure well, but postoperatively he experienced moderate bleeding. As a precaution, B. F. was to remain in the hospital for overnight observation. The child's parents were apprehensive about his condition and were quite relieved by the decision to hospitalize B. F.

A 2:00 a.m. nurse's note stated that B. F. was experiencing "some respiratory difficulty." There were no further notations in the medical record until 5:00 a.m., when B. F. was found in severe respiratory distress. Despite aggressive therapy, B. F. developed adult respiratory distress syndrome. The child died 3 weeks later.

It was determined that the child had aspirated gastric contents. The failure to assess the child systematically during the night contributed to his death. Legal action resulted in a payment of $600,000 to the parents of B. F.

Nursing Negligence Associated With Inadequate Care by the Physician

Nursing malpractice associated with inadequate care by the physician caused 1.88% of the adverse events in the pediatric setting. Failure to obtain care for a patient receiving inadequate treatment from the physician caused 3.03% of the injuries in this setting.

The patient in this subgroup was a 13-year-old male with an orthopedic problem. The patient suffered permanent peripheral nerve damage because the physician failed to treat reported symptoms of neurovascular embarrassment.

Case 10-6: Inadequate Care by the Physician

J. F., a 13-year-old boy, was injured as he collided with a teammate while playing baseball on June 26. A Salter's III fracture of the right tibial epiphysis and a fracture of the right proximal shaft of the fibula were diagnosed in the emergency department. J. F. was admitted to the hospital, and an orthopedic surgeon was called.

J. F. was not examined by the orthopedic surgeon until the morning of June 27. Approximately 4 hours later, the orthopedic surgeon performed a closed reduction of the fractures and applied a long leg cast. As the afternoon and early evening progressed, the patient complained of decreased sensation in the right foot, with numbness of the toes. He also complained of severe pain in the back of his right knee. The orthopedic surgeon was periodically apprised of the patient's condition throughout the night. Each time the nurses were instructed to "observe the patient."

By the next morning (June 28), J. F. had no sensation in his right foot and decreased sensation from the knee down to the ankle. Midmorning, the surgeon measured the pressure in the tibial compartments and determined that a surgical emergency existed. However, the fasciotomy was not performed until early afternoon.

During the next 4 days, the patient suffered severe pain and sensory alterations in the right leg. Numerous calls were placed to the physician during this period of time regarding signs and symptoms of neurovascular embarrassment. Nothing more was done for J. F.

On July 2, at the request of the family, J. F. was transferred to another hospital. Evaluation revealed complete necrosis of all muscles of the anterior and lateral compartments, as well as complete loss of function of the common peroneal nerve and incomplete loss of function of the tibial nerve. Numerous surgical procedures and skin grafting were required to save the leg.

Failure by the nursing staff to intervene on behalf of the patient to obtain adequate medical care caused a permanent partial loss of function as well as severe scarring and disfigurement of over 50% of the surface of the right lower extremity. Legal action resulted in a payment of $600,000 to the patient.

MALPRACTICE PAYMENTS

Malpractice payments in the pediatric setting ranged from $1,000 to $10,350,000. The mean payment was $1,958,962, and the median was $1,000,000.

The mean malpractice payment in cases of injury was $2,487,333 and in cases of death was $1,087,150. This difference was due to the need for lifelong care associated with the large number of pediatric patients suffering the adverse outcome of brain damage (41.50%). Table 10.8 summarizes malpractice payment data by adverse outcome.

TABLE 10.8 Malpractice Payments in the Pediatric Setting, by Adverse Outcome

Adverse Outcome	Malpractice Payments			
	No.	Range ($)	Mean ($)	Median ($)
Death	20	130,000 to 7,000,000	1,087,150	850,000
Injury	33	1,000 to 10,350,000	2,487,333	1,500,000
All deaths and injuries	53	1,000 to 10,350,000	1,958,962	1,000,000

TABLE 10.9 Malpractice Payments in the Pediatric Setting, by Nursing Care Problem (N = 53)

Problem Area	Malpractice Payments			
	No.	Range ($)	Mean ($)	Median ($)
Nursing assessment	5	75,000 to 6,875,000	1,375,000	800,000
Nursing intervention	8	130,000 to 10,350,000	3,420,000	1,815,000
Medication administration	18	1,000 to 6,500,000	1,360,777	980,000
Inadequate physician care	1	600,000	600,000	600,000
Communication	15	200,000 to 9,000,000	2,188,000	1,100,000
Equipment and products	6	104,000 to 8,100,000	1,777,933	911,000

The largest number of malpractice payments in the pediatric setting were made for medication administration problems (33.96%) and communication problems (28.30%). Table 10.9 summarizes malpractice payment data by nursing care problem.

The distribution of malpractice payments in the pediatric setting was diverse. For all adverse outcomes, the greatest number of payments were between $800,001 and $4,000,000 (48.86%), followed by $100,001 through $800,000 (32.07%), $4,000,001 through $12,000,000 (15.08%), and $1,000 through $100,000 (3.76%). Figure 10.4 presents payment distribution data for all adverse outcomes.

In cases of death, payments were clustered around the range of $100,001 to $400,000 (40.00%) and the range of $800,001 to $4,000,000 (35.00%). Figure 10.5 presents the distribution of payments for the adverse outcome of death.

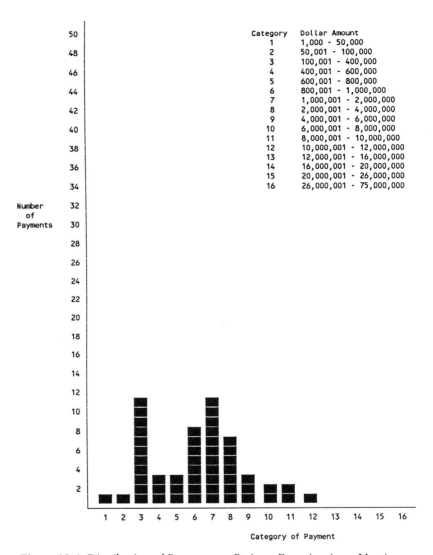

Figure 10.4. Distribution of Payments to Patients Experiencing a Nursing-Care-Related Adverse Outcome in the Pediatric Setting

For pediatric patients experiencing injury, the largest number of payments were in two categories: (a) $1,000,001 through $2,000,000

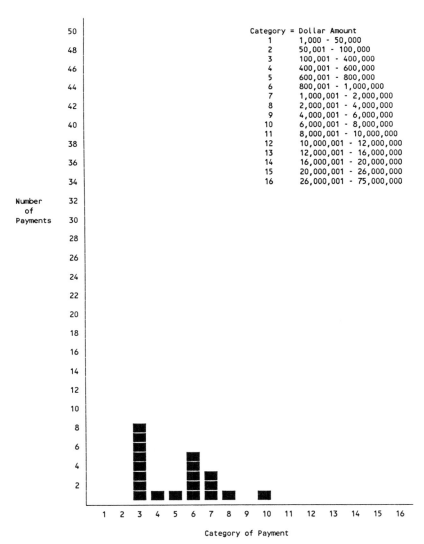

Figure 10.5. Distribution of Payments to Patients Suffering Death as a
Nursing-Care-Related Adverse Outcome in the Pediatric Setting

(24.24%) and (b) $2,000,001 through $4,000,000 (18.18%). Payments of $1,000,000 or more were made in 63.63% of the cases of

injury. Figure 10.6 summarizes data regarding malpractice payment distribution in cases of injury.

RISK PREVENTION STRATEGIES
IN THE PEDIATRIC SETTING

Risk management strategies applicable to all clinical settings as well as those common to selected nursing care problem areas will be found in Chapter 14.

Seventy-nine percent of the nursing-care-related adverse events in the pediatric setting were either death or brain damage. Problems associated with medication administration and communication were responsible for the majority of negative outcomes. Prevention of nursing-care-related injuries unique to the pediatric patient requires the nurse to ask the following questions:

- Is the physician promptly informed of important nursing assessment data (especially neurological status)?
- Are the "five rights" of medication administration respected?
- Is electronic monitoring equipment utilized correctly?
- Are the content and frequency of nursing assessment appropriate to the patient's condition (especially with regard to respiratory status)?

SUMMARY

Nursing negligence in the pediatric setting caused either death or brain damage to over three quarters of the patients. Medication errors and inadequate communication were the most common nursing care problems.

Pediatric patients ranged in age from 14 days to 17 years, and the mean age was 4.97 years. Sixty percent of the patients were male. The most common presenting problem was either systemic or local infection. Major mechanisms of injury were failure to apprise the physician of abnormal assessment findings, administration of the wrong dose of medication, and improper use of equipment and/or supplies.

Malpractice payments in the pediatric setting ranged from $1,000 to $10,350,000. The mean malpractice payment for injury ($2,487,333) was larger than the mean payment for death ($1,087,150). This was because a large number of patients suffered brain damage as an adverse outcome and will require lifelong care.

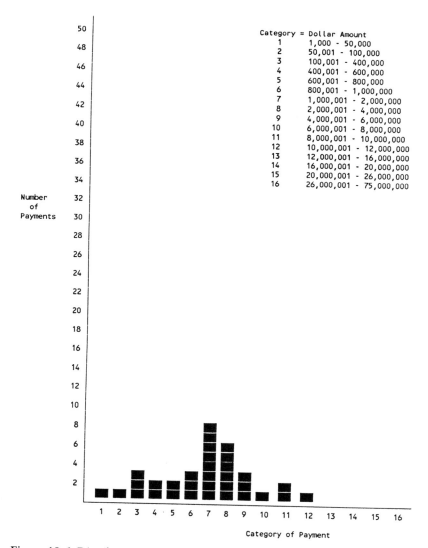

Figure 10.6. Distribution of Payments to Patients Experiencing Injury as a Nursing-Care-Related Adverse Outcome in the Pediatric Setting

11

Nursing Negligence in the Labor Room

Care of the pregnant woman in the labor room requires expert knowledge and understanding of the labor phase in the process of childbearing. In addition to the mastery of certain knowledge and skills, teamwork between the nurse and physician is essential. It is especially important in this clinical setting to keep the physician informed of the progress of the patient's labor. Accurate reporting of nursing assessment data and its documentation in the medical record are fundamental. Safe and effective nursing care requires the delivery of systematic care utilizing the framework of the nursing process.

This chapter is concerned with the adverse events experienced by the obstetrical patient during the first stage of labor: that is, from the time the patient is having regular contractions of the uterus until the cervix is fully dilated.

Patients experiencing an adverse nursing care outcome in the labor room accounted for 17.14% (128 of 747) of the malpractice cases in the database. Nursing negligence caused or contributed to 94 (73.43%) fetal/newborn injuries, 8 (6.25%) maternal injuries, 21 (16.40%) fetal/newborn deaths, and 5 (3.90%) maternal deaths in this setting. The term *fetal/newborn* is used in cases of pregnancy in which there is a childbirth-induced/associated adverse outcome that involves only the fetus or newborn infant. Adverse outcomes due to

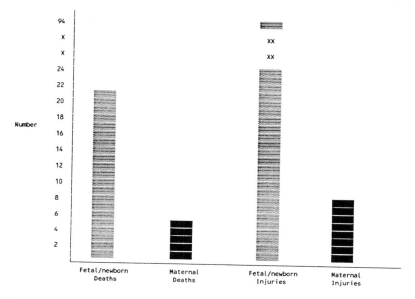

Figure 11.1. Distribution of Deaths and Injuries Caused by Negligent Nursing Care in the Labor Room

nursing negligence were particularly severe and costly in the labor room. The distribution of deaths and injuries in this setting is presented in Figure 11.1.

The primary cause of fetal/newborn injury as well as death was inadequate communication of nursing assessment data to the physician. Inadequate nursing assessment and medication administration error during this first stage of labor caused the majority of maternal injuries and deaths. Table 11.1 summarizes adverse outcomes and associated departures from the standard of care in the labor room.

PATIENT CHARACTERISTICS

Patients in this group ranged in age from 16 to 38 years. The mean age was 24.97, and the median age was 26.00 years. Table 11.2 summarizes age data for patients experiencing an adverse outcome in the labor room.

TABLE 11.1 Nursing Malpractice Adverse Outcomes and Associated Departures From the Standard of Care in the Labor Room

Adverse Outcome Category	Departure From the Standard of Care Causing the Adverse Outcome	No. of Cases	% of Category	% of Total
Injury (fetal/newborn)		94	100.00	73.43
	Inadequate communication with the physician regarding nursing assessment data	36	38.29	
	Inadequate nursing assessment	19	20.21	
	Inadequate care by the physician	18	19.14	
	Medication administration error	15	15.95	
	Inadequate nursing intervention	4	4.25	
	Unsafe environment	2	2.12	
Injury (maternal)		8	100.00	6.25
	Medication administration error	6	75.00	
	Inadequate nursing assessment	1	12.50	
	Inadequate care by the physician	1	12.50	
Death (fetal/newborn)		21	100.00	16.40
	Inadequate communication with the physician regarding nursing assessment data	16	76.19	
	Inadequate care by the physician	3	14.28	
	Inadequate nursing intervention	2	9.52	
Death (maternal)		5	100.00	3.90
	Inadequate nursing assessment	2	40.00	
	Medication administration	2	40.00	
	Inadequate care by the physician	1	20.00	

TABLE 11.2 Age of Patients Experiencing a Nursing-Care-Related Adverse Outcome in the Labor Room

Maternal Age	All Cases (N = 128)	Cases of Death		Cases of Injury	
		Maternal (N = 5)	Fetal/Newborn (N = 21)	Maternal (N = 8)	Fetal/Newborn (N = 94)
Range	16 to 38 yr.	18 to 29 yr.	17 to 33 yr.	20 to 36 yr.	16 to 38 yr.
Mean	24.97 yr.	24.40 yr.	24.57 yr.	27.75 yr.	24.86 yr.
Median	26.00 yr.	27.00 yr.	26.00 yr.	27.00 yr.	25.50 yr.

Sixty patients (46.86%) were under 25 years of age, and 41 (32.03%) were 25 years or over. The largest number of labor room patients experiencing a negative nursing care outcome were in the 25-through-27-year age group (27; 21.09%). Sixty patients (46.86%) were under 25 years of age, and 41 (32.03%) were 25 years or over.

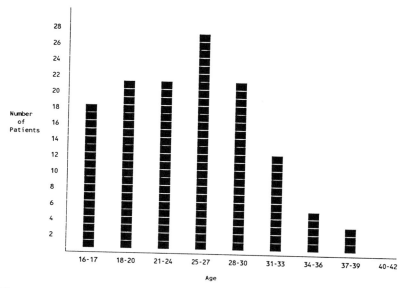

Figure 11.2. Age Distribution of Maternal Patients Experiencing a Nursing-Care-Related Adverse Outcome in the Labor Room

Figure 11.2 presents the age distribution of maternal patients experiencing an adverse outcome of nursing care in the labor room.

The majority (85.15%) of the obstetrical patients experiencing an adverse outcome in the labor room were admitted in active labor for a pregnancy without complications. The patients presenting without pregnancy complications experienced 80.95% of the fetal/newborn deaths and 92.55% of the fetal/newborn injuries. In cases of uncomplicated pregnancy, there were no maternal deaths, but 62.50% of the maternal injuries occurred in this group. On the other hand, patients admitted with complications of pregnancy experienced 37.50% of the maternal injuries, 100.00% of the maternal deaths, 19.04% of the fetal/newborn deaths, and only 7.44% of the fetal/newborn injuries. Complications of pregnancy included preeclampsia (36.84%), severe constant abdominal pain (26.31%), appendicitis (10.52%), abruptio placentae (10.52%), vaginal bleeding (10.52%), and premature labor (10.52%). Table 11.3 addresses presenting problems in the labor room.

ADVERSE NURSING CARE OUTCOMES

Nursing malpractice in the labor room setting resulted in maternal as well as fetal/newborn adverse outcomes. Fetal/newborn consequences of nursing negligence were severe brain damage (73.43%) and stillbirth (16.40%). Maternal nursing-care-related adverse events included death (3.90%), brain damage (2.34%), uterine rupture (1.56%), sensory loss (0.78%), digit amputation (0.78%), and hepatitis (0.78%). Adverse outcomes in the labor room are summarized in Table 11.4.

The most frequent nursing care problem in the labor room was communication. Failure to inform the physician of a change in maternal status or fetal status was the departure from the standard of care responsible for 40.62% of the adverse outcomes. Other deviations from the prevailing professional standard of care associated with negative outcomes were failure to obtain help for a patient not receiving adequate care from the physician (17.96%), failure to administer medications properly (17.96%), failure to assess the patient systematically (17.18%), failure to perform a nursing treatment and/or procedure properly (4.68%), and failure to provide a safe environment (1.56%). Nursing care problems and associated departures from the standard of care in the labor room are summarized in Table 11.5.

The majority of the maternal injuries were related to medication administration error. Administration of the wrong dose of medication and incorrect parenteral injection technique were the most frequent mechanisms of injury. Forty percent of the maternal deaths were related to inadequate nursing assessment. The mechanism of injury common to cases of both fetal/newborn injury and fetal/newborn death, on the other hand, was failure by the nurse to inform the physician of fetal distress in a timely manner. Table 11.6 presents the mechanisms of injury responsible for adverse outcomes in the labor room.

NURSING CARE PROBLEMS

Communication Negligence

Problems associated with communication were responsible for 40.62% of the adverse events in the labor room setting. Failure to inform the physician of a change in maternal or fetal/newborn status

TABLE 11.3 Diagnoses/Presenting Problems of Patients Experiencing a Nursing-Care-Related Adverse Outcome in the Labor Room

Patient Diagnosis/ Presenting Problem	Adverse Outcome									
	Total (N = 128)		Fetal/ Newborn Death (N = 21)		Fetal/ Newborn Injury (N = 94)		Maternal Death (N = 5)		Maternal Injury (N = 8)	
	No.	%	No.	%	No.	%	No.	%	No.	%
Pregnancy and labor without complications	109	85.15	17	80.95	87	92.55	0	0.00	5	62.50
Pregnancy and/or labor with complications	19	14.84	4	19.04	7	7.44	5	100.00	3	37.50

TABLE 11.4 Type of Adverse Outcome Caused by Nursing Malpractice in the Labor Room (N = 128)

Adverse Outcome Caused by Nursing Malpractice	No. of Cases	% of Cases
Stillborn child	21	16.40
Brain-damaged baby	94	73.43
Maternal death	5	3.90
Maternal brain damage	3	2.34
Maternal uterine rupture	2	1.56
Maternal sensory loss: vision	1	0.78
Maternal digit amputation	1	0.78
Maternal hepatitis infection	1	0.78

TABLE 11.5 Nursing Care Problems and Associated Departures From the Standard of Care in the Labor Room

Problem Area	Departure From the Standard of Care	No. of Cases	% of Cases
Communication	Failure to inform the physician of a change in maternal or fetal condition	52	40.62
Inadequate care by the physician	Failure to obtain help for a patient not receiving adequate care from the physician	23	17.96
Medication administration	Failure to administer medication(s) properly	23	17.96
Nursing assessment	Failure to assess the patient systematically	22	17.18
Nursing intervention	Failure to perform a nursing treatment or procedure properly	6	4.68
Environmental safety	Failure to provide a safe environment	2	1.56

TABLE 11.6 Mechanisms of Injury Responsible for Nursing-Care-Related Adverse Outcomes in the Labor Room

	Adverse Outcome						
	Maternal Injuries (N = 8)		Fetal/ Newborn Injuries (N = 94)		Maternal Deaths (N = 5)		Fetal/ Newborn Deaths (N = 21)
Mechanism of Injury	No.	%	No.	%	No.	%	No.	%
Inadequate nursing action related to failure by the physician to attend the patient promptly	0	0.00	0	0.00	1	20.00	0	0.00
Inadequate nursing action related to failure by the physician to act in the presence of maternal distress	1	12.50	0	0.00	0	0.00	0	0.00
Inadequate nursing action related to failure by the physician to act in the presence of fetal distress	0	0.00	18	19.14	0	0.00	3	14.28
Failure by the nurse to inform the physician promptly of fetal distress per monitor tracings	0	0.00	35	37.23	0	0.00	16	76.19
Failure to inform the physician promptly of abnormal maternal nursing assessment findings	0	0.00	1	1.06	0	0.00	0	0.00
Pitocin administered in the presence of fetal distress	1	12.50	14	14.89	0	0.00	0	0.00
Wrong medication dose administered	2	25.00	0	0.00	1	20.00	0	0.00
Incorrect parenteral injection technique	2	25.00	0	0.00	0	0.00	0	0.00
Wrong medication administered	1	12.50	0	0.00	0	0.00	0	0.00
Medication omitted	0	0.00	1	1.06	1	20.00	0	0.00
Delay in transfer to tertiary hospital	0	0.00	2	1.12	0	0.00	0	0.00
Inadequate maternal nursing assessment	1	12.50	0	0.00	2	40.00	0	0.00
Inadequate fetal nursing assessment	0	0.00	19	20.21	0	0.00	0	0.00
Nursing procedure or treatment not executed properly	0	0.00	4	4.25	0	0.00	2	9.52

caused 38.29% of the fetal/newborn injuries and 76.19% of the fetal/newborn deaths. No maternal injuries or deaths were attributed to this departure from the standard of care.

The mean age of obstetrical patients in this subgroup was 24.50 years, and the median age was 26.00 years. Of these patients, 84.62% presented with a normal pregnancy, and 15.38% exhibited complications.

Adverse outcomes due to nursing negligence in this subgroup were fetal/newborn brain damage (69.23%) and stillbirth (30.76%). The mechanism of injury was failure by the nurse to inform the physician (a) of fetal distress per electronic monitoring (96.15%) or (b) of abnormal maternal assessments (3.84%).

Case 11-1: Communication Negligence

R. H., a 26-year-old married mother of two children, presented to the hospital in active labor. One hour after admission, her membranes ruptured spontaneously, and meconium staining of the fluid was obvious. In addition, electronic fetal monitoring at this time indicated fetal distress. These observations were not reported to the physician.

Three hours later, the physician examined R. H. while making "routine rounds." Fetal distress was noted at this time by the physician, and an emergency cesarean section was performed.

Failure to communicate signs of fetal distress to the physician caused the child to be born in a severely depressed state with Apgar scores of 0 and 1. The umbilical cord was wrapped around the baby's neck two times, and there was also a "true knot" in the cord. The child suffers cerebral palsy, spastic quadriplegia, and developmental delay. Legal action resulted in a payment of $2,250,000 for lifelong care of the child.

Nursing Negligence Associated With Inadequate Care by the Physician

The problem of inadequate care by the physician and associated nursing negligence was responsible for 17.96% of the adverse events in the labor room. Failure by the nurse to obtain help for the patient not receiving adequate care from a physician caused 12.50% of the maternal injuries, 19.14% of the fetal/newborn injuries, 20.00% of the maternal deaths, and 14.28% of the fetal/newborn deaths in this setting.

The mean age of patients in this subgroup was 22.65 years, and the median age was 22.00. Of these patients, 91.31% were admitted to the labor room with a normal pregnancy, and only 8.69% presented with complications.

The predominant adverse outcome of nursing negligence was the birth of a baby with brain damage (78.26%). Other negative outcomes included stillbirth (13.04%), maternal infection (4.34%), and maternal death (4.34%).

The basic mechanism of injury in this subgroup was failure by the nurse to obtain help for the patient because of inadequate care by the physician. Most of the situations involved failure by the physician to intervene appropriately after being informed of fetal distress (43.47%). Thirty percent of the incidents occurred because the physician failed to arrive promptly at the hospital to attend the patient after such a request by the nurse. Other causes of adverse events included inability to locate the physician or failure by the physician to return telephone calls (17.39%) and failure by the physician to intervene after being informed of maternal distress (8.69%).

Case 11-2: Inadequate Care by the Physician

A 21-year-old primigravida presented to the hospital at 8:30 a.m. in early labor. Indications of fetal distress were noted at 1:00 p.m., and the physician was promptly informed of the problem. The physician asked the nurse to "keep an eye on the patient" until he could "get away" from his child's birthday party. The fetal distress persisted, and two additional calls were made to the physician. However, the physician did not arrive at the hospital until 5:00 p.m.

Failure to inform the nursing supervisor of the situation and failure to contact another physician to facilitate a timely cesarean section caused the baby to be born with severe brain damage. Legal action resulted in a payment of $6,000,000 to provide for lifelong care for the child.

Medication Administration Negligence

Medication administration problems were responsible for 17.96% of the adverse events in the labor room. Failure to administer medications properly caused 40.00% of the maternal deaths, 75.00% of the maternal injuries, and 15.95% of the fetal/newborn injuries in this setting.

The mean age of patients in this subgroup was 25.04, and the median age was 27.00 years. Of these patients, 82.61% presented with a normal pregnancy, and 17.39% suffered complications prior to admission.

The birth of a brain-damaged baby accounted for 65.21% of the nursing-care-related injuries in this subgroup. The remaining adverse outcomes involved maternal injuries that included brain damage

(13.04%), death (8.69%), loss of peripheral vision (4.34%), amputation of a digit (4.34%), and uterine rupture (4.34%).

The administration of medication when contraindicated was the mechanism of injury responsible for 65.21% of the adverse events. The continued administration of pitocin in the presence of documented fetal distress caused the majority of these negative incidents.

Administration of the wrong dose of a medication was the mechanism of injury in 13.04% of the negative outcomes in this subgroup. It was particularly disturbing to note that all of these incidents involved the administration of magnesium sulfate in a dose 5 to 10 times greater than the maximum recommended dose. In addition, all of the patients receiving the excessive dose of magnesium sulfate had documented signs of toxicity prior to the administration of the medication. These signs were ignored, and the result was either maternal brain damage or maternal death. Other mechanisms of injury in this subgroup included omission of medication (13.04%), incorrect parenteral administration technique (4.34%), and administration of the wrong medication (4.34%).

Case 11-3: Medication Administration Negligence

E. V., a 23-year-old woman, was admitted to the hospital with borderline pregnancy-induced hypertension. The patient's first pregnancy 2 years previously was uneventful. However, E. V. and her husband were apprehensive about the hospitalization.

Magnesium sulfate was administered by intravenous infusion. Two hours after the infusion commenced, E. V. manifested classical signs and symptoms of magnesium sulfate poisoning. The rate of the infusion was decreased, but the nurse provided no further care in terms of patient assessment. Twenty-nine minutes later, E. V. was found in full cardiopulmonary arrest. Resuscitation was successful but E. V. sustained severe brain damage. The baby was delivered stillborn.

A markedly elevated blood level of magnesium sulfate was found after the cardiopulmonary arrest. Investigation revealed that the nurse who cared for E. V. was a "float." This nurse was not knowledgeable about the therapeutic dosage range of magnesium sulfate. Eight times the prescribed dosage had been administered to E. V.

E. V. remains in a persistent vegetative state because of failure to administer the correct dosage of magnesium sulfate. Legal action resulted in a payment of $3,500,000 for the lifelong care of the patient.

Nursing Assessment Negligence

Problems associated with nursing assessment were responsible for 17.18% of the adverse events in the labor room. Failure to assess the patient systematically caused 40.00% of the maternal deaths, 12.50% of the maternal injuries, and 20.21% of the fetal/newborn injuries in this setting.

Patients in this subgroup had a mean age of 27.22 and a median age of 27.00 years. Of these patients, 86.64% presented with a normal pregnancy, and 13.36% were admitted with a history of complications.

The most frequent adverse outcome was the birth of a baby with brain damage (86.36%). The remainder of the negative events in this subgroup were maternal death (9.09%) and uterine rupture (4.54%).

The mechanism of injury for all adverse outcomes was inadequate nursing assessment. Failure to detect fetal distress in a timely manner because of infrequent assessment of fetal monitor tracings was the cause of 54.54% of the incidents. The remaining nursing-care-related negative outcomes were due to failure to apply the fetal monitor when indicated (18.18%), inappropriate discontinuance of the fetal monitor (9.09%), and inadequate maternal cardiovascular status assessment (18.18%).

Case 11-4: Nursing Assessment Negligence

A 27-year old primigravida was admitted to the hospital in active labor. A pitocin drip was administered when the labor became prolonged. Later, when a brow presentation was diagnosed, the pitocin drip was discontinued. Electronic fetal monitoring was also discontinued at this time. However, shortly before the fetal monitoring was discontinued, the strips indicated loss of beat-to-beat variability. The child was born by cesarean section, with Apgar scores of 5-5-7 as rated by the physician. The delivery room nurse, however, gave Apgar scores of 1-1-2.

Failure to assess the fetal heart rate during the 2 hours before the birth resulted in the failure to detect fetal hypoxia. The child is profoundly retarded with severe motor deficits. He is 10 years old and does not walk or speak. He must be fed by gastrostomy tube. Legal action resulted in a payment of $1,730,000 for continuing care.

Nursing Intervention Negligence

Problems associated with nursing intervention were responsible for 4.68% of the adverse events in the labor room. Failure to perform a nursing treatment or procedure properly caused 4.25% of the fetal injuries and 9.52% of the fetal deaths in this setting.

The average age of patients in this subgroup was 24.50, and the median was 25.50 years. All of the patients presented to the labor room with a normal pregnancy.

Adverse events due to nursing negligence were severe and resulted in fetal brain damage (66.66%) and stillbirth (33.33%). Mechanisms of injury included improper application of the fetal monitor (33.33%), administration of an enema when clearly contraindicated (33.33%), failure to perform a vaginal examination properly (16.66%), and inappropriate discontinuance of maternal supplemental oxygen (16.66%).

Case 11-5: Nursing Intervention Negligence

A 25-year-old primigravida was admitted to the hospital in labor. The birth was expected to be a breech delivery, and the "routine enema" was not ordered by the physician for this patient. However, T. H. was given an enema by a nurse and was left alone in the bathroom. Twenty minutes later, the patient ran into the hallway saying "something is wrong, something is hanging down." A nurse examined T. H. and found a prolapsed umbilical cord. The child was delivered promptly by emergency cesarean section, but not before sustaining hypoxia.

Failure to ensure that the patient did not receive the "routine" enema contributed to the baby's sustaining brain damage. The child is a spastic quadriplegic, and legal action resulted in a payment of $1,150,000 for lifelong care.

Environmental Safety Negligence

Problems associated with environmental safety caused 1.56% of the adverse events in the labor room. Failure to provide a safe environment was responsible for 2.12% of the fetal/newborn injuries in this setting.

Both mean and median maternal ages in this subgroup were 22.00 years. All patients presented to the labor room with a complicated pregnancy. Nursing negligence resulted in severe fetal/newborn injury in the form of brain damage. The mechanism of injury common to all incidents was a delay in the transfer of the obstetrical patient to a tertiary care facility. The delay, in all situations, was excessive, and the nursing staff did not intervene to facilitate transfer.

Case 11-6: Environmental Safety Negligence

On two separate occasions (June 23 and 24), an 18-year-old primigravida presented to the hospital with vaginal bleeding and cramping. She was examined and discharged because active labor was not evident. On June 25, C. F. was admitted to the hospital in active labor. The physician ordered electronic fetal monitoring. In addition, an order was written for immediate transfer of the patient to a tertiary care facility because of premature labor. However, the order to transfer the patient was not executed promptly because the labor and delivery suite was "very busy." In addition, a fetal monitor was not available for C. F. because "all monitors were in use." Fetal heart rate was assessed only one time, and that was at the time of admission.

The patient delivered 6 hours later, before the transfer could take place, and the child was born 8 to 10 weeks premature. Failure to assess fetal heart rate and failure to transfer the patient promptly to a facility appropriate to need contributed to cerebral palsy secondary to hypoxia during the birth process. The child is confined to a wheelchair and suffers slight cognitive impairment. Legal action resulted in a payment of $450,000 to help provide care for the child.

MALPRACTICE PAYMENTS

Nursing negligence resulted in a mean payment of $3,812,023 in the labor room setting. The median payment was $1,715,000.

Malpractice payments in the labor room were considerably larger for cases of injury than for cases of death. The high incidence of brain damage as an adverse outcome was the primary reason for this finding. Mean payments for fetal/newborn and maternal injury were $4,834,361 and $2,175,125, respectively, whereas mean payments for fetal/new-born and maternal death were $505,857 and $991,000, respectively. Table 11.7 summarizes malpractice payments by adverse outcome.

The largest number of malpractice payments were made for nursing care problems associated with communication. Payments related to communication negligence ranged from $3,000 to $72,650,000. Table 11.8 presents payment data for all nursing care problem areas.

The majority of the payments for labor room adverse outcomes were in two categories: $1,000,001 to $2,000,000 (26; 20.31%) and $2,000,001 to $4,000,000 (26; 20.31%). There were 48 (37.50%) payments between $1,000 and $1,000,000. Eighty payments were $1,000,001 or larger: 56.25% were in the range of $1,000,001 through $10,000,000, and 6.25% were in the range of $10,000,001 through $75,000,000. Figure 11.3 presents the distribution of malpractice payments to patients experiencing an adverse outcome of nursing care in the labor room.

The largest number of payments in this setting for maternal and fetal/newborn deaths respectively were between $400,001 and $600,000 and between $100,001 and $400,000. Figure 11.4 shows the distribution of malpractice payments for cases of death.

Payments for maternal and fetal/newborn injuries were substantial. The largest number of both maternal and fetal/newborn injury payments, on the other hand, were distributed between $1,000,001 and $2,000,000 (24.50%) and between $2,000,001 and $4,000,000 (23.52%). Maternal payments for nursing-care-related injury were grouped in two general categories: $100,001 through $400,000 (37.50%) and $1,000,001 through $8,000,000 (62.50%). Payments for fetal/newborn injury were grouped in three general categories: $50,001 through $1,000,000 (23.40%), $1,000,001 through $10,000,000 (68.08%), and $10,000,001 through $75,000,000 (8.51%). Figure 11.5 presents the distribution of all payments for cases of injury.

RISK PREVENTION STRATEGIES
IN THE LABOR ROOM SETTING

Risk management strategies applicable to all clinical settings as well as those common to selected nursing care problem areas will be found in Chapter 14.

TABLE 11.7 Malpractice Payments in the Labor Room, by Adverse
Outcome

Adverse	Malpractice Payments			
Outcome	No.	Range ($)	Mean ($)	Median ($)
Death (maternal)	5	500,000 to 2,260,000	991,000	600,000
Death (fetal/ newborn)	21	3,000 to 3,000,000	505,857	200,000
Injury (maternal)	8	150,000 to 8,000,000	2,175,125	1,150,000
Injury (fetal/ newborn)	94	55,000 to 72,650,000	4,834,361	2,145,000
All deaths and injuries	128	3,000 to 72,650,000	3,812,023	1,715,000

TABLE 11.8 Malpractice Payments in the Labor Room, by Nursing Care
Problem Area

Problem Area	Malpractice Payments			
	No.	Range ($)	Mean ($)	Median ($)
Nursing assessment	22	55,000 to 8,440,000	2,061,545	1,860,000
Environmental safety	2	450,000 to 10,240,000	5,345,000	5,345,000
Nursing intervention	6	200,000 to 7,500,000	2,250,000	1,037,500
Medication administration	23	150,000 to 22,000,000	3,746,565	1,840,000
Inadequate physician care	23	200,000 to 49,200,000	4,640,043	1,500,000
Communication	52	3,000 to 72,650,000	4,340,826	1,665,000

Maternal as well as fetal/newborn adverse outcomes due to nursing
malpractice in the labor room setting were severe. The babies born to
73% of the labor room patients were severely brain damaged. Prevention of nursing-care-related injuries unique to the labor room patient
requires the nurse to ask the following questions:

- Is the fetal monitor applied properly?
- Is fetal distress detected promptly and reported immediately to the
  physician?

(text continued on page 220)

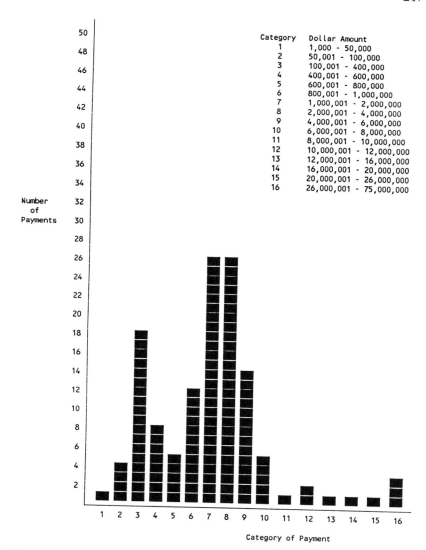

Figure 11.3. Distribution of Payments to Patients Experiencing a Nursing-Care-Related Adverse Outcome of in the Labor Room

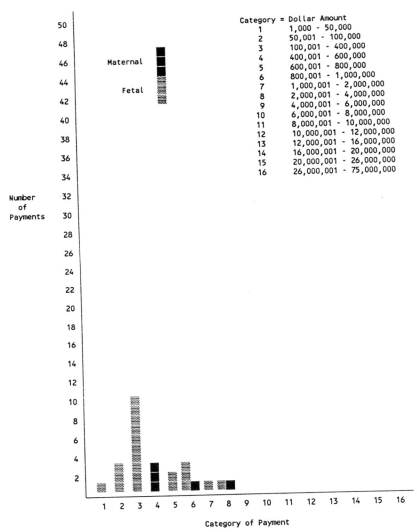

Figure 11.4. Distribution of Payments for Maternal and Fetal/Newborn Deaths Due to Negligent Nursing Care in the Labor Room

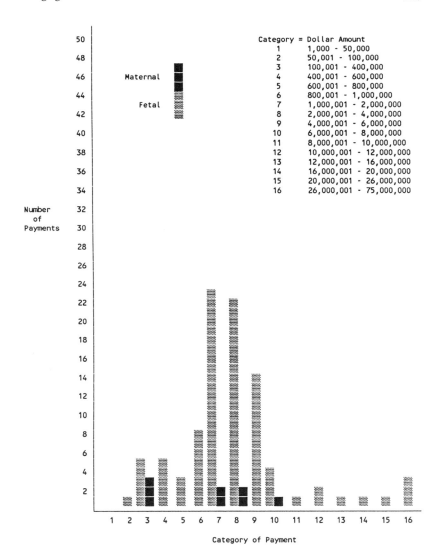

Figure 11.5. Distribution of Payments for Maternal and Fetal/Newborn Injuries Due to Negligent Nursing Care in the Labor Room

- Does the physician appropriately intervene in cases of fetal/newborn and/or maternal distress?
- Does the physician respond promptly in cases of fetal/newborn and/or maternal distress?
- Is pitocin discontinued immediately in the presence of fetal distress?
- Are the "five rights" of medication administration respected, especially when administering magnesium sulfate?
- Is transfer to a tertiary care facility executed promptly in high-risk situations?

SUMMARY

The majority of the catastrophic adverse outcomes in the labor room were associated with inadequate communication, inadequate care by the physician, inadequate nursing assessment, and medication administration error. Fetal/newborn brain damage occurred in 73.43% of the cases.

Obstetrical patients experiencing a nursing-care-related adverse outcome ranged in age from 16 to 38 years. The mean age was 24.97, and the median was 26.00 years. Eighty-five percent of the patients presented to the labor room with a normal, uncomplicated pregnancy. Maternal injuries were primarily due to medication errors, and the majority of fetal injuries were due to failure to inform the physician of fetal distress (per monitor) in a timely manner. Maternal deaths, on the other hand, were essentially due to inadequate nursing assessment, whereas fetal/newborn deaths were due, again, to the failure by the nurse to inform the physician of fetal distress (per monitor) in a timely manner.

The mean malpractice payment in the labor room setting was $3,812,023. Payments for injury, both fetal/newborn and maternal, were considerably higher than those for death. The high incidence of brain damage caused by nursing negligence, with the consequent need for lifetime assistance with activities of daily living, was the major reason for the difference in the payments.

12

Nursing Malpractice in the Delivery Room

Care of the obstetrical patient in the delivery room setting involves the second and third stages of labor. The second stage of labor begins with complete dilatation of the cervix and ends with the birth of the fetus. The third stage of labor is the period from the birth of the fetus through the expulsion of the placenta. Basic responsibilities of the nurse in this setting are related to surgical asepsis, accurate execution of nursing interventions, the proper use of equipment and products, communication with the physician, and ensuring that the patient receives care consistent with the prevailing professional standard.

Patients experiencing an adverse incident in the delivery room accounted for 2.81% (21 of 747) of the nursing negligence cases in the database. Nursing negligence caused or contributed to 15 (71.42%) fetal/newborn injuries, 5 (23.80%) maternal injuries, and 1 (4.76%) fetal/newborn death in this setting. The term *fetal/newborn* is used in cases of pregnancy in which there is a childbirth-induced/associated adverse outcome that involves only the fetus or newborn infant. Figure 12.1 presents the distribution of deaths and injuries in the delivery room.

Inadequate communication with the physician regarding nursing assessment data was the major departure from the standard of nursing care associated with both fetal/newborn death and injury. Maternal injury was primarily related to inadequate nursing intervention.

221

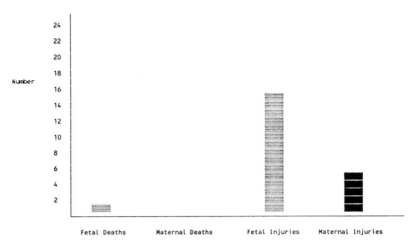

Figure 12.1. Distribution of Deaths and Injuries Due to Negligent Nursing Care in the Delivery Room

Table 12.1 summarizes nursing malpractice adverse outcomes and associated departures from the standard of care in the delivery room.

PATIENT CHARACTERISTICS

Patients experiencing a nursing-care-related adverse outcome in the delivery room ranged in age from 18 to 43 years. Both mean and median ages were 27.00 years. Table 12.2 presents age data for delivery room patients.

Fifty-two percent of the patients were distributed in three age categories: 22 through 24 years (19.04%), 25 through 27 years (14.28%), and 28 through 30 years (19.04%). Figure 12.2 displays maternal age distribution data.

The majority (61.90%) of the patients presented to the delivery room with a normal, uncomplicated pregnancy. However, 66.66% of the fetal/newborn injuries and all of the fetal/newborn deaths occurred in cases of normal pregnancy. Patients presenting with complications of pregnancy constituted 38.09% of this group. Of the patients with

TABLE 12.1 Nursing Malpractice Adverse Outcomes and Associated
Departures From the Standard of Care in the Delivery Room

Adverse Outcome Category	Departure From the Standard of Care Causing the Adverse Outcome	No. of Cases	% of Category	% of Total
Injury (fetal/newborn)		15	100.00	71.42
	Inadequate communication with the physician regarding nursing assessment data	10	66.66	
	Improper use of equipment	2	13.33	
	Inadequate nursing intervention	2	13.33	
	Inadequate care by the physician	1	6.66	
Injury (maternal)		5	100.00	23.80
	Inadequate nursing intervention	4	80.00	
	Improper use of equipment	1	20.00	
Death (fetal/newborn)		1	100.00	4.76
	Inadequate communication with the physician regarding nursing assessment data	1	100.00	

TABLE 12.2 Age of Patients Experiencing a Nursing-Care-Related Adverse
Outcome in the Delivery Room

Maternal Age	All Cases (N = 21)	Cases of Death		Cases of Injury	
		Maternal (N = 0)	Fetal/Newborn (N = 1)	Maternal (N = 5)	Fetal/Newborn (N = 15)
Range	18 to 43 yr.	N/A	43 yr.	22 to 36 yr.	18 to 33 yr.
Mean	27.00 yr.	N/A	43 yr.	30.00 yr.	24.93 yr.
Median	27.00 yr.	N/A	43 yr.	31.00 yr.	26.00 yr.

complications, 88.00% of the cases were characterized as high-risk pregnancies, and a cesarean section was ultimately performed. One high-risk patient in this group was not in labor, and the physician was misinformed by the nurse about the patient's condition. The physician was told that the patient was bleeding as well as being fully effaced and dilated. The patient was subjected to a cesarean section that resulted in the birth of an extremely premature baby. Table 12.3 summarizes the presenting problems of patients experiencing a nursing-care-related adverse outcome in the delivery room.

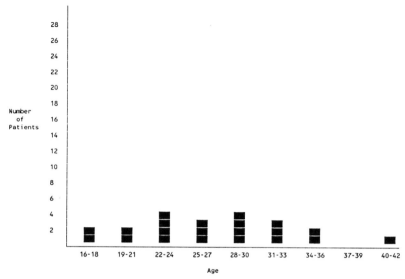

Figure 12.2. Age Distribution of Maternal Patients Experiencing a Nursing-Care-Related Adverse Outcome in the Delivery Room

ADVERSE NURSING
CARE OUTCOMES

Fetal/newborn brain damage was the most common nursing-care-related adverse event (52.38%) in this setting. Other negative outcomes in the delivery room included newborn Erb's palsy (19.04%), maternal retained sponge(s) (14.28%), stillbirth (4.76%), maternal sacroiliac sprain (4.76%), and maternal uterine rupture (4.76%). Table 12.4 summarizes adverse outcomes in the delivery room setting.

Inadequate communication with the physician was the predominant nursing care problem associated with unfavorable outcomes in the delivery room. Failure by the nurse to inform the physician of a change in maternal or fetal condition was the departure from the standard of care responsible for 52.38% of the adverse incidents. Problems associated with nursing intervention, equipment, and inadequate care by the physician were responsible for the remaining nursing-care-related

TABLE 12.3 Diagnoses/Presenting Problems of Patients Experiencing a
Nursing-Care-Related Adverse Outcome in the Delivery Room

Patient Diagnosis/ Presenting Problem	Total (N = 21)		Fetal/Newborn Death (N = 1)		Fetal/Newborn Injury (N = 15)		Maternal Death (N = 0)		Maternal Injury (N = 5)	
	No.	%	No.	%	No.	%	No.	%	No.	%
Pregnancy without complications	13	61.90	1	100.00	10	66.66	0	0.00	2	40.00
Pregnancy and/or labor with complications	8	38.09	0	0.00	5	33.33	0	0.00	3	60.00

TABLE 12.4 Type of Adverse Outcome Caused by Nursing Malpractice in
the Delivery Room (0 = 21)

Adverse Outcome Caused by Nursing Malpractice	No. of Cases	% of Cases
Newborn with Erb's palsy	4	19.04
Stillborn	1	4.76
Fetal/newborn brain damage	11	52.38
Maternal sacroiliac sprain	1	4.76
Maternal retained sponge(s)	3	14.28
Maternal uterine rupture	1	4.76

TABLE 12.5 Nursing Care Problems and Associated Departures From the
Standard of Care in the Delivery Room

Problem Area	Departure From the Standard of Care	No. of Cases	% of Cases
Communication	Failure to inform the physician of a change in maternal or fetal condition	11	52.38
Nursing intervention	Failure to perform a nursing treatment or procedure properly	6	28.57
Equipment	Failure to use equipment properly	3	14.28
Inadequate care by the physician	Failure to obtain help for a patient not receiving adequate care from the physician	1	4.76

negative outcomes. All nursing care problems, along with associated
departures from the standard of care, are summarized in Table 12.5.

The mechanism of injury responsible for the majority of maternal adverse events was retained sponges (60.00%). Fetal/newborn injuries and deaths were primarily related to a delivery by the nurse or an attempt to delay the delivery (33.33%). In both of these situations, the physician was present in the hospital but was not informed of the impending delivery. All mechanisms of injury responsible for adverse outcomes are presented in Table 12.6.

TABLE 12.6 Mechanisms of Injury Responsible for Nursing-Care-Related Adverse Outcomes in the Delivery Room

	Adverse Outcome							
Mechanism of Injury	Maternal Injuries (N = 5)		Fetal/Newborn Injuries (N = 15)		Maternal Deaths (N = 0)		Fetal/Newborn Deaths (N = 1)	
	No.	%	No.	%	No.	%	No.	%
Retained sponge(s)	3	60.00	0	0.00	0	0.00	0	0.00
Application of excessive fundal pressure	1	20.00	2	13.33	0	0.00	0	0.00
Fetal monitor not functional	0	0.00	2	13.33	0	0.00	0	0.00
Stirrups not locked	1	20.00	0	0.00	0	0.00	0	0.00
Physician present in hospital but not informed of impending delivery (delivery by nurse or attempt to delay delivery)	0	0.00	5	33.33	0	0.00	1	100.00
Physician misinformed that the patient is in active labor	0	0.00	1	6.66	0	0.00	0	0.00
Pediatrician not called for a high-risk delivery as per hospital policy	0	0.00	4	26.66	0	0.00	0	0.00
Inadequate care by the physician	0	0.00	1	6.66	0	0.00	0	0.00

NURSING CARE PROBLEMS

Communication Negligence

Problems associated with communication were responsible for 52.38% of the adverse events in the delivery room. Failure by the nurse to inform the physician of a change in maternal or fetal condition caused or contributed to 66.66% of the fetal/newborn injuries and all of the fetal/newborn deaths in this setting.

Both mean and median ages of patients in this subgroup were 27.00 years. Of these patients, 54.55% presented with a normal pregnancy, and 45.45% were considered high risk.

Nursing negligence in this subgroup caused or contributed to fetal/newborn brain damage (72.72%), newborn Erb's palsy (18.18%), and stillbirth (9.09%). The dominant mechanism of injury was delivery by the nurse or delay of delivery. In all cases, the physician was present in the hospital but was not informed of the impending delivery (54.54%). Failure by the nurse to call a pediatrician for a high-risk delivery as directed by hospital policy was responsible for 36.36% of the incidents. The remaining 9.09% of the negative outcomes were caused by the physician's performing a cesarean section on a patient who was not in labor. The physician did not examine the patient, and the decision to perform a cesarean section was based upon erroneous nursing assessment data communicated by the nurse.

Case 12-1: Communication Negligence

L. L., a 22-year-old woman, was taken to the operating room for an appendicitis at 21 weeks gestation. The surgery was uneventful, and she recovered well. The pregnancy progressed in a normal manner.

At 28 weeks gestation, L. L. experienced a small amount of bloody spotting and two sharp abdominal pains 5 minutes apart. She presented to the hospital at the request of her physician. A nursing assessment was performed upon admission. However, information about contractions and effacement was omitted.

Thirty minutes later, another nurse performed a vaginal examination and told L. L. that she was "10 centimeters dilated and ready to deliver." L. L., the mother of three children, stated that except for the earlier abdominal pain she was not having contractions. In addition, the patient commented that she did not feel as if she was in labor.

The physician, however, was informed that the patient was having contractions every 5 minutes, was completely dilated, was bleeding, and had the urge to push. Dr. F. ordered the patient to be prepared for a cesarean section.

Incorrect patient assessment information was communicated to the physician, and he did not verify the information by examination of the patient. The physician delivered a 2-pound, 11-ounce baby.

Failure by the nursing staff to provide accurate assessment data contributed to the birth of a premature infant who suffered severe brain damage. The child is profoundly retarded, quadriplegic, deaf, and blind. Legal action resulted in a payment of $5,750,000 for lifelong care.

Nursing Intervention Negligence

Problems associated with nursing intervention caused 28.57% of the adverse events in the delivery room. Failure by the nurse to perform a nursing treatment or procedure properly was responsible for 80.00% of the maternal injuries and 13.33% of the fetal/newborn injuries in this setting.

The mean age of patients in this subgroup was 26.50 years, and the median age was 24.50 years. Fifty percent of the patients in this subgroup delivered vaginally; the remaining patients delivered by cesarean section.

Maternal adverse outcomes due to nursing negligence in this subgroup were the need for additional surgery (75.00%) and ruptured uterus (25.00%). All fetal/newborn adverse outcomes were related to the development of Erb's palsy. Mechanisms of injury related to maternal negative outcomes were retained sponges secondary to an absent or incomplete sponge count (75.00%) and excessive fundal pressure (25.00%). Excessive fundal pressure was also the mechanism of injury contributing to all fetal/newborn injuries.

Case 12-2: Nursing Intervention Negligence

M. A., a 27-year-old married woman, was admitted to the hospital for a sixth cesarean section delivery. A healthy baby was born, and M. A.'s hospitalization was uneventful.

Four months after the delivery, M. A. experienced abdominal pain and a persistent low-grade temperature elevation. Evaluation and x-ray examination revealed a retained surgical sponge.

A large abdominal abscess was found during surgical exploration. Tissue damage was extensive and necessitated excision of a 1-foot portion of the terminal ilium along with excision of the proximal third of the colon. A temporary colostomy was created to permit healing. After a 1-year period, the colostomy was successfully reversed. However, M. A. faces the possibility of future surgery if adhesions cause bowel obstruction.

Investigation revealed that a laparotomy sponge was left in M. A.'s abdomen because both the scrub nurse and the circulating nurse failed to execute accurate sponge counts. Legal action resulted in a $1,240,000 payment to the patient.

Equipment and Products Negligence

Problems associated with equipment and products were responsible for 14.28% of the adverse events in the delivery room. Failure by the nurse to use equipment and/or product(s) properly caused 20.00% of the maternal injuries and 13.33% of the fetal/newborn injuries in this setting.

The mean age of patients in this subgroup was 25.66 years, and the median was 28.00 years. All patients presented to the delivery room with a normal, uncomplicated pregnancy and delivered vaginally.

Adverse outcomes due to negligent use of equipment and/or products caused or contributed to fetal/newborn brain damage (66.66%) and maternal sacroiliac sprain (33.33%). A nonfunctional fetal monitor was the mechanism of injury related to the cases of brain damage. The sacroiliac sprain was caused by the sudden and forceful falling of a patient's leg due to failure by the nurse to lock the stirrups on the delivery room table.

Case 12-3: Equipment Negligence

J. H., a 28-year-old married mother of two children, presented to the hospital after her membranes ruptured. Labor was induced with pitocin and progressed slowly.

Thirty minutes prior to her transfer to the delivery room, early signs of fetal distress, according to the monitor tracing, were evident. At 5:30 p.m., J. H. was taken to a delivery room where it was known that the fetal monitor was inoperable. No attempt was made to obtain a functional monitor, even though early signs of fetal distress had been observed.

Vacuum extraction and fundal pressure were unsuccessful in delivering the fetus. Pitocin was again administered. There was no further attempt to obtain a functional electronic fetal monitor. More vacuum extraction was attempted with the application of fundal pressure by two nurses. The child was finally delivered at 6:45 p.m. and had an Apgar score of 0 at 1 minute and 1 at 5 minutes.

Failure to provide for fetal monitoring contributed to the child's sustaining severe brain damage. He is profoundly retarded and has severe cerebral palsy. Legal action resulted in a payment of $4,400,000 for the lifelong care of the child.

Nursing Negligence Associated
With Inadequate Care by the Physician

Problems of inadequate care by the physician and related nursing negligence were responsible for 4.76% of the adverse events in the delivery room. Failure by the nurse to obtain assistance for a patient who was not receiving adequate care by the physician caused or contributed to 6.66% of the fetal/newborn injuries in this setting.

The one patient in this subgroup was 31 years old and presented to the delivery room with a normal pregnancy. The adverse outcome of fetal/newborn brain damage was the result of delivery by an inexperienced physician. The nurse in this case failed to summon help for the inexperienced physician when the delivery became prolonged and difficult.

Case 12-4: Inadequate Care by the Physician

M. V., a 31-year-old pregnant woman, was admitted to the hospital at 2:30 a.m. after her membranes ruptured at home. The patient weighed 351 pounds, and three of her last five children had weighed over 10 pounds at birth.

Active labor began that day at 8:00 a.m. Dr. W., who had delivered her last two children, examined the patient at 11:30 a.m., when she was 4 centimeters dilated. Pelvimetry revealed an adequate pelvic size for vaginal delivery.

At 2:30 p.m., Dr. W. left the hospital to join friends for a game of golf. Dr. O., an inexperienced new associate of Dr. W., was asked to assume the care and treatment of the patient. Pitocin was administered, and the patient was taken to the delivery room at 3:25 p.m.

Dr. O. delivered the head of the baby but had difficulty with delivery of the shoulders. Forceps were applied, and after 3 to 5 minutes Dr. O. left the delivery room to "answer a page." After waiting for Dr. O. to return, a resident physician who was assisting with the delivery finally delivered a 13.5-pound baby with difficulty.

Failure to obtain adequate care by a competent physician, in accordance with established hospital policy guidelines, caused the child to sustain neurovascular damage to the right brachial plexus and to suffer Erb's palsy. Legal action resulted in a payment of $3,500,000 for the care of the handicapped child.

MALPRACTICE PAYMENTS

Malpractice payments in the delivery room ranged from $50,000 to $49,271,000. The mean payment for all deaths and injuries was $4,754,952, and the median was $1,240,000.

The mean and median payments in cases of fetal/newborn injury were $6,417,533 and $2,700,000, respectively. Fetal brain damage was the most common adverse event in the delivery room setting, and the large payments were consistent with the need for lifelong assistance with activities of daily living. Payments for maternal injury were small in comparison to those for fetal/newborn injury. Mean and median payments for maternal injury were $518,200 and $215,000, respectively. These payments reflected the less serious nature of maternal injuries in this setting. Table 12.7 summarizes malpractice payment data by adverse outcome.

The largest number of malpractice payments made in the delivery room setting were for problems associated with communication. Nursing care problems related to equipment and products were responsible for the greatest dollar range of payments—namely, $66,000 through $49,300,000. Table 12.8 exhibits malpractice payments by nursing care problem.

TABLE 12.7 Malpractice Payments in the Delivery Room, by Adverse
Outcome

Adverse		Malpractice Payments		
Outcome	No.	Range ($)	Mean ($)	Median ($)
Death (maternal)	0	0	0	0
Death (fetal/newborn)	1	1,000,000	1,000,000	1,000,000
Injury (maternal)	5	66,000 to 1,240,000	518,200	215,000
Injury (fetal/newborn)	15	50,000 to 49,271,000	6,417,533	2,700,000
All deaths and injuries	21	50,000 to 49,271,000	4,754,952	1,240,000

TABLE 12.8 Malpractice Payments in the Delivery Room, by Nursing Care
Problem

Problem Area		Malpractice Payments (N = 21)		
	No.	Range ($)	Mean ($)	Median ($)
Nursing intervention	6	50,000 to 1,240,000	449,500	168,500
Inadequate physician care	1	3,500,000	3,500,000	3,500,000
Communication	11	220,000 to 12,500,000	3,629,000	2,100,000
Equipment and products	3	66,000 to 49,300,000	18,120,000	4,400,000

There was a varied distribution of malpractice payments made in
this setting. Payments of $1,000,000 or less were made in 47.61% of
the cases, and those in excess of $1,000,000 were made in 52.38% of
the cases. Figure 12.3 presents the distribution of payments made for
all adverse outcomes in the delivery room.

Only one fetal/newborn death occurred in the delivery room; this
resulted in a $1,000,000 payment. There were no maternal deaths.

Eighty percent of the malpractice payments for maternal injury were
$1,000,000 or less. Only one third of the payments for fetal/newborn
injury were $1,000,000 or less, and the remaining two thirds were
greater than $1,000,000. Figure 12.4 displays the distribution of
malpractice payments for cases of injury in the delivery room.

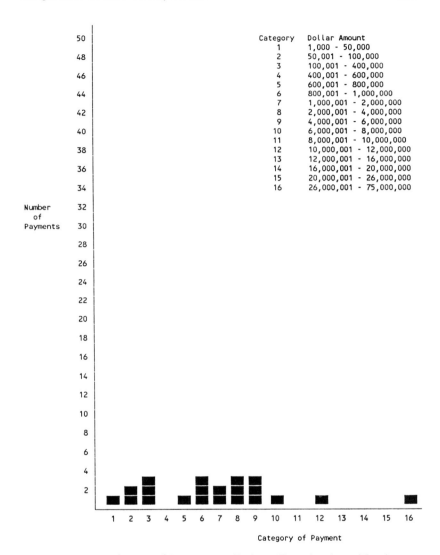

Figure 12.3. Distribution of Payments to Patients Experiencing a Nursing-Care-Related Adverse Outcome in the Delivery Room

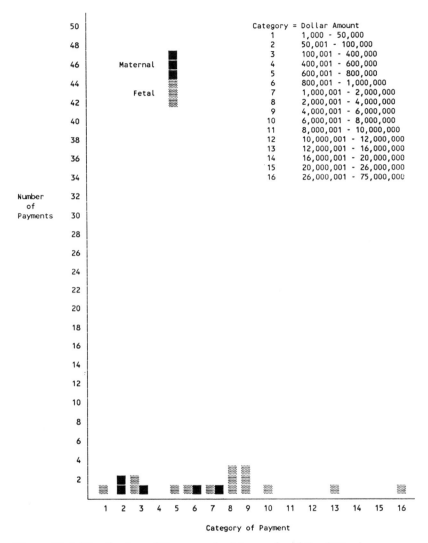

Figure 12.4. Distribution of Payments for Maternal and Fetal/Newborn
Injuries Due to Negligent Nursing Care in the Delivery Room

RISK PREVENTION STRATEGIES
IN THE DELIVERY ROOM SETTING

Risk management strategies applicable to all clinical settings as well as those common to selected nursing care problem areas will be found in Chapter 14.

Communication problems between the nurse and the physician were responsible for the majority of the delivery room adverse events. Prevention of nursing-care-related injuries in the delivery room requires the nurse to ask the following questions:

- Is fetal monitoring equipment maintained and cared for according to the manufacturer's instructions?
- Are problems with fetal monitoring equipment reported promptly so repairs can be made?
- Is the physician informed promptly of impending delivery?
- Is a pediatrician called promptly when the delivery becomes high risk?
- Is fetal monitoring promptly instituted when indicated?
- Is there an accurate accounting for all sponges, instruments, and other foreign bodies?
- Is fundal pressure applied without excessive force?

SUMMARY

The most frequent departure from the prevailing professional standard of nursing care in the delivery room setting was that of failure by the nurse to inform the physician of a change in maternal or fetal condition. Fetal/newborn injury was the primary aftermath of nursing malpractice in this setting.

Delivery room patients ranged in age from 18 to 43 years. Both mean and median ages were 27.00 years. Almost 62% (61.90%) of the patients in this setting presented with a normal pregnancy. Of interest, however, is that 66.66% of the fetal/newborn injuries and all of the fetal/newborn deaths occurred to patients admitted for an uncomplicated, normal pregnancy.

Maternal nursing-care-related injuries were less severe than those of the fetus/newborn. Fetal/newborn adverse outcomes, on the other hand, were grave and included death, brain damage, and newborn Erb's palsy. Problems associated with communication were responsible for the bulk of the negative outcomes in the delivery room. The most common mechanisms of injury in this setting were retained sponges, failure to inform the physician of impending delivery, and failure to obtain the services of a pediatrician for a high-risk delivery.

The mean payment for all adverse incidents in the delivery room was $4,754,952. The mean payment for fetal/newborn injury was $6,417,533, and the mean for maternal injury was $518,200. The high incidence of fetal/newborn brain damage as an adverse event in this setting accounted for the large payment differences.

13

Nursing Malpractice in the Newborn Nursery

During pregnancy, the fetus is nourished and protected in the mother's uterus. At birth the fetus/neonate encounters the most profound physiologic changes that occur at any period of its lifetime. Adaptation to extrauterine existence is facilitated by both immediate and continuing nursing care in the newborn nursery. The nurse must protect the newborn from exposure and injury. Systematic nursing assessment, in addition to providing for the physical needs of the infant, is vital during this period. The infant's natal day is the most hazardous time during the postnatal period. Thus it is important that the nurse provide systematic and continuous care to the newborn during the first 24 hours.

The newborn nursery population for the database was limited to neonates that did not experience an adverse event during the childbirth process. The database included healthy newborns as well as those experiencing physiological alterations at admission to the nursery or in the immediate newborn period.

Newborns experiencing an adverse nursing care outcome in the newborn nursery accounted for 6.96% (52 of 747) of the malpractice cases in the database. Nursing negligence caused or contributed to 8 (15.38%) deaths and 44 (84.61%) injuries in this setting.

The majority of the deaths were due to medication administration error, inadequate nursing intervention, and inadequate nursing assessment. Injuries were most frequently related to inadequate nursing intervention and an unsafe environment. Table 13.1 summarizes adverse outcomes and associated departures from the standard of care in the newborn nursery.

Adverse nursing care outcomes were devastating because 76.91% of the incidents in the newborn nursery resulted in either severe brain damage or death.

PATIENT CHARACTERISTICS

Seventy-five percent of the newborns suffering an adverse outcome of nursing care in the nursery were well babies. The remaining 25.00% of the newborn infants were well at birth but developed physiological problems at admission or in the immediate newborn period related to low birth weight (85.00%), congenital heart problems (7.50%), and temperature regulation problems (7.50%). Table 13.2 contains a summary of admission status of newborns experiencing adverse nursing care outcomes.

ADVERSE NURSING CARE OUTCOMES

The predominant adverse outcomes in the newborn nursery were brain damage (61.53%) and death (15.38%). Infants discharged to the wrong parents but later returned to the correct family were responsible for 5.76% of the adverse nursing care incidents. Other nursing-care-related injuries were amputation of digit(s), 5.76%; sensory loss (sight), 3.84%; chemical burn, 3.84%; respiratory system damage, 1.92%; and central nervous system infection, 1.92%. Table 13.3 describes data regarding type of adverse outcome experienced by infants in the newborn nursery.

Failure to perform a nursing treatment or procedure properly was the departure from the standard of nursing care responsible for 25.00% of the adverse incidents in the nursery setting. Other nursing care problems included those associated with environmental safety (17.30%), nursing assessment (17.30%), medication administration (15.38%), communication (13.46%), equipment and/or products (5.76%), inadequate care by the physician (3.84%), and nosocomial infection (1.92%). Table 13.4 contains data regarding nursing care problems and associated departures from the standard of care in the newborn nursery.

TABLE 13.1 Nursing Malpractice Adverse Outcomes and Associated
Departures From the Standard of Care in the Newborn
Nursery

Adverse Outcome Category	Departure From the Standard of Care Causing the Adverse Outcome	No. of Cases	% of Category	% of Total
Injury		44	100.00	84.61
	Inadequate nursing intervention	11	25.00	
	Unsafe environment	9	20.45	
	Inadequate nursing assessment	7	15.90	
	Inadequate communication with the physician regarding nursing assessment data	7	15.90	
	Medication administration error	5	11.36	
	Inadequate care by the physician	2	4.54	
	Improper use of equipment	2	4.54	
	Failure to prevent nosocomial infection	1	2.27	
Death		8	100.00	15.38
	Medication administration error	3	37.50	
	Inadequate nursing intervention	2	25.00	
	Inadequate nursing assessment	2	25.00	
	Improper use of equipment	1	12.50	

TABLE 13.2 Admitting Status of Infants Experiencing a
Nursing-Care-Related Adverse Outcome

	Adverse Outcome					
	Total (N = 52)		Death (N = 8)		Injury (N = 44)	
Admitting Status	No.	%	No.	%	No.	%
Normal newborn	39	75.00	3	37.50	36	81.81
Newborn developing problems at admission or shortly thereafter	13	25.00	5	62.50	8	18.18

The dominant mechanisms of injury in this setting were inadequate
nursing assessment (15.90%) and inadequate communication of assessment findings to the physician (15.90%). Deaths in the newborn
nursery were primarily due to the administration of the wrong medication (37.50%), suffocation by formula accumulation in the pharynx
(25.00%), and inadequate nursing assessment (25.00%). All mechanisms of injury responsible for newborn nursery adverse outcomes are
summarized in Table 13.5.

TABLE 13.3 Type of Adverse Outcome Caused by Nursing Malpractice in the Newborn Nursery (N = 52)

Adverse Outcome Caused by Nursing Malpractice	No. of Cases	% of Cases
Brain damage	32	61.53
Death	8	15.38
Emotional distress to parent(s)	3	5.76
Amputation of digits	3	5.76
Sensory loss: sight	2	3.84
Respiratory system damage	1	1.92
Burn	2	3.84
Central nervous system infection	1	1.92

TABLE 13.4 Nursing Care Problems and Associated Departures From the Standard of Care in the Newborn Nursery

Problem Area	Departure From the Standard of Care	No. of Cases	% of Cases
Nursing intervention	Failure to perform a nursing treatment or procedure properly	13	25.00
Environmental safety	Failure to provide a safe environment	9	17.30
Nursing assessment	Failure to assess the patient systematically	9	17.30
Medication administration	Failure to administer medication(s) properly	8	15.38
Communication	Failure to inform the physician of a change in the patient's condition	7	13.46
Equipment and products	Failure to use equipment and/or products properly	3	5.76
Inadequate physician care	Failure to obtain help for a patient not receiving adequate care from the physician	2	3.84
Nosocomial infection	Failure to prevent infection	1	1.92

NURSING CARE PROBLEMS

Nursing Intervention Negligence

Problems associated with nursing interventions were responsible for 25.00% of the adverse outcomes in the newborn nursery. Failure to perform a nursing treatment or procedure properly caused 25.00% of the injuries and 25.00% of the deaths in this setting. In this subgroup, 53.84% of the newborns were normal, and 46.15% were considered to have physiological alterations.

TABLE 13.5 Mechanisms of Injury Responsible for Nursing-Care-Related Adverse Outcomes in the Newborn Nursery

	Adverse Outcome			
	Infant Injury (N = 44)		Infant Death (N = 8)	
Mechanism of Injury	No.	%	No.	%
Omission of physician orders	1	2.27	0	0.00
Inadequate identification of an infant (infant given to the wrong parents)	3	6.81	0	0.00
Suffocation by formula in the pharynx	0	0.00	2	25.00
Careless use of scissors, causing digit amputation	2	4.54	0	0.00
Improper use of tape, causing digit amputation	1	2.27	0	0.00
Excess oxygen administered	2	4.54	0	0.00
Inappropriate removal from warmer	1	2.27	0	0.00
Delayed cardiopulmonary resuscitation	1	2.27	0	0.00
Endotracheal tube inadequately secured	1	2.27	0	0.00
Air in central venous pressure line	1	2.27	0	0.00
Baby dropped by nurse	4	9.09	0	0.00
Inappropriate transfer to well baby nursery and/or delay in transfer to neonatal intensive care	3	6.81	0	0.00
Inadequate nursing assessment	7	15.90	2	25.00
Administration of the wrong medication	2	4.54	3	37.50
Administration of the wrong dose of a medication	2	4.54	0	0.00
Incorrect parenteral administration technique	1	2.27	0	0.00
Failure to inform the physician promptly of abnormal assessment findings	7	15.90	0	0.00
Improper use of equipment or equipment not available	2	4.54	1	12.50
Inadequate care by the physician	2	4.54	0	0.00
Inadequate infection control	1	2.27	0	0.00

The majority of the newborn adverse outcomes involved either brain damage (38.46%) or death (15.38%). Other newborn injuries included loss of sight (15.38%) and digit amputation (7.69%). The remaining 23.07% of the negative outcomes were related to the emotional distress of the infant's parent(s). This emotional distress was caused by the infant's being given to the wrong parent(s) at discharge from the hospital.

Mechanisms of injury in this subgroup were quite varied. They included inadequate identification of the infant (23.07%), suffocation by milk in the pharynx (15.38%), administration of excess oxygen (15.38%), omission of the physician's order (7.69%), premature removal from warmer/incubator (7.69%), amputation of digits due to careless use of scissors when changing the intravenous infusion site (7.69%), delay in cardiopulmonary resuscitation (7.69%), inadequate securing of an endotracheal tube (7.69%), and introduction of air into a central venous line (7.69%).

Case 13-1: Nursing Intervention Negligence

Baby E. was born by emergency cesarean section. She was admitted to the newborn nursery in "good condition."

Fifteen hours after birth, a nurse attempted to discontinue an intravenous infusion that was located in the child's right hand. While cutting off the dressing and protective splint with scissors, the nurse partially amputated Baby E.'s thumb at the proximal interphalangeal joint. The thumb was surgically reattached, but the child developed a wound infection. The infection required additional surgical procedures, and the child suffered permanent limitation of motion in the thumb and a sensory deficit.

Failure to perform the nursing intervention with appropriate care caused injury to Baby E. Legal action resulted in a payment of $275,000 to the child's parents.

Environmental Safety Negligence

Problems associated with environmental safety were responsible for 17.30% of the adverse events in the newborn nursery. Failure to provide a safe environment resulted in 20.45% of the injuries in this setting. Of the newborns in this subgroup, 88.89% were well babies, and only 11.11% developed a physiological alteration.

Nursing-care-related adverse outcomes in this subgroup included brain damage (77.77%) and amputation of digit(s) (22.22%). Mechanisms of injury included dropping the newborn (44.44%), inappropriate transfer to the well baby nursery or delay in transfer to the neonatal intensive care unit (33.33%), careless use of scissors in the vicinity of the newborn (11.11%), and hand restraint by tape, resulting in loss of circulation (11.11%).

Case 13-2: Environmental Safety Negligence

Baby Y., a healthy newborn, was admitted to the nursery after an uncomplicated vaginal delivery. A nurse, while holding the infant in her arms during feeding, fell asleep seated in a chair. The baby fell out of the nurse's arms and dropped to the floor. The baby sustained a skull fracture that was complicated by a subdural hematoma.

The nurse who was caring for the infant was working a double shift. She worked as a "courtesy to the hospital," even though she was "dead tired." Failure to provide a safe environment for Baby Y. caused the infant to suffer permanent brain damage manifested by severe speech delay, cognitive deficit, and a learning disorder. Legal action resulted in a payment of $1,280,000 for the continuing care of Baby Y.

Nursing Assessment Negligence

Problems associated with nursing assessment caused 17.30% of the adverse events in the newborn nursery. Failure to assess the infant systematically resulted in 15.90% of the injuries and 25.00% of the deaths in this setting. All infants in this subgroup were considered healthy, normal newborns.

Adverse outcomes due to nursing negligence were brain damage (77.77%) and death (22.22%). The mechanism of injury was inadequate assessment. Specifically, inadequate assessment involved failure to assess systematically respiratory status (55.55%), neurological status (22.22%), and blood glucose (22.22%).

Case 13-3: Nursing Assessment Negligence

Baby B. was admitted to the newborn nursery after an uneventful delivery. It was noted that at approximately 6 hours of age, the infant began to experience respiratory distress. He was not assessed, however, for a period of 2 hours after the problem was first noted.

At the time of the next assessment, the infant was found in full cardiopulmonary arrest. Resuscitation was successful, but the child suffered hypoxic encephalopathy.

Failure to assess the baby systematically, especially after respiratory distress was noted, in all probability caused the brain damage. Legal action resulted in a payment of $5,640,000 for lifelong care of the child.

Medication Administration Negligence

Problems associated with medication administration resulted in 15.38% of the adverse events in the newborn nursery. Failure to administer medications properly caused 11.36% of the injuries and 37.50% of the deaths in this setting. Of the infants in this subgroup, 62.50% developed physiological problems after admission, and 37.50% were considered normal, well babies at admission.

The predominant adverse outcomes due to negligent nursing care in this subgroup were brain damage (37.50%) and death (37.50%). Respiratory system damage (12.50%) and chemical burns (12.50%) accounted for the remaining negative outcomes.

The most common mechanism of injury was administration of the wrong medication or the wrong intravenous infusion solution (62.50%). The wrong medication was administered frequently because it had a similar name to the prescribed medication. Administration of the wrong intravenous infusion solution was caused by a combination of two circumstances: The pharmacy department sent the wrong solution to the newborn nursery labeled with the infant's name, and the nurse failed to read the label of the solution before administering it. When the wrong intravenous infusion solution was administered, in most cases, the solution administered was very different from the one prescribed. The remaining tragic incidents of administering the wrong medication were the result of the nurse's diluting a medication for intravenous administration with potassium chloride rather than normal saline solution or sterile water.

The wrong dosage of a medication or of intravenous infusion solution was the mechanism of injury in 25.00% of the adverse nursing care outcomes. The magnitude of the errors in the newborn nursery were most alarming. Fifty to 65 times the ordered dosage was administered. The remaining 12.50% of the negative outcomes were due to incorrect parenteral administration technique.

Case 13-4: Medication Administration Negligence

Baby C., born after an uneventful labor and delivery, was admitted to the newborn nursery in "good condition." Twelve hours later, at

2:00 p.m., the infant developed acute respiratory distress. She was intubated and mechanically ventilated. Seconal 1.5 milligrams, intravenous push, was ordered every 4 to 6 hours as needed.

In the early morning hours, a nurse administered 1.4 milliliters of Seconal, approximately 75 milligrams. This overdose of medication resulted in Baby C.'s remaining on mechanical ventilation longer than required by her condition. The prolonged mechanical ventilation resulted in chronic reversible obstructive airway disease and an asthmatic condition. Legal action resulted in a payment of $100,000 to the child's parents.

Communication Negligence

Problems associated with communication were responsible for 13.46% of the adverse incidents in the newborn nursery. Failure to inform the physician of a change in the infant's condition caused 15.90% of the injuries in this setting. All newborns in this subgroup were healthy infants.

All adverse outcomes due to nursing negligence resulted in severe brain damage. The mechanism of injury was inadequate communication of neurological status changes (71.42%) or of respiratory status changes (28.57%).

Case 13-5: Communication Negligence

Ms. S., the mother of a healthy 4-year-old child, gave birth to Baby F. Both pregnancy and the labor and delivery were uneventful.

Baby F.'s 1-minute Apgar score was 7. Deductions of 1 and 2 were made for slow and irregular respiration and systemic cyanosis, respectively. At 5 minutes, the Apgar score was unchanged.

The child was admitted to the newborn nursery at 12:11 p.m., and "mild breathing trouble" was reported to the pediatrician. At 12:30 p.m., chest retractions and grunting sounds were noted, along with "mild cyanosis." Eighty-five percent oxygen was administered by hood, and the child began to "pink up." Shortly thereafter, symptoms indicating acute respiratory distress were evident. The child became cyanotic and developed hypotonic muscle tone. The pediatrician was not informed of the child's continuing respiratory problems until 2:00 p.m.

The physician came to the hospital to examine the child at 2:15 p.m. A right tension pneumothorax was diagnosed, and a chest tube was inserted. The child's condition improved.

The tension pneumothorax was due to a congenital cyst on the lung, causing a pleural tear with inspiration at birth. The accumulation of air in the right chest cavity severely impaired perfusion and ventilation.

Failure to inform the physician promptly of respiratory problems and the consequent delay in the evacuation of the air in the pleural cavity caused Baby F. to suffer brain damage. This resulted in spastic quadriplegia and a developmental disability. Legal action resulted in a payment of $500,000 for the continuing care of the child.

Equipment and Product Negligence

Problems associated with equipment and products accounted for 5.76% of the adverse events in the newborn nursery. Failure to use equipment and/or products properly caused 4.54% of the injuries and 12.50% of the deaths in this setting. Of the newborns, 66.66% were normal, and 33.33% developed physiological problems.

Adverse outcomes in this subgroup were evenly divided among brain damage (33.33%), electric shock and burns (33.33%), and death (33.33%). Mechanisms of injury included unavailability of resuscitation equipment, electric shock from a malfunctioning cardiac monitor, and failure to activate cardiac monitor alarms.

Case 13-6: Equipment Negligence

Baby C. was admitted to the newborn nursery in "excellent condition" after an uneventful delivery. Four hours after admission, a brief period of cyanosis along with an irregular heart rhythm was noted. This was reported to the physician, and Baby C. was placed on a cardiac monitor.

The monitor alarm sounded when all of the nurses were involved with feeding of the infants. The alarm was "assumed" to be false and was ignored for approximately 15 minutes. When the infant was finally attended, he was in a state of full cardiopulmonary arrest.

Failure to respond to the cardiac monitor alarm resulted in Baby C.'s sustaining severe brain damage. He expired 2 days later. Legal action resulted in a payment of $350,000 to the child's parents.

Nursing Negligence Associated
With Inadequate Care by the Physician

Inadequate care by the physician and associated nursing negligence were responsible for 3.84% of the adverse events in the newborn nursery. Failure to obtain care for an infant who was not receiving adequate care from a physician resulted in 4.54% of the injuries in this setting. All of the infants in this subgroup were admitted to the nursery as well babies.

Nursing-care-related injury consisted of severe brain damage. In all cases, abnormal nursing assessment data were reported by the nurse to the physician. However, the physician did not alter the treatment plan. The nurse continued to observe the infant's condition deteriorating but did not attempt to procure additional care for the patient in accordance with hospital policy and procedures.

Case 13-7: Inadequate Care by the Physician

A healthy newborn infant was admitted to the nursery after a normal delivery. Approximately 20 hours later, the nursing staff noted that Baby J. was jaundiced, irritable, and "jittery." In addition, the infant did not take feedings. The physician was informed, and she ordered a septic workup.

Three and one-half hours later, laboratory results indicating bacterial infection were communicated to the physician. She did not order antibiotics or change any of the "routine newborn care" orders.

The infant's condition deteriorated. The physician was informed but did not alter the treatment plan. Six hours later, Baby J. began to have seizures.

Another physician was finally called to evaluate the child. By this time, however, Baby J. was suffering from severe acute meningitis.

Failure by the nursing staff to follow hospital policy to obtain adequate medical care for the infant caused a delay in antibiotic therapy. This resulted in severe brain damage manifested by spastic quadriparesis, mental retardation, and cortical blindness. Legal action resulted in a payment of $6,620,000 for lifelong care for Baby J.

Nosocomial Infection

Problems associated with nosocomial infection caused 1.92% of the adverse events in the newborn nursery. The failure to prevent infection was responsible for 2.27% of the injuries in this setting. The newborn in this subgroup was healthy upon admission but later developed a central nervous system infection with consequent brain damage. Poor hand-washing technique was the mechanism of injury.

Case 13-8: Nosocomial Infection

A healthy newborn was admitted to the nursery. Approximately 3 weeks after discharge, Baby D. developed Citrobacter meningitis.

Three months earlier, two infants had experienced a *Citrobacter diversus* meningitis. It was determined that poor hand-washing technique was responsible for the spread of the meningitis. Baby D. suffered brain damage as a result of the infection and is now a spastic quadriplegic with a cognitive disability. Legal action resulted in a payment of $1,000,000 to the child's parents for his continuing care.

MALPRACTICE PAYMENTS

Malpractice payments in the newborn nursery were substantial. The mean payment for all adverse outcomes was $3,342,673, and the median was $1,000,000. There was a considerable difference between the malpractice payments for cases of injury and death. Mean payments for injury were $3,877,227, whereas those for cases of death were $402,625. This difference was due to the large number of nursing-care-related adverse outcomes resulting in brain damage, with the consequent need for lifetime assistance with activities of daily living. Table 13.6 summarizes malpractice payments in the newborn nursery by adverse event.

The largest number of malpractice payments were made for problems associated with nursing intervention. Table 13.7 presents malpractice payments by nursing care problem.

Payments greater than $1,000,000 were made in 50.00% of the malpractice cases in the newborn nursery. These large payments were widely distributed as follows: 32.68%, $1,000,001 through $4,000,000; 9.61%, $4,000,001 through $8,000,000; 1.92%, $8,000,001 through $10,000,000; 3.84%, $16,000,001 through $20,000,000; and 1.92%, $26,000,001 through $75,000,000. Figure 13.1 presents the distribution of malpractice payments in the newborn nursery.

TABLE 13.6 Malpractice Payments in the Newborn Nursery, by Adverse Outcome

Adverse Outcome	Malpractice Payments			
	No.	Range ($)	Mean ($)	Median ($)
Death	8	90,000 to 606,000	402,625	387,500
Injury	44	22,000 to 56,000,000	3,877,227	1,300,000
All deaths and injuries	52	22,000 to 56,000,000	3,342,673	1,000,000

TABLE 13.7 Malpractice Payments in the Newborn Nursery, by Nursing Care Problem

Problem Area	Malpractice Payments (N = 52)			
	No.	Range ($)	Mean ($)	Median ($)
Nursing assessment	9	375,000 to 5,640,000	2,493,888	1,500,000
Environmental safety	9	50,000 to 2,900,000	1,341,111	1,350,000
Nursing intervention	13	22,000 to 56,000,000	6,542,923	500,000
Medication administration	8	90,000 to 2,340,000	676,375	417,500
Inadequate physician care	2	850,000 to 6,620,000	3,735,000	3,735,000
Communication	7	500,000 to 19,190,000	5,530,000	3,650,000
Infection	1	1,000,000	1,000,000	1,000,000
Equipment	3	35,000 to 1,270,000	551,666	350,000

In cases of death, all payments were less than $1,000,000. Fifty percent of the payments in death were between $100,001 and $400,000, and the remaining payments were in the following dollar categories: 25.00%, $400,001 through $600,000; 12.50%, $1,000 through $50,000; and 12.50%, $600,001 through $800,000. Figure 13.2 contains payment distribution data for cases of death.

On the other hand, 59.09% of the payments for newborn injury were greater than $1,000,000: 47.72% were $1,000,001 through $6,000,000; 4.54% were $6,000,001 through $10,000,000; and 6.81% were $16,000,001 through $75,000,000. Figure 13.3 presents data regarding the distribution of payments in the nursery setting for newborn injuries.

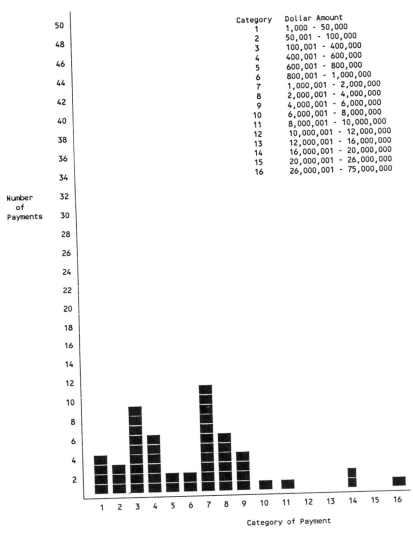

Figure 13.1. Distribution of Payments in the Nursery Setting for Newborns Experiencing a Nursing-Care-Related Adverse Outcome

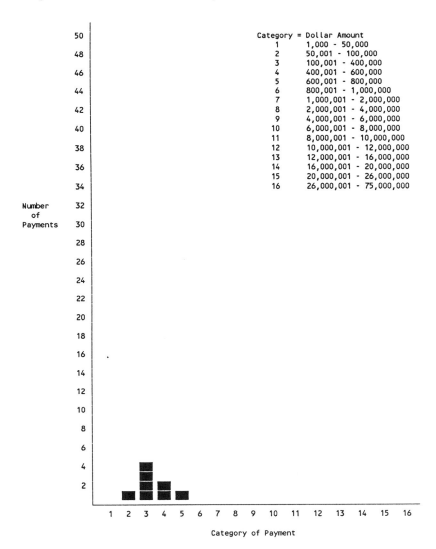

Figure 13.2. Distribution of Payments in the Nursery Setting for Newborns Suffering Death as a Nursing-Care-Related Adverse Outcome

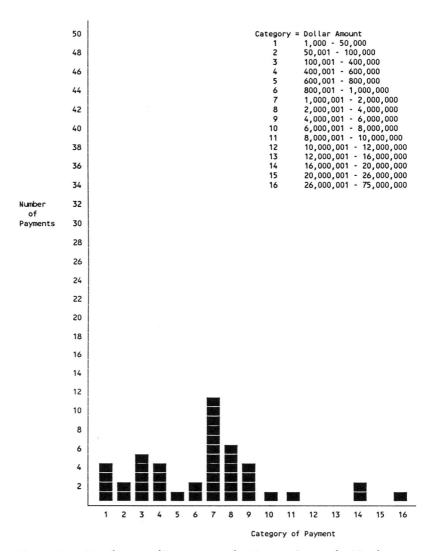

Figure 13.3. Distribution of Payments in the Nursery Setting for Newborns Experiencing Injury as a Nursing-Care-Related Adverse Outcome

RISK PREVENTION STRATEGIES IN
THE NEWBORN NURSERY SETTING

Risk management strategies applicable to all clinical settings as well as those common to selected nursing care problem areas will be found in Chapter 14.

Nursing negligence in the newborn nursery caused devastating outcomes. Prevention of nursing-care-related injuries unique to the newborn nursery setting requires that the nurse ask the following questions:

• Are the infant and parent(s) properly identified prior to placing the infant into the care of the parent(s)?
• Is the infant assessed systematically, especially after feeding?
• When staff are executing a nursing intervention requiring the use of scissors, are the infant's digits protected from scissors injury?
• Is adhesive tape applied carefully to extremities to avoid circulatory obstruction?
• Are normal, healthy newborn infants assessed systematically (especially respiratory status)?
• Are the "five rights" of medication administration respected (especially in reference to intravenous infusions)?
• Is the correct intravenous infusion solution administered?
• Is the correct solution used in diluting a medication for intravenous administration?
• Is proper hand-washing technique used at all times?
• Is the infant handled carefully to avoid dropping it?

SUMMARY

Nursing negligence in the nursery setting resulted in severe injury or death. The majority of the adverse outcomes were related to inadequate nursing intervention, inadequate nursing assessment, medication administration error, and an unsafe environment.

Seventy-five percent of the newborns in this setting were considered normal, well babies. These infants experienced 81.81% of the total injuries and 37.50% of the total deaths. The 25.00% of the newborns developing physiological problems at admission or in the immediate newborn period, on the other hand, experienced 62.50% of the total deaths and only 18.18% of the total injuries.

Adverse nursing care outcomes were severe, with 61.53% of the infants experiencing brain damage and 15.38% suffering death. Four mechanisms of injury were responsible for the majority of adverse outcomes: administration of the wrong medication, inadequate nursing assessment, failure to inform the physician promptly of abnormal assessment findings, and a baby dropped by the nurse.

Fifty percent of the malpractice payments in this setting were $1,000,001 or larger. Severe brain damage with the consequent need for lifetime care was the reason for the majority of the large payments in this setting. The mean payment for nursing-care-related injury was $3,877,227, whereas the mean for death was only $402,625.

$\sqrt{14}$

Risk Management Strategies

Risk-free nursing care is impossible because nurses are human and they make mistakes. Nurses function in a complex and stressful environment. Recognizing the importance of patient safety and participating in an effective hospital risk management system will contribute, however, to reducing or preventing unnecessary error. Prevention of adverse patient care outcomes is proactive because it will save lives.

Nursing-care-related patient injury as well as death can be minimized or prevented by utilizing the nursing process in planning patient care. Communication, both verbal and written, is fundamental to the nursing process. Patient assessment that is continuous and systematic is an integral part of the nursing process. It provides the foundation for the identification and definition of patient needs and problems. Patient care goals and desired objectives are established, and a plan of care is developed. A safe biological and physical environment is necessary for the implementation of the care plan. Nursing care to meet patient needs must be delivered in accordance with the prevailing professional standards of practice. Safe and effective nursing care is promoted by attention to principles of safe medication administration, accurate execution of nursing treatments and procedures, and the appropriate use of equipment and supplies. Finally, the care is evaluated in relation to achieving the desired outcomes. Hospital policies and procedures provide important guidance in this process.

The nurse is a key member of the risk management team in the hospital setting because he or she is the only member of the health care team responsible for the patient 24 hours a day. In addition, the nurse is in the best position to learn from the patient, family members, and visitors because of the daily patient contact. The importance of good communication, both verbal and written, cannot be overemphasized in the prevention of adverse events. Adverse patient care outcomes can be reduced or avoided when the nurse recognizes situations in which negligent actions are most likely to occur.

The risk management strategies in this chapter focus on the prevention of adverse nursing care incidents. A professional attitude and a solid knowledge base are key ingredients for providing safe nursing care. The following are guidelines for developing and maintaining a professional attitude:

- Be responsible, diligent, and studious.
- Be committed to expanding your knowledge base. The secret to a long, safe nursing career is to reduce the "don't know" category as much as possible.
- Commit assessment variables, nursing care procedures, etc., to memory; this frees up mental capacity to deal with unforeseen events. The more you know, the more you will have to offer the patient.
- Use colleagues; frequently they have information you need.
- Return to basics if confused.
- Be open-minded to constructive criticism.
- Ask for help when overloaded; do not try to do everything yourself.
- Do not become complacent. Never take anything for granted, never become relaxed, question everything, and stay alert.
- Learn from the mistakes of others. Review all accidents/adverse outcomes and ask, What would I have done? How could I have avoided this accident/adverse outcome?
- Be able to adapt.
- Never enter a clinical area with a head full of personal problems. Leave them outside the clinical area or stay outside yourself.
- Eliminate distractions and maintain an alert, vigilant mental state.
- Be able to recognize the onset of personal inattention or that of colleagues.
- Listen to others and find out how they do things. Then you can reevaluate your own habit patterns.
- Develop an awareness of potential risks in the hospital setting.
- Understand the importance of good verbal communication.

- Understand the importance of the medical record in the hospital setting.
- Understand the importance of informed consent and patient rights.

To effectively provide patient care, the nurse must observe the following guidelines:

- Use hospital policies and procedures so everyone knows what to expect.
- Stick to hospital policies and procedures unless they are obviously inadequate.
- Mentally prepare strategies to deal with difficult patient care situations.
- The focus of your interest must be on patient care. You must want to do a good job.
- Be able to adapt. No two patient care situations are exactly alike.
- Plan ahead for normal patient care needs and be prepared for unexpected contingencies.
- Keep patient care options open. Never become committed to a single course of action.
- Always have available both a plan and a contingency plan.
- Be totally aware of everything about the patient, particularly when subtle changes are occurring.
- If anything seems out of the ordinary with regard to a patient or if the patient does not seem to be the way you think he or she should be, check it out.
- Awareness is the sum total of many little things that vary with the condition of the patient. Review all the little things that make up the total.
- If you have any doubt about any aspect of patient care, ask questions. Get answers to questions before rendering care.
- Be especially vigilant when everything is going well.
- Be alert because trouble can begin when everything is normal with the patient; everybody seems to relax then.
- Avoid complacency when giving patient care. The minute you think something will not go wrong, it will.
- Look at the big picture when providing patient care; do not become fixed on anything.
- Communicate pertinent information about the patient.
- Remember that any time the patient's condition changes, new risks must be monitored and managed.

- If you get rushed or overloaded, slow down, even if it means slightly delaying care.
- Pay attention to your sixth sense. If something feels wrong, it probably is.
- Almost nothing needs to be done in a hurry when providing patient care; think things through.

PREVENTION OF
DOCUMENTATION PROBLEMS

Problems associated with documentation of patient care in the medical record were evident in the majority of the 747 malpractice cases reviewed. The medical record is the instrument that provides for continuity of patient care by containing vital information about the patient's condition, the type and kind of care provided, and the patient's response to the care. The medical record is like the flight data recorder in an airplane.

The cases in the database revealed that documentation problems occurred in all the clinical areas of the hospital. Recurrent problems included (a) inadequate or incomplete documentation in the medical record, (b) the absence of documentation in the medical record, (c) all or a part of the medical record missing, (d) alteration of the medical record, (e) falsification in the medical record, and (f) fabrication of entries in the medical record.

The act of documenting patient assessment and nursing care in the medical record is inseparable from the act of actually providing the nursing care. The importance of documentation in maintaining an accurate and timely medical record cannot be overemphasized. Documentation of care is as critical and important to the patient as the actual delivery of the nursing care. The nurse can prevent documentation problems by ensuring that all nursing entries in the medical record are

- Objective, factual, specific, and professionally stated
- Accurate, clear, concise, and complete
- Timely and in proper sequence
- Legible
- Written using approved abbreviations, correct grammar, and correct spelling
- Signed on the right side of the page with the first initial, full last name, and title

All nursing entries in the medical record from hospital admission to discharge must demonstrate

- The continuous collection of patient data
- The continuous care and treatment of the patient
- The nursing process
  1. Initial and ongoing assessments
  2. Definition of patient needs/problems
  3. Nursing interventions
  4. Treatments, procedures, diagnostic tests
  5. Notation of visits by other members of the health care team
  6. Patient response to treatment
  7. Pertinent statements made by the patient
  8. Comfort and safety measures
  9. Patient teaching
  10. Nursing discharge summary (patient condition, teaching measures, special instructions, etc.)

For effective documentation and the prevention of adverse events, the nurse must review periodically

- Hospital policies and procedures concerning documentation
- Standards set by various professional organizations such as the American Nurses' Association and the Joint Commission on Accreditation of Health Care Organizations

All nursing notations in the medical record should reveal

- What is being done
- What is seen
- What is felt
- What is heard
- Both normal and abnormal assessment data
- Any aspect of nursing care omitted, along with the reason for the omission
- Content of telephone calls concerning patient care

- Potentially harmful patient actions such as
  1. Refusal of prescribed treatments
  2. Refusal of medications or misuse of prescribed medications
  3. Refusal to follow instructions or physician's orders
  4. Failure to provide a complete and accurate health history and health status information
  5. Interference with the delivery of health care or any behavior that hinders the delivery of care (e.g., tampering with equipment such as intravenous infusion apparatus)
  6. Use of unauthorized items and substances such as a heating pad, tobacco, alcoholic beverages, and medications
  7. Leaving the hospital against advice
- Potentially harmful acts committed by the patient's visitor or family member, such as tampering with wound dressings, tampering with equipment, preventing or delaying the delivery of health care, providing unauthorized items or substances, and assisting the patient with actions contrary to the treatment plan

It is helpful for the nurse to remember the following:

- Nursing care and documentation go hand in hand.
- Nursing care and documentation cannot be separated.
- Nursing care and documentation are one act.
- Documentation of nursing care is as important as providing the actual nursing care.
- Gaps in documentation suggest that the patient was neglected.
- Complete documentation in all sections of the medical record concerned with nursing care (e.g., medication administration record, intake and output sheet, graphic record).
- Document and sign for only the actual nursing care you provided to the patient.
- Document only after the nursing care has been provided to the patient.
- If a documentation error is made, a single line is drawn through the error and the word *error* is written above the line. This is initialed, and the correction follows.
- Alter the medical record only if absolutely necessary and only for patient care purposes.
- Any medical record alteration must include the date, time, reason for alteration, and signature with title of the person making the alteration.

- An addition to the record or a late entry can be made if absolutely necessary, but this entry must
  1. Be made as promptly as possible
  2. Have the date and time
  3. Be headed "addendum [or late entry] to the nurse's notes of [date and time]"
  4. State the reason for the addendum
  5. Contain the signature and title of the person making the addendum
- Never obliterate or erase any entry in a medical record.
- Never remove a page or destroy a section of the medical record.
- Never insert corrections and/or additional information between lines, in margins, or between other entries.
- In the event of legal action, absolutely avoid correcting or revising a medical record even if there is a reason.
- In the event that an incident report is made, do not include it in the medical record, and do not refer to filing the incident report in the medical record (unless instructed otherwise by the hospital).
- If an unusual occurrence involves a patient, document the incident in the medical record in a factual, detailed, and objective manner.
- All pages of the medical record used for documentation identify
  1. The patient by name
  2. The medical record number
  3. The nursing unit or room number
- Every entry in the medical record contains
  1. Complete date
  2. Accurate time
- Telephone and verbal orders are only taken when the physician cannot attend the patient.
- Draw a line through any empty spaces in front of your signature to prevent subsequent additions.

INCIDENT REPORTS FOR RISK ANALYSIS AND PREVENTION

At one time, the incident report was frequently thought of as a punitive tool for disciplinary action. However, today the incident report (also called the *situation, event,* or *occurrence report*) is a management tool and is a very important element of the risk management system. Its function is to gather data so that actual or potential problems can be identified. All persons functioning in the contemporary hospital setting must use the incident report to communicate atypical occurrences.

When an incident involves the patient, factual, detailed, and objective knowledge of the incident is documented in the medical record. Opinions and speculation are to be avoided. However, the incident report, in almost all hospital settings, does not become a part of the patient's medical record, and reference to filing it is not made in the medical record. The reason for this is that the incident report is an internal management tool used to improve safety and the quality of patient care.

PREVENTION OF
MEDICATION ADMINISTRATION PROBLEMS

Accurate administration of medication is a fundamental nursing responsibility. Medication errors, however, are not uncommon in the hospital setting and pose a great danger to the patient. One of the biggest perils the nurse faces in practice is medication administration error. A wide range of deviations from a prescribed order is possible. Mistakes occur when principles of safe medication preparation and administration are ignored. All medication administration errors can and should be prevented. Safe administration of medication requires that the nurse

- Compare the medication with the order in the medical record
- Evaluate the medication order for appropriateness in the context of the patient's history, condition, and current treatment
- Possess a thorough knowledge of the medication to be administered
- Read the medication label three times (adapt the procedure to the system your hospital uses)
- Review the "five rights" of medication administration
  1. The right patient
  2. The right medication
  3. The right route
  4. The right time
  5. The right dose

- Listen to and investigate if the patient questions a medication (always heed the patient's warning!)
- Evaluate the patient's response to the medication
- Possess knowledge of drug interactions when multiple medications are administered

The nurse can further prevent medication errors by assuring that the physician's order for a medication is

- Valid
- Complete and containing
    1. The name of the patient to receive the therapeutic measure(s)
    2. The date and time the order is written
    3. The name of the therapeutic agent to be administered
    4. The dosage or concentration of the agent
    5. The time and frequency the agent is to be administered
    6. The route of administration
    7. The signature of the physician
- Clarified, reaffirmed, or revised if it is not clear and understandable
- Questioned if it is suspected to be incorrect or unsafe
- Not executed if it is considered incorrect or unsafe
- Accepted by telephone or verbally only if the physician cannot attend the patient and if the order is
    1. Recorded in the medical record verbatim with the date and time of the order
    2. Verified by reading the order verbatim back to the physician
    3. Complete
    4. Countersigned by the physician as soon as possible

PREVENTION OF NURSING ASSESSMENT PROBLEMS

Systematic nursing assessment is a vital nursing responsibility and is crucial to the nursing process. The initial nursing assessment and nursing history provide the foundation for proper formulation of the nursing care plan. An initial nursing assessment should include such data as the following:

- Patient's chief complaint: onset of illness, complete description of symptoms and condition
- Past medical history
- Social and family history
- Behavioral status
- Respiratory status
- Circulatory status
- Neurologic status
- Body temperature
- Integumentary and wound status (when applicable)
- Renal function and fluid status
- Gastrointestinal status
- Weight and height
- Musculoskeletal status
- Endocrine and metabolic status
- Sensory and perceptual status
- Immune status

After the initial assessment, the nurse is obligated to monitor the biopsychosocial status of the patient continuously. This is a most important responsibility because the nurse is the only member of the health care team with the patient 24 hours a day. The nurse must listen carefully to the patient and must not ignore any patient concern or complaint.

Most nursing assessments do not require a physician's order and are independent nursing actions. The frequency of nursing assessment as well as the content is based upon the patient's condition and/or needs. Such systematic observations may include

- Respiratory status assessment
  1. Patency of airway
  2. Respiratory rate
  3. Respiratory rhythm
  4. Respiratory character
  5. Breath sounds
  6. Ease of respiration
  7. Duration of inspiration vs. expiration
  8. General chest expansion
  9. Presence/absence of intercostal retractions

    10. Posture of the patient and facial expression
    11. Presence/absence of fatigue with breathing
    12. Effectiveness and frequency of cough
    13. Sputum amount and character
    14. Percussion of chest, noting intensity, pitch, quality, duration, and equality of sound
    15. Arterial blood gas interpretation
    16. Tidal volume
    17. Minute volume
    18. Vital capacity

- Circulatory status assessment
    1. Pulse rate
    2. Pulse rhythm
    3. Pulse quality
    4. Blood pressure
    5. Skin color
    6. Skin temperature
    7. Central venous pressure and other hemodynamic line measurements
    8. Circulation in extremities (peripheral pulses, temperature and color of extremity, blanching sign, motor and sensory function)

- Body temperature status assessment
- Neurologic status assessment
    1. Response to stimuli
    2. Orientation
    3. Level of consciousness
    4. Response to commands
    5. Pupillary response (size, equality, and reaction to light)
    6. Ocular movements—noting if eyes move, if movement is conjugate (together) or disconjugate (separate), and direction of eye movement when head rotated (doll's head maneuver)
    7. Motor and sensory function (movement and strength in extremities, abnormal sensations)
    8. Reflexes
    9. Behavioral changes
    10. Headache or seizure activity

- Integumentary and wound status assessment
    1. Description of trauma
    2. Character of drainage

    3. Amount of drainage

    4. Condition of dressings and/or suture lines

    5. Condition of skin

- Renal status assessment
  1. Urinary output
  2. Character of urine
- Fluid status assessment
  1. Intake (amount, kind, route, rate)
  2. Intake vs. output
  3. Estimated or actual fluid loss
- Pain status assessment
  1. Qualitative aspects
  2. Quantitative aspects
  3. Topographic aspects
  4. Temporal aspects
  5. General level of comfort
- Gastrointestinal status assessment
  1. Appearance of abdomen
  2. Bowel sounds
  3. Presence/absence of nausea, emesis
- Musculoskeletal status assessment
  1. Sensory and motor function
  2. Mobility
- Endocrine and metabolic status assessment
- Sensory and perceptual status assessment
- Immune status assessment
- Psychosocial status assessment

The nurse is not only responsible for determining the frequency and content of nursing assessment but accountable for the decision.

PREVENTION OF
ENVIRONMENTAL SAFETY PROBLEMS

Patients in the hospital setting are prime candidates for environmental injury because of such risk factors as advanced age, equilibrium problems secondary to medications, unfamiliar surroundings, a weakened condition due to disease and/or treatment(s), impaired mobility, impaired sensory perceptions, and altered mental status. Falls are not uncommon in this setting. A fundamental nursing responsibility, then, is to protect the hospitalized patient from avoidable injury by providing a safe environment. Safety measures such as the proper use of restraints, bedside rails, night-lights, provision of assistance with ambulation, and placement of beds in the low position near the floor are nursing obligations.

Assessment and evaluation of the patient's needs related to the physical environment of the hospital are an important part of the nursing care plan. Nursing interventions specific to the environmental safety needs of the patient must be implemented. Environmental safety problems can be avoided by

- Systematic and timely assessment/observation of the patient
- Provision of prompt assistance to the ambulatory/nonambulatory patient as needed
- Use of safety devices such as side rails
- Proper application of restraints when indicated, along with frequent observation of the patient (at least every hour) and frequent removal of the restraint(s) (at least every 4 hours)

PREVENTION OF
NOSOCOMIAL INFECTION PROBLEMS

A hospital-acquired or nosocomial infection is an infection that is not present or incubating at the time the patient is admitted to the hospital. Nosocomial infection is a serious threat to the hospitalized patient because the hospital harbors a large number and variety of virulent organisms. Many microorganisms are resistant to antibiotics. Patients entering the hospital are at an increased risk of acquiring infection not only because of exposure to a wide variety and increased concentration of microbial agents but because of a decreased resistance to infection due to illness, invasive procedures, and invasive treatments.

Nurses have a duty to provide a safe biological environment for the hospitalized patient by avoiding actions that transmit microorganisms, by eliminating reservoirs of infection, and by controlling portals of entry and exit of microorganisms. Prevention of infection is a primary nursing obligation. The nurse must do the following:

- Apply sound aseptic practices to patient care
- Eliminate or contain sources of infection
- Interrupt the mechanism(s) of transmission of infection
- Protect all patients, especially those who are susceptible from infection
- Maintain the integrity of the patient's skin
- Use meticulous hand-washing technique when caring for patients
- Prevent the introduction of microorganisms in portals of entry created by invasive procedures, instrumentation, and/or vascular system lines

PREVENTION OF
COMMUNICATION PROBLEMS

Communication problems, specifically failure by the nurse to apprise the physician of a significant change in the patient's condition or of critical nursing assessment data, have caused too many adverse patient outcomes. Delay in communicating observations has increased the risk of a negative outcome for many patients and in a number of instances has altered the patient's ultimate outcome. Effective communication is the foundation for the delivery of competent nursing care.

The physician is dependent upon communication from the nurse in the hospital setting because the nurse is the only member of the health care team with the patient 24 hours a day. Documentation of critical observations is not enough; observations must be communicated in a timely manner so that action may be taken. Prevention of adverse outcomes due to communication problems are dependent upon the nurse's observance of the following guidelines:

- Report a change in the patient's condition to the physician.
- Report significant patient assessment data to the physician.
- Report if the patient's condition fails to improve in response to treatment.
- Contact the physician about any significant patient care concern.
- Contact the physician as patient care needs dictate. Do not be intimidated or hesitant to call the physician in the middle of the night and/or on weekends and/or on holidays.
- Follow hospital policies and procedures for reporting the behavior of a physician if he or she is known to be angered by a telephone call about a patient's condition.

- Consult with a colleague for advice if there is a question about communicating patient needs/problems.
- Place a telephone call to the physician even if you are in doubt about the necessity of the communication regarding patient needs/problems.
- Always question information.
- Develop effective listening skills.
- Share information with colleagues.
- Let everyone know what you are thinking, planning, and doing because surprises have no place in patient care.
- Keep all health care team members informed of nursing assessment data and the status of the patient's condition.
- Never assume anything. All critical information must be verified and cross-checked.
- Discuss complex patient care situations with those involved. Talk through what you are going to do. Everyone should participate.
- Develop an assertive attitude, and openly communicate concerns to colleagues.

PREVENTION OF NURSING NEGLIGENCE ASSOCIATED WITH INADEQUATE CARE BY THE PHYSICIAN

The nurse must recognize situations when the care provided to the patient by a physician departs from prevailing professional standards of practice. Under these circumstances, the nurse is expected to recognize the inadequate care and to intervene on behalf of the patient. However, the nurse is not demanded or expected to practice medicine. In the hospital setting, the nurse is responsible and accountable for negative outcomes associated with inadequate care by the physician.

Prevention of nursing-care-related adverse outcomes associated with inadequate care by the physician include

- Informing the physician of a patient care problem and expecting appropriate action
- Recognizing inadequate care by the physician
- Utilizing hospital policies and procedures to obtain appropriate care for the patient receiving inadequate care
- Persisting in obtaining suitable care for the patient

PREVENTION OF NURSING
INTERVENTION PROBLEMS

Nursing intervention problems can be avoided by proficient execution of nursing treatments and/or procedures. Independent nursing interventions—that is, those initiated by the nurse without the need for a physician's order—have a great potential for creating malpractice problems. Many of the independent interventions such as skin care and vital signs are frequently neglected or performed with less care by the nurse because they are considered "routine" or "unimportant." Patient condition, of course, dictates the type and frequency of independent nursing interventions required, and the nurse is the only member of the health care team qualified to make the determination.

Dependent nursing treatments and procedures such as medication prescription or urinary catheterization, on the other hand, require a physician's order. To ensure safe execution of these interventions, the nurse must not only have a complete and accurate order but perform the treatment or procedure with technical proficiency.

Nursing procedures and treatments are changing rapidly. They are becoming more sophisticated as well as complicated. The nurse is accountable and responsible for keeping abreast of advances in nursing practice. A nurse's expert knowledge along with hospital policies and procedures to provide guidance ensures proper application and execution of nursing treatments and procedures.

Nursing intervention problems are avoided by

- Possessing a valid and complete physician's order for dependent nursing treatments and procedures (see risk reduction strategies concerning physician orders)
- Questioning a physician's order that does not seem appropriate to patient care needs
- Performing all treatments and procedures with caution and care, using proper techniques
- Following hospital procedures for nursing intervention
- Procuring help if one is unsure about executing a treatment or procedure
- Consistently updating knowledge and skills

PREVENTION OF EQUIPMENT
AND PRODUCT PROBLEMS

Misuse or careless use of equipment is a major cause of adverse incidents in the hospital setting. Also, the use of malfunctioning or poorly maintained equipment contributes to negative outcomes. The nurse must be knowledgeable about the proper operation and care of equipment used for patient care. This responsibility is especially important today because of the ever-changing, wide array of sophisticated instrumentation available. Hospital-based in-service education programs and information provided by manufacturers, in addition to nursing periodicals and textbooks, are important resources for information about equipment. For safe use of equipment the nurse must

- Possess knowledge about the safe operation of equipment used for patient care
- Use equipment in accordance with the manufacturer's instructions
- Use equipment only for its intended and specified purpose
- Ensure that equipment is properly used and maintained
- Avoid the use of defective or malfunctioning equipment
- Ensure that all safety features of equipment such as alarms are employed during use
- Adjust the controls on a piece of equipment only after
  1. Looking at the piece of equipment
  2. Knowing the function of the piece of equipment
  3. Knowing why he or she wants to adjust the controls of the equipment

Adverse patient care outcomes, in the hospital setting, have resulted from the use of products for purposes other than those intended by the manufacturer. In addition, death or injury of the patient has been the consequence of careless use or application of products. For safe use of products, the nurse must

- Be knowledgeable about the product
- Use the product in accordance with the manufacturer's instructions
- Use the product only for its specified and intended purpose
- Avoid the use of a defective or improperly packaged (e.g., broken safety seal) product

SUMMARY

Prevention of adverse patient care outcomes in the hospital setting begins with the application of the nursing process to patient care. A safe physical and biological environment is necessary for the implementation of the nursing care plan. Systematic patient assessment, along with the delivery of nursing care interventions that conform to prevailing professional standards of nursing care, will ensure quality patient care. Documentation of the nursing care in the medical record is as important to the well-being of the patient as the actual delivery of the care because this will ensure the continuity of care.

Identification by the nurse of actual or potential risks in the hospital setting will reduce or eliminate unnecessary errors in the care of the patient. This is a crucial responsibility because the nurse is the only member of the health care team that remains with the patient 24 hours a day.

References

American Hospital Association. (1993). *Hospital statistics.* Chicago: American Hospital Publishing.

Brennan, T. A., Leape, L. L., Laird, N. M., Hebert, L. E., Localio, A. R., Lawthers, A. G., Newhouse, J. P., Weiler, P. C., & Hiatt, H. H. (1991). Incidence of adverse events and negligence in hospitalized patients: Results of the Harvard Medical Practice Study I. *New England Journal of Medicine, 324,* 370-376.

Danzon, P. M. (1985). *Medical malpractice: Theory, evidence and public policy.* Cambridge, MA: Harvard University Press.

Donahue v. Port (1993). 92-CIV-4477 (C.P. Lackawanna Co., Pennsylvannia.)

Freeland, W. G. (1973). *Report of the Secretary's Commission on Medical Malpractice.* Washington, DC: U.S. Dept. of Health, Education, and Welfare.

Harvard Medical Practice Study. (1990). *Patients, doctors, and lawyers: Medical injury, malpractice litigation, and patient compensation in New York: The report of the Harvard Medical Practice Study to the state of New York.* Cambridge, MA: Author.

Hiatt, H. H., Barnes, B. A., Brennan, T. A., Laird, N. M., Lawthers, A. G., Leape, L. L., Localio, A. R., Newhouse, J. P., Peterson, L. M., & Thorpe, K. E. (1989). A study of medical injury and medical malpractice: An overview. *New England Journal of Medicine, 321,* 480-484.

Leape, L. L., Brennan, T. A., Laird, N. M., Lawthers, A. G., Localio, A. R., Barnes, B. A., Hebert, L., Newhouse, J. P., Weiler, P. C., & Hiatt, H. H. (1991). The nature of adverse events in hospitalized patients: Results of the Harvard Medical Practice Study II. *New England Journal of Medicine, 324,* 377-384.

Localio, A. R., Lawthers, A. G., Brennan, T. A., Laird, N. M., Hebert, L. E., Peterson, L. M., Newhouse, J. P., Weiler, P. C., & Hiatt, H. H. (1991). Relation between malpractice claims and adverse events due to negligence: Results of the Harvard Medical Practice Study III. *New England Journal of Medicine, 325,* 245-251.

McDonough, W. J., & Rioux, M. (1989). Increasing number of nurses named as sole defendants in malpractice suits. *Forum, 10*(1), 4-5, 12.

Mills, D. H. (Ed.). (1977). *Medical insurance feasibility study.* Sacramento: California Medical Association and California Hospital Association.

1993's largest verdicts. (1994). *National Law Journal, 16*(18), S1, S8-9.

Pabst, Jr., W. R. (1973). *An analysis of an American Hospital Association professional liability survey* (U.S. Dept. of Health, Education, and Welfare Report No. SCMM-WP-AH). Washington, DC: Government Printing Office.

Patterson, R. M., & Robinson, R. E. (Eds.). (1982). *Drugs in litigation: Damage awards involving prescription and nonprescription drugs.* Indianapolis: Allan Smith.

Pocincki, L. S., Dogger, S. J., & Schwartz, B. (1973). *The incidence of iatrogenic injuries* (U.S. Dept. of Health, Education, and Welfare Report No. SCMM-ER-GE-11). Washington, DC: Government Printing Office.

Rudov, M. H., Myers, T. I., & Mirabella, A. (1973). *Medical malpractice insurance claims files closed in 1970* (U.S. Dept. of Health, Education, and Welfare Report). Washington, DC: Government Printing Office.

Taragin, M., Willett, L. R., Wilczek, A. P., Trout, R., & Carson, J. L. (1992). The influence of standard of care and severity of injury on the resolution of medical malpractice claims. *Annals of Internal Medicine, 117,* 780-784.

U.S. Bureau of Statistics. (1993). *Statistical abstract of the United States.* Washington, DC: Government Printing Office.

U.S. General Accounting Office. (1986). *Medical malpractice: Six state case studies show claims and insurance costs still rise despite reforms* (General Accounting Office Publication No. HRD-87-21). Washington, DC: Government Printing Office.

Washington v. New York City Health and Hospitals Corp. (1993). 8608/89 (Superior Court, Bronx Co., N.Y., 1993).

World Almanac and Book of Facts. (1993). New York: Press Publishing.

Index

Admitting diagnosis, 27, 60-61, 80, 97-100, 122-124, 140-141, 160, 184-185, 205, 222-223, 238
Adverse outcome, definition, 10, 20
Adverse outcomes, 20-21, 56-57, 62, 78, 80-81, 95-101, 120, 125, 139, 141-143, 158, 161, 182, 185-186, 202, 206, 221, 224, 237-238
Age data, 21-24, 58, 79, 96, 121-122, 140, 159-160, 182-184, 203-205, 222
Air Line Pilots Association (ALPA), accident investigation, 2
Algorithmic error, 12
American Nurses' Association (ANA), 1, 4, 9, 259
Amputation, 3, 27, 66, 83, 106, 108, 147, 166, 167, 169, 172, 190, 194, 211, 241, 242
Appellate court, 17
Arithmetic error, calculations, 12
Assessment, 263-266
   body temperature, 265
   circulatory status, 265
   endocrine-metabolic status, 266
   fluid status, 266

   gastrointestinal status, 266
   immune status, 266
   integumentary-wound status, 265-266
   musculoskeletal status, 266
   neurologic status, 265
   pain status, 266
   psychosocial status, 266
   renal status, 266
   respiratory status, 264-265
   sensory and perceptual status, 266
   See also Nursing assessment
Attitude, professional, 256-257

Body temperature assessment, 265
Bowel necrosis, 166
Brain damage, 3, 27, 65, 66, 68, 71, 83, 85, 87, 88, 89, 104, 108, 109, 111, 130, 146, 147, 148, 149, 150, 151, 166, 167, 170, 172, 175, 190, 191, 192, 193, 194, 208, 209, 210, 212, 213, 214, 227, 229, 230, 241, 242, 243, 244, 245, 246, 247
Breach of duty, negligence, 14

About the Author

Janet Pitts Beckmann is Affiliate Professor at the School of Nursing of the University of Washington, as well as an independent consultant. She holds a Ph.D. from the University of Washington in higher education (college and university administration) and physiology biophysics, and an M.N. from Emory University in medical-surgical nursing. Previously she has served as Dean and Associate Professor at the School of Nursing of the University of Alabama in Huntsville and as an Associate Dean and Associate Professor at the University of Miami School of Nursing. She has been a member of the Editorial Board of the *Journal of Nursing Education* and an accreditation visitor for the National League of Nursing. She authored the book *Nursing Malpractice: Implications for Clinical Practice and Nursing Education* (1995).

The major portion of her career has been devoted to clinical practice and nursing education. For the past 15 years, she has served as a consultant to attorneys on nursing standards and has been a pioneer nursing expert witness and possesses a vast body of knowledge regarding nursing malpractice. It is her desire now to stimulate the nursing profession to face the reality of the need to maintain accepted nursing standards and to begin to address the problem of nursing negligence.